John William Stanhope Hows

**Golden Leaves from the British Poets**

John William Stanhope Hows

**Golden Leaves from the British Poets**

ISBN/EAN: 9783743312616

Manufactured in Europe, USA, Canada, Australia, Japa

Cover: Foto ©ninafisch / pixelio.de

Manufactured and distributed by brebook publishing software
(www.brebook.com)

John William Stanhope Hows

**Golden Leaves from the British Poets**

# GOLDEN LEAVES

## FROM THE

# BRITISH POETS

COLLECTED BY

JOHN W. S. HOWS

NEW YORK
JAMES G. GREGORY 540 BROADWAY.
M DCCC LXIV

Entered according to Act of Congress, in the year 1864,

By JAMES G. GREGORY,

In the Clerk's Office of the District Court of the United States for the Southern District of New York.

C. A. ALVORD, STEREOTYPER AND PRINTER.

# PREFACE.

IN adding another compilation from the Poets to the many already before the public, it seems necessary to offer some distinctive claim to originality as an apology for the temerity of the attempt. This collection so far differs from previous ones, that no arbitrary or individual preferences have controlled the Selections; they are exclusively those specimens of "THE BRITISH POETS," which, by long-established consent, have become "*Household words*" in our language, as exponents of all that is beautiful in thought, expression, and feeling. To collect these into one *portable* volume, that might with ease be made the companion of the Railroad car, the Steamboat, and the shady nook of a country retreat; and from its elegance of typographical and mechanical beauty, would entitle it to a place on the Parlour table for reference and family use, seemed an experiment that might find favour with the reading public. The necessarily prescribed limits of this volume would not admit of the adoption of all those Gems, even of minor poems, which have become stereotyped, as it were, in the affections of the general reader; especial care, however, has been taken to admit only those which have been recognized as the purest and most brilliant droppings from "the wells of English undefiled." The period of Shakespeare and his contemporaries has been chosen for the commencement of the Selections; our language then assumed its almost definite shape, and its literature may be considered then to have achieved some of its greatest triumphs. Subsequent Poets, as far as practicable, have been arranged to follow in the order of their succession, down to the latest candidate for poetic fame at the publication of this volume.

The Selections have been arranged consecutively under their appropriate authors, affording greater facilities for reference, and concentrating more distinctly the interest on each individual Poet, than could be obtained by a miscellaneous distribution: a species of unity and individuality is thus preserved, that we trust will be found acceptable to the reader.

The Collector, in acknowledging the adaptation

of the Title of an English compilation of very limited extent, intended chiefly for the introduction of Pictorial Illustrations, confesses the expressiveness of the name so completely harmonized with the design he contemplated, in furnishing a *Series* of Compilations that should be indeed "GOLDEN LEAVES" from the works of Standard Authors, that he could not resist its adoption. The second volume of the Series is prepared, and will be issued immediately, under the title of "GOLDEN LEAVES FROM THE AMERICAN POETS."

J. W. S. H.

NEW YORK, June 22, 1864.

# CONTENTS.

**WILLIAM SHAKESPEARE.**     PAGE
- Spring and Winter .................................................... 1
- Love's Perjuries ..................................................... 2
- True Love ............................................................ 3
- Soul and Body ........................................................ 4
- Youth and Age ........................................................ 4
- Blow, blow, thou Winter Wind ......................................... 5
- Under the Greenwood Tree ............................................. 6

**EDMUND SPENSER.**
- Prothalamion ......................................................... 7

**SIR PHILIP SIDNEY.**
- Love is dead ......................................................... 13
- A Ditty .............................................................. 14

**SIR WALTER RALEIGH.**
- The Silent Lover ..................................................... 15
- Lines written the Night before his Death ............................. 16

**CHRISTOPHER MARLOWE.**
- The Passionate Shepherd to his Love .................................. 17

**SIR HENRY WOTTON.**
- Character of a Happy Life ............................................ 18

## CONTENTS.

### Ben Jonson.
|  | PAGE |
|---|---|
| The Noble Nature | 19 |
| Hymn to Diana | 19 |
| To the Memory of my beloved Master, William Shakespeare, and what he hath left us | 20 |
| On the Portrait of Shakespeare. Under the Frontispiece to the first edition of his Works: 1623 | 23 |

### George Wither.
| Christmas | 23 |
|---|---|

### George Herbert.
| Virtue | 27 |
|---|---|
| Sunday | 27 |

### Sir John Suckling.
| The Bride. (From "The Ballad upon a Wedding.") | 30 |
|---|---|

### Robert Herrick.
| Gather the Rose-buds | 31 |
|---|---|
| Cherry Ripe | 31 |
| To Daffodils | 32 |
| To Blossoms | 32 |
| To Primroses, filled with Morning Dew | 33 |

### Abraham Cowley.
| The Epicure | 34 |
|---|---|
| The Grasshopper | 35 |

### Edmund Waller.
| "Go, lovely Rose!" | 36 |
|---|---|
| Old Age and Death | 37 |

### Andrew Marvell.
| Thoughts in a Garden | 38 |
|---|---|

### John Milton.
| Lycidas | 40 |
|---|---|
| L'Allégro | 47 |
| Il Penseroso | 52 |

## CONTENTS.

**Izaak Walton.**
    The Angler's Wish .................................................. 58

**John Dryden.**
    Alexander's Feast .................................................. 59
    Ode to Saint Cecilia ............................................... 64

**Alexander Pope.**
    Messiah ............................................................ 66
    The Universal Prayer .............................................. 70
    The Dying Christian to his Soul ................................... 72

**Joseph Addison.**
    A Hymn: "When all thy Mercies, O my God" ..................... 73
    Ode: "The Spacious Firmament" ................................... 75

**John Gay.**
    The Poet and the Rose ............................................. 76
    Black-eyed Susan .................................................. 77

**Matthew Prior.**
    The Garland ....................................................... 79

**John Pomfret.**
    The Choice ........................................................ 80

**Thomas Parnell.**
    The Hermit ........................................................ 86

**William Collins.**
    Ode on the Passions ............................................... 94
    Dirge in Cymbeline, sung by Guiderus and Arviragus over Fidele, supposed to be dead ....................................... 98
    How Sleep the Brave .............................................. 99

**Thomas Gray.**
    Elegy written in a Country Churchyard ........................... 100
    The Epitaph ...................................................... 104
    Hymn to Adversity ............................................... 105

## CONTENTS.

**Allan Ramsay.**                                       PAGE
    Lochaber no more ................................................ 107

**James Thomson.**
    Universal Hymn to the Seasons ........................... 108
    Lavinia .................................................................. 112

**David Mallet.**
    William and Margaret ........................................ 116

**John Logan.**
    To the Cuckoo .................................................. 119

**Oliver Goldsmith.**
    Extracts from "The Deserted Village" ............... 120
    Retaliation ....................................................... 128

**Tobias Smollett.**
    Ode to Leven-water ......................................... 137

**Bishop Percy.**
    "O, Nanny, wilt thou gang wi' me" ................. 138
    The Friar of Orders Gray ................................. 139

**James Beattie.**
    Description of Edwin, the Minstrel Boy ............ 143

**Sir William Jones.**
    A Persian Song of Hafiz ................................... 148

**James Merrick.**
    The Chameleon ................................................ 150

**Lady Anne Lindsay.**
    Auld Robin Gray .............................................. 152

**Henry Carey.**
    Sally in Our Alley ............................................ 154

**Thomas Chatterton.**
    The Bristow Tragedy ....................................... 156

## CONTENTS.

**WILLIAM COWPER.**
  Verses supposed to be written by Alexander Selkirk, during his solitary abode in the Island of Juan Fernandez .................................................................. 170
  The Pulpit ............................................................ 172
  The Poplar Field ..................................................... 173
  To Mary Unwin ........................................................ 174

**ANNA LETITIA BARBAULD.**
  Hymn to Content...................................................... 176

**MATTHEW GREGORY LEWIS**
  The Maniac ........................................................... 178

**HENRY KIRKE WHITE.**
  The Star of Bethlehem ................................................ 181
  To an Early Primrose ................................................. 182

**ROBERT BURNS.**
  The Cotter's Saturday Night .......................................... 183
  Tam O'Shanter. A Tale ................................................ 190
  My Luve is like a Red, Red Rose ...................................... 197
  John Anderson ........................................................ 198
  Highland Mary ........................................................ 198
  To Mary in Heaven .................................................... 200
  A Man's a Man for a' that ............................................ 201

**MRS. PIOZZI.**
  The Three Warnings ................................................... 203

**WILLIAM WORDSWORTH.**
  Laodamia ............................................................. 207
  To the Daisy ......................................................... 213
  To the Skylark ....................................................... 214
  The Daffodils ........................................................ 215
  The Education of Nature .............................................. 216
  The Lost Love ........................................................ 218
  A Portrait ........................................................... 218
  By the Sea ........................................................... 219

## SAMUEL TAYLOR COLERIDGE.

 Rime of the Ancient Mariner. In Seven Parts............ 220
 Genevieve ......................................................... 244
 Work without Hope............................................. 247

## ROBERT SOUTHEY.

 The Scholar ....................................................... 248
 The Well of St. Keyne ........................................ 249
 Jaspar ............................................................... 251

## THOMAS CAMPBELL.

 Hohenlinden....................................................... 257
 The Soldier's Dream ........................................... 259
 Lord Ullin's Daughter ......................................... 260
 Battle of the Baltic............................................. 262
 Valedictory Stanzas to John Philip Kemble............... 265

## SIR WALTER SCOTT.

 The Lay of the Last Minstrel ................................ 268
 Marmion. The Trial of Constance ........................ 272
 The Death of Marmion........................................ 284
 The Lady of the Lake. Meeting of Ellen and Fitzjames 292
 Rokeby. Wilfrid, the Youthful Visionary ................ 303

## JAMES HOGG.

 To the Skylark .................................................. 306

## HORACE SMITH.

 To an Egyptian Mummy ....................................... 307

## THOMAS MOORE.

 Paradise and the Peri. (From "Lalla Rookh.")......... 310
 The Death of Hafed and Hinda.............................. 328
 Beauty, Wit, and Gold......................................... 338
 Reason, Folly, and Beauty ................................... 339
 Those Evening Bells............................................. 340
 A Canadian Boat-song ......................................... 341

## LORD BYRON.

Extracts from "Childe Harold." Ancient Greece......... 342
Evening on Lake Leman ..................................... 344
Storm on Lake Leman............................................ 345
The Coliseum. The Dying Gladiator ...................... 345
The Dream................................................................ 347
The Shipwreck. (From "Don Juan.")...................... 353
"There's not a joy the world can give" .................. 355

## LEIGH HUNT.

Spring in Ravenna. (From "Rimini.")..................... 357
Abou Ben Adhem .................................................. 358

## PERCY BYSSHE SHELLEY.

To the Skylark ....................................................... 358
The Sensitive Plant ............................................... 362
The Poet's Dream ................................................. 366

## JOHN KEATS.

The Eve of St. Agnes............................................ 367
Bards of Passion .................................................. 381
Lines on the Mermaid Tavern................................ 383

## JOHN WILSON (CHRISTOPHER NORTH).

Extracts from "City of the Plague" ........................ 384

## "BARRY CORNWALL" (BRYAN W. PROCTOR).

The Sea................................................................. 387

## REV. GEORGE CROLY.

The Seventh Plague of Egypt ............................... 388

## BISHOP HEBER.

Passage of the Red Sea. (From "Palestine.")......... 392
Missionary Hymn.................................................... 395

## MRS. HEMANS.

The Landing of the Pilgrim Fathers in New England... 397
The Homes of England .......................................... 398
Washington's Statue............................................... 400

## CONTENTS.

**Thomas Davis.**
 The Welcome.................................................... 401

**John Sterling.**
 Shakespeare..................................................... 402

**Walter Savage Landor.**
 The Maid's Lament............................................ 403
 The Brier........................................................ 404

**Allan Cunningham.**
 "Awake, my Love!"............................................ 405
 "A wet Sheet and a flowing Sea".......................... 406

**Thomas Haynes Bailey.**
 The Soldier's Tear............................................. 407
 "Oh, no! we never mention her"........................... 408
 "I'd be a Butterfly"............................................ 409
 "She wore a Wreath of Roses"............................. 410

**Rev. Charles Wolfe.**
 The Burial of Sir John Moore at Corunna................ 411

**John Keble.**
 Advent Sunday................................................. 413
 The Flowers of the Field..................................... 415

**Richard Monckton Milnes.**
 The Voice of the People..................................... 417

**Thomas Hood.**
 The Dream of Eugene Aram................................ 419
 The Song of the Shirt........................................ 426
 The Bridge of Sighs.......................................... 429

**Mrs. Caroline Norton.**
 Twilight......................................................... 432
 "We have been Friends together"......................... 439
 The Fallen Leaves............................................ 440

## SAMUEL LOVER.
Rory O'More; or, Good Omens .................................. 442
The Angel's Whisper .................................................. 443

## THOMAS BABINGTON MACAULAY.
The Battle of Ivry ....................................................... 444

## MRS. ELIZABETH BARRETT BROWNING.
The Cry of the Children ............................................. 448

## ROBERT BROWNING.
How they brought the good news from Ghent to Aix ... 454
The Statue and the Bust ............................................. 456

## ALFRED TENNYSON.
Locksley Hall ............................................................. 466
The May Queen .......................................................... 478
Lady Clara Vere de Vere ............................................. 487
Extracts from "In Memoriam" ................................... 490
The Bugle Song .......................................................... 496
Come into the Garden, Maud .................................... 497
The Charge of the Light Brigade, at Balaklava ........... 500
Idyls of the King. Vivien ............................................ 502

## MARY HOWITT.
Cornfields .................................................................. 508

## WILLIAM MOTHERWELL.
Jeanie Morrison ......................................................... 509
My Heid is like to rend, Willie .................................... 513

## MRS. CAROLINE ANNE SOUTHEY.
The Mariner's Hymn .................................................. 515
The Pauper's Death-bed ............................................. 517

## ELIZA COOK.
The Old Arm-chair ..................................................... 518
Song of the Hempseed ............................................... 519

## CONTENTS.

**CHARLES KINGSLEY.**
    Song of the River..................................................... 523

**ALEXANDER SMITH.**
    A Song (from a Life-Drama)................................. 524

**JEAN INGELOW.**
    The Brides of Enderby; or, the High Tide............... 526

**EDWIN ARNOLD.**
    The Knight's Grave ................................................ 532

**GERALD MASSEY.**
    The Kingliest Kings ............................................... 535

**SYDNEY DOBELL.**
    "How's my Boy?"..................................................... 536

**WALTER THORNBURY.**
    The Two Norse Kings: a Yorkshire Legend ............ 538

**ROBERT BUCHANAN.**
    The Story of Pygmalion........................................... 539

**RICHARD CHENEVIX TRENCH.**
    Be patient ............................................................... 544

**MISS ADELAIDE ANNE PROCTOR.**
    A Doubting Heart ................................................... 545

# GOLDEN LEAVES.

## William Shakespeare.

### SPRING AND WINTER.

#### SPRING.

I.  WHEN daisies pied, and violets blue,
      And lady-smocks all silver-white,
And cuckoo-buds of yellow hue,
    Do paint the meadows with delight,
The cuckoo then, on every tree,
Mocks married men, for thus sings he,
        Cuckoo;
Cuckoo, cuckoo,—O word of fear,
Unpleasing to a married ear!

II. When shepherds pipe on oaten straws,
     And merry larks are ploughmen's clocks,
When turtles tread, and rooks and daws,
     And maidens bleach their summer smocks,
The cuckoo then, on every tree,
Mocks married men, for thus sings he,
        Cuckoo;
Cuckoo, cuckoo,—O word of fear,
Unpleasing to a married ear!

### WINTER.

III. When icicles hang by the wall,
    And Dick the shepherd blows his nail,
And Tom bears logs into the hall,
    And milk comes frozen home in pail,
When blood is nipp'd, and ways be foul,
Then nightly sings the staring owl,
    To-who,
Tu-whit, to-who; a merry note,
While greasy Joan doth keel the pot.

IV. When all aloud the wind doth blow,
    And coughing drowns the parson's saw,
And birds sit brooding in the snow,
    And Marian's nose looks red and raw,
When roasted crabs hiss in the bowl,
Then nightly sings the staring owl,
    To-who,
Tu-whit, to-who; a merry note,
While greasy Joan doth keel the pot.

---

### LOVE'S PERJURIES.

ON a day, alack the day!
    Love, whose month is ever May,
Spied a blossom passing fair,
Playing in the wanton air:
Through the velvet leaves the wind
All unseen 'gan passage find;
That the lover, sick to death,
Wish'd himself the heaven's breath.

Air, quoth he, thy cheeks may blow;
Air, would I might triumph so!
But, alack, my hand is sworn
Ne'er to pluck thee from thy thorn:
Vow, alack, for youth unmeet;
Youth so apt to pluck a sweet.
Do not call it sin in me
That I am forsworn for thee:
Thou for whom e'en Jove would swear
Juno but an Ethiope were,
And deny himself for Jove,
Turning mortal for thy love.

---

### TRUE LOVE.

LET me not to the marriage of true minds
   Admit impediments. Love is not love
Which alters when it alteration finds,
   Or bends with the remover to remove:—

O no! it is an ever-fixèd mark
   That looks on tempests, and is never shaken;
It is the star to every wandering bark
   Whose worth's unknown, although his height be taken.

Love's not Time's fool, though rosy lips and cheeks
   Within his bending sickle's compass come;
Love alters not with his brief hours and weeks,
   But bears it out ev'n to the edge of doom:—

If this be error, and upon me proved,
I never writ, nor no man ever loved.

## SOUL AND BODY.

POOR Soul, the centre of my sinful earth,
    Fool'd by those rebel powers that thee array,
Why dost thou pine within, and suffer dearth,
    Painting thy outward walls so costly gay?

Why so large cost, having so short a lease,
    Dost thou upon thy fading mansion spend?
Shall worms, inheritors of this excess,
    Eat up thy charge? is this thy body's end?

Then, Soul, live thou upon thy servant's loss,
    And let that pine to aggravate thy store;
Buy terms divine in selling hours of dross;
    Within be fed, without be rich no more:—

So shalt thou feed on death, that feeds on men,
And death once dead, there's no more dying then.

---

## YOUTH AND AGE.

CRABBED Age and Youth
    Cannot live together:
Youth is full of pleasance,
Age is full of care;
Youth like summer morn,
Age like winter weather,
Youth like summer brave,
Age like winter bare:
Youth is full of sport,
Age's breath is short,

Youth is nimble, Age is lame:
Youth is hot and bold,
Age is weak and cold,
Youth is wild, and Age is tame:—
Age, I do abhor thee,
Youth, I do adore thee;
O! my Love, my Love is young!
Age, I do defy thee—
O sweet shepherd, hie thee,
For methinks thou stay'st too long.

---

## BLOW, BLOW, THOU WINTER WIND.

BLOW, blow, thou winter wind,
　　Thou art not so unkind
As man's ingratitude;
Thy tooth is not so keen
Because thou art not seen,
Although thy breath be rude.
Heigh ho! sing heigh ho! unto the green holly:
Most friendship is feigning, most loving mere folly:
　　Then, heigh ho! the holly!
　　This life is most jolly.

Freeze, freeze, thou bitter sky,
Thou dost not bite so nigh
As benefits forgot:
Though thou the waters warp,
Thy sting is not so sharp
As friend remember'd not.

Heigh ho! sing heigh ho! unto the green holly:
Most friendship is feigning, most loving mere folly:
    Then, heigh ho! the holly!
    This life is most jolly.

---

## UNDER THE GREENWOOD TREE.

    UNDER the greenwood tree
      Who loves to lie with me,
    And tune his merry note
    Unto the sweet bird's throat—
Come hither, come hither, come hither!
    Here shall he see
    No enemy
But winter and rough weather.

    Who doth ambition shun
    And loves to live i' the sun,
    Seeking the food he eats
    And pleased with what he gets—
Come hither, come hither, come hither!
    Here shall he see
    No enemy
But winter and rough weather.

## Edmund Spenser.

### PROTHALAMION.

CALM was the day, and through the trembling air
   Sweet-breathing Zephyrus did softly play—
A gentle spirit, that lightly did delay
Hot Titan's beams, which then did glister fair;
When I (whom sullen care,
Through discontent of my long fruitless stay
In princes' court, and expectation vain
Of idle hopes, which still do fly away
Like empty shadows, did afflict my brain)
Walk'd forth to ease my pain
Along the shore of silver-streaming Thames;
Whose rutty bank, the which his river hems,
Was painted all with variable flowers,
And all the meads adorn'd with dainty gems
Fit to deck maidens' bowers,
And crown their paramours
Against the bridal-day, which is not long:
   Sweet Thames! run softly, till I end my song.

There in a meadow by the river's side
A flock of nymphs I chancèd to espy,
All lovely daughters of the flood thereby,
With goodly greenish locks all loose untied
As each had been a bride;
And each one had a little wicker basket
Made of fine twigs, entrailèd curiously,
In which they gather'd flowers to fill their flasket,

And with fine fingers cropt full feateously
The tender stalks on high.
Of every sort which in that meadow grew
They gather'd some; the violet, pallid blue,
The little daisy that at evening closes,
The virgin lily and the primrose true:
With store of vermeil roses,
To deck their bridegrooms' posies
Against the bridal-day, which was not long:
 Sweet Thames! run softly, till I end my song.

 With that I saw two swans of goodly hue
Come softly swimming down along the lee;
Two fairer birds I yet did never see;
The snow which doth the top of Pindus strow
Did never whiter show,
Nor Jove himself, when he a swan would be
For love of Leda, whiter did appear;
Yet Leda was (they say) as white as he,
Yet not so white as these, nor nothing near;
So purely white they were
That even the gentle stream, the which them bare,
Seem'd foul to them, and bade his billows spare
To wet their silken feathers, lest they might
Soil their fair plumes with water not so fair,
And mar their beauties bright
That shone as Heaven's light
Against their bridal-day, which was not long;
 Sweet Thames! run softly, till I end my song.

 Eftsoons the nymphs, which now had flowers their fill,
Ran all in haste to see that silver brood
As they came floating on the crystal flood;

Whom when they saw, they stood amazèd still
Their wondering eyes to fill;
Them seem'd they never saw a sight so fair
Of fowls, so lovely, that they sure did deem
Them heavenly born, or to be that same pair
Which through the sky draw Venus' silver team;
For sure they did not seem
To be begot of any earthly seed,
But rather angels, or of angels' breed;
Yet were they bred of summer's heat, they say,
In sweetest season, when each flower and weed
The earth did fresh array;
So fresh they seem'd as day,
Even as their bridal-day, which was not long:
 Sweet Thames! run softly, till I end my song.

 Then forth they all out of their baskets drew
Great store of flowers, the honour of the field,
That to the sense did fragrant odours yield,
All which upon those goodly birds they threw
And all the waves did strew,
That like old Peneus' waters they did seem
When down along by pleasant Tempe's shore
Scatter'd with flowers, through Thessaly they stream,
That they appear, through lilies' plenteous store,
Like a bride's chamber-floor.
Two of those nymphs meanwhile two garlands bound
Of freshest flowers which in that mead they found,
The which presenting all in trim array,
Their snowy foreheads therewithal they crown'd;
Whilst one did sing this lay
Prepared against that day,

Against their bridal-day, which was not long:
   Sweet Thames! run softly, till I end my song.

"Ye gentle birds! the world's fair ornament,
And Heaven's glory, whom this happy hour
Doth lead unto your lovers' blissful bower,
Joy may you have, and gentle hearts content
Of your love's complement;
And let fair Venus, that is queen of love,
With her heart-quelling son upon you smile,
Whose smile, they say, hath virtue to remove
All love's dislike, and friendship's faulty guile
Forever to assoil.
Let endless peace your steadfast hearts accord,
And blessed plenty wait upon your board;
And let your bed with pleasures chaste abound,
That fruitful issue may to you afford
Which may your foes confound,
And make your joys redound
Upon your bridal-day, which is not long:
   Sweet Thames, run softly, till I end my song."

So ended she; and all the rest around
To her redoubled that her undersong,
Which said their bridal-day should not be long:
And gentle Echo from the neighbour ground
Their accents did resound.
So forth those joyous birds did pass along
Adown the lee that to them murmur'd low,
As he would speak but that he lack'd a tongue,
Yet did by signs his glad affection show,
Making his stream run slow.

And all the fowl which in his flood did dwell
'Gan flock about these twain, that did excel
The rest, so far as Cynthia doth shend
The lesser stars.  So they, enrangèd well,
Did on those two attend,
And their best service lend
Against their wedding-day, which was not long:
    Sweet Thames! run softly, till I end my song.

    At length they all to merry London came,
To merry London, my most kindly nurse,
That to me gave this life's first native source,
Though from another place I take my name,
An house of ancient fame:
There when they came whereas those bricky towers
The which on Thames broad agèd back do ride,
Where now the studious lawyers have their bowers,
There whilome wont the Templar-knights to bide,
Till they decay'd through pride;
Next whereunto there stands a stately place,
Where oft I gainèd gifts and goodly grace
Of that great lord, which therein wont to dwell,
Whose want too well now feels my friendless case;
But ah! here fits not well
Old woes, but joys to tell
Against the bridal-day, which is not long:
    Sweet Thames! run softly, till I end my song.

    Yet therein now doth lodge a noble peer,
Great England's glory and the world's wide wonder,
Whose dreadful name late thro' all Spain did thunder,
And Hercules' two pillars standing near
Did make to quake and fear:

Fair branch of honour, flower of chivalry!
That fillest England with thy triumphs' fame,
Joy have thou of thy noble victory,
And endless happiness of thine own name
That promiseth the same;
That through thy prowess and victorious arms
Thy country may be freed from foreign harms,
And great Eliza's glorious name may ring
Through all the world, fill'd with thy wide alarms
Which some brave Muse may sing
To ages following,
Upon the bridal-day, which is not long:
    Sweet Thames! run softly, till I end my song.

From those high towers this noble lord issùing
Like radiant Hesper, when his golden hair
In th' ocean billows he hath bathèd fair,
Descended to the river's open viewing
With a great train ensuing.
Above the rest were goodly to be seen
Two gentle knights of lovely face and feature,
Beseeming well the bower of any queen,
With gifts of wit and ornaments of nature
Fit for so goodly stature,
That like the twins of Jove they seem'd in sight
Which deck the baldric of the Heavens bright;
They too, forth pacing to the river's side,
Received those two fair brides, their love's delight;
Which, at th' appointed tide,
Each one did make his bride
Against their bridal-day, which is not long:
    Sweet Thames! run softly, till I end my song.

## Sir Philip Sidney.

### LOVE IS DEAD.

RING out your bells, let mourning shews be spread,
    For Love is dead!
  All Love is dead, infected
    With plague of deep disdain,
Worth, or not worth, rejected,
    And faith fair scorn doth gain.
      From so ungrateful fancy,
      From such a female frenzy,
      From them that use men thus,
      Good Lord deliver us.

Weep, neighbours, weep, do you not hear it said
    That Love is dead?
  His death-bed peacock's folly,
    His winding-sheet is shame,
His will, false seeming holy,
    His sole executor blame.
      From so ungrateful fancy,
      From such a female frenzy,
      From them that use men thus,
      Good Lord deliver us.

Let dirge be sung, and trentals richly read,
    For Love is dead:
  And wrong his tomb ordaineth
    My mistress' marble heart;
Which epitaph containeth,
    Her eyes were once his dart.

>   From so ungrateful fancy,
>   From such a female frenzy,
>   From them that use men thus,
>     Good Lord deliver us.
>
> Alas! I lie, rage has this error bred—
>   Love's not dead.
> Love is not dead but sleepeth
>   In her unmatchèd mind,
> Where she his counsel keepeth
>   Till one desert she find.
>     Therefore from so vile fancy,
>     To call such wit a frenzy,
>     Who Love can temper thus,
>       Good Lord deliver us.

---

### A DITTY.

> MY true-love hath my heart, and I have his,
>   By just exchange one to the other given:
> I hold his dear, and mine he cannot miss,
>   There never was a better bargain driven:
>     My true-love hath my heart, and I have his.
>
> His heart in me keeps him and me in one,
>   My heart in him his thoughts and senses guides:
> He loves my heart, for once it was his own,
>   I cherish his because in me it bides:
>     My true-love hath my heart, and I have his.

## Sir Walter Raleigh.

### THE SILENT LOVER.

PASSIONS are likened best to floods and streams:
   The shallow murmur, but the deep are dumb;
So when affections yield discourse, it seems
   The bottom is but shallow whence they come.
They that are rich in words, in words discover
That they are poor in that which makes a lover.

   Wrong not, sweet empress of my heart!
      The limit of true passion,
   With thinking that he feels no smart,
      That sues for no compassion;

   Since if my plaints serve not to approve
      The conquest of thy beauty,
   It comes not from defect of love,
      But from excess of duty:

   For, knowing that I sue to serve
      A saint of such perfection,
   As all desire, but none deserve,
      A place in thy affection,

   I rather choose to want relief
      Than venture the revealing:
   Where glory recommends the grief,
      Despair distrusts the healing.

Thus those desires that aim too high
  For any mortal lover,
When reason cannot make them die,
  Discretion doth them cover.

Yet, when discretion doth bereave
  The plaints that they should utter,
Then thy discretion may perceive
  That silence is a suitor.

Silence in love betrays more woe
  Than words, though ne'er so witty;
A beggar that is dumb, you know,
  May challenge double pity!

Then wrong not, dearest to my heart!
  My true, though secret passion;
He smarteth most that hides his smart,
  And sues for no compassion.

---

## LINES

#### WRITTEN THE NIGHT BEFORE HIS DEATH.

EVEN such is Time, that takes on trust
  Our youth, our joys, our all we have,
And pays us but with age and dust;
  Who in the dark and silent grave,
When we have wandered all our ways,
Shuts up the story of our days!

## Christopher Marlowe.

**THE PASSIONATE SHEPHERD TO HIS LOVE.**

COME live with me and be my Love,
And we will all the pleasures prove
That hills and valleys, dale and field,
And all the craggy mountains yield.

There will we sit upon the rocks
And see the shepherds feed their flocks,
By shallow rivers, to whose falls
Melodious birds sing madrigals.

There will I make thee beds of roses
And a thousand fragrant posies,
A cap of flowers, and a kirtle
Embroider'd all with leaves of myrtle.

A gown made of the finest wool,
Which from our pretty lambs we pull,
Fair linèd slippers for the cold,
With buckles of the purest gold.

A belt of straw and ivy buds,
With coral clasps and amber studs:
And if these pleasures may thee move,
Come live with me and be my Love.

Thy silver dishes for thy meat
As precious as the gods do eat,
Shall on an ivory table be
Prepared each day for thee and me.

The shepherd swains shall dance and sing
For thy delight each May-morning:
If these delights thy mind may move,
Then live with me and be my Love.

---

## Sir Henry Wotton.

### CHARACTER OF A HAPPY LIFE.

HOW happy is he born and taught
    That serveth not another's will;
Whose armour is his honest thought,
    And simple truth his utmost skill!

Whose passions not his masters are,
    Whose soul is still prepared for death,
Not tied unto the world with care
    Of public fame, or private breath;

Who envies none that chance doth raise
    Or vice; Who never understood
How deepest wounds are given by praise;
    Nor rules of state, but rules of good;

Who hath his life from rumours freed,
    Whose conscience is his strong retreat;
Whose state can neither flatterers feed,
    Nor ruin make accusers great;

Who God doth late and early pray
    More of his grace than gifts to lend;
And entertains the harmless day
    With a well-chosen book or friend;

—This man is freed from servile bands
  Of hope to rise, or fear to fall;
Lord of himself, though not of lands;
  And having nothing, yet hath all.

---

## Ben Jonson.

### THE NOBLE NATURE.

IT is not growing like a tree
  In bulk, doth make Man better be;
Or standing long an oak, three hundred year,
To fall a log at last, dry, bald, and sere:
  A lily of a day
  Is fairer far in May,
Although it fall and die that night—
It was the plant and flower of Light.
In small proportions we just beauties see;
And in short measures life may perfect be.

---

### HYMN TO DIANA.

DRINK to me only with thine eyes,
  And I will pledge with mine;
Or leave a kiss but in the cup,
  And I'll not look for wine.
The thirst that from the soul doth rise
  Doth ask a drink divine;
But might I of Jove's nectar sup,
  I would not change for thine.

I sent thee late a rosy wreath,
    Not so much honouring thee
As giving it a hope that there
    It could not wither'd be;
But thou thereon didst only breathe
    And sent'st it back to me;
Since when it grows, and smells, I swear,
    Not of itself but thee!

---

## TO THE MEMORY OF MY BELOVED MASTER, WILLIAM SHAKESPEARE, AND WHAT HE HATH LEFT US.

TO draw no envy, Shakespeare, on thy name,
    Am I thus ample to thy book and fame;
While I confess thy writings to be such
As neither man nor Muse can praise too much.
'Tis true, and all men's suffrage. But these ways
Were not the paths I meant unto thy praise;
For silliest ignorance on these would light,
Which, when it sounds, at best but echoes right;
Or blind affection, which doth ne'er advance
The truth, but gropes, and urges all by chance;
Or crafty malice might pretend this praise,
And think to ruin, where it seem'd to raise.
But thou art proof against them, and, indeed,
Above the ill fortune of them, or the need.
I therefore will begin: Soul of the age!
The applause, delight, the wonder of our stage!
My Shakespeare, rise! I will not lodge thee by
Chaucer, or Spenser, or bid Beaumont lie

A little further off, to make thee room:
Thou art a monument without a tomb,
And art alive still, while thy book doth live,
And we have wits to read, and praise to give.
That I not mix thee so, my brain excuses,
I mean with great but disproportion'd Muses:
For if I thought my judgment were of years,
I should commit thee surely with thy peers,
And tell how far thou didst our Lyly outshine,
Or sporting Kyd or Marlowe's mighty line.
And though thou had small Latin and less Greek,
From thence to honour thee I will not seek
For names; but call forth thund'ring Eschylus,
Euripides, and Sophocles to us,
Pacuvius, Accius, him of Cordova dead,
To live again, to hear thy buskin tread,
And shake a stage: or when thy socks were on,
Leave thee alone for the comparison
Of all, that insolent Greece or haughty Rome
Sent forth, or since did from their ashes come.
Triumph, my Britain, thou hast one to show,
To whom all scenes of Europe homage owe.
He was not of an age, but for all time!
And all the Muses still were in their prime,
When, like Apollo, he came forth to warm
Our ears, or like a Mercury, to charm!
Nature herself was proud of his designs,
And joy'd to wear the dressing of his lines!
Which were so richly spun, and woven so fit,
As, since, she will vouchsafe no other wit.
The merry Greek, tart Aristophanes,
Neat Terence, witty Plautus, now not please;

But antiquated and deserted lie,
As they were not of nature's family.
Yet must I not give nature all; thy art,
My gentle Shakespeare, must enjoy a part.
For though the poet's matter nature be,
His art doth give the fashion; and, that he
Who casts to write a living line, must sweat
(Such as thine are) and strike the second heat
Upon the Muses' anvil; turn the same,
And himself with it, that he thinks to frame;
Or for the laurel, he may gain a scorn;
For a good poet's made as well as born.
And such wert thou! Look how the father's face
Lives in his issue, even so the race
Of Shakespeare's mind and manners brightly shines
In his well-turned and true-filed lines:
In each of which he seems to shake a lance,
As brandish'd at the eyes of ignorance.
Sweet Swan of Avon! what a sight it were
To see thee in our water yet appear,
And make those flights upon the banks of Thames
That so did take Eliza and our James!
But stay, I see thee in the hemisphere
Advanced, and made a constellation there!
Shine forth, thou Star of Poets, and with rage,
Or influence, chide, or cheer the drooping stage,
Which since thy flight from hence hath mourned like night,
And despairs day, but for thy volume's light!

## ON THE PORTRAIT OF SHAKESPEARE.

[Under the frontispiece to the first edition of his works: 1623.]

THIS figure that thou here seest put,
   It was for gentle Shakespeare cut,
Wherein the graver had a strife
With nature, to outdo the life:
O could he but have drawn his wit,
As well in brass, as he hath hit
His face; the print would then surpass
All that was ever writ in brass:
But since he cannot, reader, look
Not on his picture, but his book.

---

## George Wither.

### CHRISTMAS.

SO now is come our joyful'st feast;
   Let every man be jolly;
Each room with ivy leaves is drest,
   And every post with holly.
Though some churls at our mirth repine,
Round your foreheads garlands twine,
Drown sorrow in a cup of wine,
   And let us all be merry.

Now all our neighbours' chimneys smoke,
   And Christmas blocks are burning;
Their ovens they with baked meats choke,
   And all their spits are turning.

Without the door let sorrow lie;
And if for cold it hap to die,
We'll bury't in a Christmas pie,
    And evermore be merry.

Now every lad is wondrous trim,
    And no man minds his labour;
Our lasses have provided them
    A bagpipe and a tabor;
Young men and maids, and girls and boys,
Give life to one another's joys;
And you anon shall by their noise
    Perceive that they are merry.

Rank misers now do sparing shun;
    Their hall of music soundeth;
And dogs thence with whole shoulders run,
    So all things there aboundeth.
The country folks, themselves advance,
With crowdy-muttons out of France;
And Jack shall pipe, and Jill shall dance,
    And all the town be merry.

Ned Squash hath fetcht his bands from pawn,
    And all his best apparel;
Brisk Nell hath bought a ruff of lawn
    With droppings of the barrel;
And those that hardly all the year
Had bread to eat, or rags to wear,
Will have both clothes and dainty fare,
    And all the day be merry.

Now poor men to the justices
  With capons make their errants;
And if they hap to fail of these,
  They plague them with their warrants:
But now they feed them with good cheer,
And what they want they take in beer,
For Christmas comes but once a year,
  And then they shall be merry.

Good farmers in the country nurse
  The poor, that else were undone;
Some landlords spend their money worse,
  On lust and pride at London.
There the roysters they do play,
Drab and dice their lands away,
Which may be ours another day,
  And therefore let's be merry.

The client now his suit forbears,
  The prisoner's heart is eased;
The debtor drinks away his cares,
  And for the time is pleased.
Though others' purses be more fat,
Why should we pine, or grieve at that?
Hang sorrow! care will kill a cat,
  And therefore let's be merry.

Hark! now the wags abroad do call
  Each other forth to rambling:
Anon you'll see them in the hall,
  For nuts and apples scrambling.

Hark! how the roofs with laughter sound!
Anon they'll think the house goes round,
For they the cellar's depth have found,
    And there they will be merry.

The wenches with their wassail-bowls
    About the streets are singing;
The boys are come to catch the owls,
    The wild mare in is bringing.
Our kitchen-boy hath broke his box,
And to the dealing of the ox
Our honest neighbours come by flocks,
    And here they will be merry.

Now kings and queens poor sheepcotes have,
    And mate with everybody;
The honest now may play the knave,
    And wise men play the noddy.
Some youths will now a mumming go,
Some others play at Rowland-ho,
And twenty other gambols mo,
    Because they will be merry.

Then, wherefore, in these merry days,
    Should we, I pray, be duller?
No, let us sing some roundelays,
    To make our mirth the fuller:
And, while we thus inspired sing,
Let all the streets with echoes ring;
Woods and hills, and every thing,
    Bear witness we are merry.

## George Herbert.

### VIRTUE.

SWEET day! so cool, so calm, so bright,
    The bridal of the earth and sky;
The dews shall weep thy fall to-night;
    For thou must die.

Sweet rose! whose hue, angry and brave,
Bids the rash gazer wipe his eye;
Thy root is ever in its grave;
    And thou must die.

Sweet spring! full of sweet days and roses;
A box where sweets compacted lie;
Thy music shows ye have your closes;
    And all must die.

Only a sweet and virtuous soul,
Like season'd timber never gives;
But, though the whole world turn to coal,
    Then chiefly lives.

---

### SUNDAY.

O DAY most calm, most bright,
    The fruit of this, the next world's bud,
The indorsement of supreme delight,
Writ by a Friend, and with His blood;
The couch of time, care's balm and bay:
The week were dark, but for thy light;
    Thy torch doth show the way.

The other days and thou
Make up one man; whose face *thou* art,
Knocking at heaven with thy brow:
The workydays are the back-part;
The burden of the week lies there,
Making the whole to stoop and bow,
  Till thy release appear.

Man had straightforward gone
To endless death: but thou dost pull
And turn us round, to look on One,
Whom, if we were not very dull,
We could not choose but look on still;
Since there is no place so alone,
  The which He doth not fill.

Sundays the pillars are,
On which heaven's palace archèd lies:
The other days fill up the spare
And hollow room with vanities.
They are the fruitful beds and borders
In God's rich garden: that is bare,
  Which parts their ranks and orders.

The Sundays of man's life,
Threaded together on Time's string,
Make bracelets to adorn the wife
Of the eternal glorious King.
On Sunday heaven's gate stands ope;
Blessings are plentiful and rife—
  More plentiful than hope.

This day my Saviour rose,
And did enclose this light for His;

That, as each beast his manger knows,
Man might not of his fodder miss.
Christ hath took in this piece of ground,
And made a garden there for those
    Who want herbs for their wound.

    The rest of our creation
Our great Redeemer did remove
With the same shake, which at His passion
Did the earth and all things with it move.
As Sampson bore the doors away,
Christ's hands, though nail'd, wrought our salvation,
    And did unhinge that day.

    The brightness of that day
We sullied by our foul offence:
Wherefore that robe we cast away,
Having a new at His expense,
Whose drops of blood paid the full price
That was required to make us gay,
    And fit for paradise.

    Thou art a day of mirth:
And where the week-days trail on ground,
Thy flight is higher, as thy birth:
O let me take thee at the bound,
Leaping with thee from seven to seven,
Till that we both, being toss'd from earth,
    Fly hand in hand to heaven!

## Sir John Suckling.

**THE BRIDE.**

(From "The Ballad upon a Wedding.")

HER finger was so small, the ring
Would not stay on, which they did bring;
  It was too wide, *a peck;*
And to say truth (for out it must),
It look'd like the great collar (*just*)
  About our young colt's neck.

*Her feet beneath her petticoat,*
*Like little mice, stole in and out,*
  *As if they fear'd the light;*
*But oh! she dances such a way!*
*No sun upon an Easter Day*
  *Is half so fine a sight.*

Her cheeks so rare a white was on,
No daisy bears comparison
  (Who sees them is undone),
For streaks of red were mingled there,
Such as are on a Katherine pear,
  *The side that's next the sun.*

*Her lips were red, and one was thin*
*Compar'd to that was next her chin,*
  *Some bee had stung it newly;*
But (Dick) her eyes so *guard* her face,
I durst no more upon *them* gaze,
  Than on the sun in July.

## Robert Herrick.

**GATHER THE ROSE-BUDS.**

GATHER ye rose-buds as ye may,
   Old Time is still a-flying;
And this same flower that smiles to-day,
   To-morrow will be dying.

The glorious lamp of heav'n, the sun,
   The higher he's a-getting,
The sooner will his race be run,
   And nearer he's to setting.

The age is best which is the first,
   When youth and blood are warmer;
But being spent, the worse and worst
   Time still succeed the former.

Then be not coy, but use your time,
   And while ye may, go marry;
For having lost but once your prime,
   You may forever tarry.

---

**CHERRY RIPE.**

CHERRY ripe, ripe, ripe, I cry,
   Full and fair ones — come and buy;
If so be you ask me where
They do grow? — I answer, There,
Where my Julia's lips do smile —
There's the land, or cherry-isle;
Whose plantations fully show
All the year where cherries grow.

## TO DAFFODILS.

Fair daffodils, we weep to see
    You haste away so soon:
As yet the early-rising Sun
    Has not attain'd his noon.
        Stay, stay,
    Until the hasting day
        Has run
    But to the even-song;
And, having pray'd together, we
    Will go with you along.

We have short time to stay, as you,
    We have as short a Spring;
As quick a growth to meet decay
    As you, or any thing.
        We die,
    As your hours do, and dry
        Away
    Like to the Summer's rain;
Or as the pearls of morning's dew
    Ne'er to be found again.

---

## TO BLOSSOMS.

Fair pledges of a fruitful tree,
    Why do ye fall so fast?
    Your date is not so past,
But you may stay yet here awhile
    To blush and gently smile,
        And go at last.

What, were ye born to be
　　An hour or half's delight,
　　And so to bid good-night?
'Twas pity Nature brought ye forth
　　Merely to show your worth,
　　　　And lose you quite.

But you are lovely leaves, where we
　　May read how soon things have
　　Their end, though ne'er so brave:
And after they have shown their pride
　　Like you, awhile, they glide
　　　　Into the grave.

---

### TO PRIMROSES,

#### FILLED WITH MORNING DEW.

WHY do ye weep, sweet babes? Can tears
　　Speak grief in you,
　　　Who were but born
　　　Just as the modest morn
　　Teemed her refreshing dew?
Alas! ye have not known that shower
　　That mars a flower;
　　　Nor felt th' unkind
　　　Breath of a blasting wind;
　　Nor are ye worn with years;
　　　Or warped, as we,
　　　Who think it strange to see
Such pretty flowers, like to orphans young,
Speaking by tears before ye have a tongue.

Speak, whimpering younglings, and make known
  The reason why
   Ye droop and weep.
   Is it for want of sleep,
  Or childish lullaby?
Or, that ye have not seen as yet
  The violet?
   Or brought a kiss
   From that sweetheart to this?
  No, no; this sorrow, shown
  By your tears shed,
  Would have this lecture read:—
"That things of greatest, so of meanest worth,
Conceived with grief are, and with tears brought forth."

---

### Abraham Cowley.

#### THE EPICURE.

FILL the bowl with rosy wine,
 Around our temples roses twine,
And let us cheerfully awhile,
Like the wine and roses, smile.
Crown'd with roses, we contemn
Gyges' wealthy diadem.
To-day is ours; what do we fear?
To-day is ours; we have it here.
Let's treat it kindly, that it may
Wish at least with us to stay.
Let's banish business, banish sorrow;
To the gods belongs to-morrow.

## THE GRASSHOPPER.

HAPPY insect, what can be
 In happiness compar'd to thee?
Fed with nourishment divine,
The dewy morning's gentle wine!

Nature waits upon thee still,
And thy verdant cup does fill;
'Tis fill'd wherever thou dost tread,
Nature self's thy Ganymede.

Thou dost drink, and dance, and sing,
Happier than the happiest king!
All the fields which thou dost see,
All the plants belong to thee;

All that summer hours produce,
Fertile made with early juice.
Man for thee does sow and plough;
Farmer he, and landlord thou!

Thou dost innocently enjoy;
Nor does thy luxury destroy.
The shepherd gladly heareth thee,
More harmonious than he.

Thee country hinds with gladness hear,
Prophet of the ripen'd year!
Thee Phœbus loves, and does inspire;
Phœbus is himself thy sire.

To thee, of all things upon earth,
Life is no longer than thy mirth.
Happy insect! happy thou,
Dost neither age nor winter know.

But when thou'st drunk, and danced, and sung
Thy fill, the flowery leaves among
(Voluptuous and wise withal,
Epicurean animal!),

Satiated with thy summer feast,
Thou retir'st to endless rest.

---

## Edmund Waller.

### "GO, LOVELY ROSE!"

GO, lovely Rose!
   Tell her, that wastes her time and me,
  That now she knows,
When I resemble her to thee,
How sweet and fair she seems to be.

  Tell her that's young
And shuns to have her graces spied,
  That hadst thou sprung
In deserts, where no men abide,
Thou must have uncommended died.

Small is the worth
Of beauty from the light retired:
Bid her come forth,
Suffer herself to be desired,
And not blush so to be admired.

Then die! that she
The common fate of all things rare
May read in thee:
How small a part of time they share
That are so wondrous sweet and fair!

---

## OLD AGE AND DEATH.

THE seas are quiet when the winds give o'er;
So calm are we when passions are no more.
For then we know how vain it was to boast
Of fleeting things, too certain to be lost.
Clouds of affection from our younger eyes
Conceal that emptiness which age descries.

The soul's dark cottage, batter'd and decay'd,
Lets in new light through chinks that time has made:
Stronger by weakness, wiser men become,
As they draw near to their eternal home.
Leaving the old, both worlds at once they view,
That stand upon the threshold of the new.

## Andrew Marvell.

### THOUGHTS IN A GARDEN.

HOW vainly men themselves amaze
　To win the palm, the oak, or bays,
And their incessant labours see
Crown'd from some single herb or tree,
Whose short and narrow-vergèd shade
Does prudently their toils upbraid;
While all the flowers and trees do close
To weave the garlands of Repose.

Fair Quiet, have I found thee here,
And Innocence, thy sister dear?
Mistaken long, I sought you then
In busy companies of men:
Your sacred plants, if here below,
Only among the plants will grow:
Society is all but rude
To this delicious solitude.

No white nor red was ever seen
So amorous as this lovely green.
Fond lovers, cruel as their flame,
Cut in these trees their mistress' name:
Little, alas, they know or heed
How far these beauties her exceed!
Fair trees! where'er your barks I wound,
No name shall but your own be' found.

When we have run our passion's heat,
Love hither makes his best retreat:

The gods, who mortal beauty chase,
Still in a tree did end their race:
Apollo hunted Daphne so,
Only that she might laurel grow:
And Pan did after Syrinx speed,
Not as a nymph, but for a reed.

What wondrous life is this I lead!
Ripe apples drop about my head;
The luscious clusters of the vine
Upon my mouth do crush their wine;
The nectarine and curious peach
Into my hands themselves do reach;
Stumbling on melons, as I pass,
Ensnared with flowers, I fall on grass.

Meanwhile the mind from pleasure less
Withdraws into its happiness;
The mind, that ocean where each kind
Does straight its own resemblance find;
Yet it creates, transcending these,
Far other worlds, and other seas;
Annihilating all that's made
To a green thought in a green shade.

Here, at the fountain's sliding foot,
Or at some fruit-tree's mossy root,
Casting the body's vest aside,
My soul into the boughs does glide;
There, like a bird, it sits and sings,
Then whets and claps its silver wings,
And, till prepared for longer flight,
Waves in its plumes the various light.

Such was the happy garden state,
While man there walked without a mate:
After a place so pure and sweet,
What other help could yet be meet?
But 'twas beyond a mortal's share
To wander solitary there:
Two paradises are in one,
To live in paradise alone.

How well the skilful gard'ner drew
Of flowers, and herbs, this dial new!
Where, from above, the milder sun
Does through a fragrant zodiac run:
And, as it works, th' industrious bee
Computes its time as well as we.
How could such sweet and wholesome hours
Be reckoned, but with herbs and flowers?

---

## John Milton.

### LYCIDAS.

YET once more, O ye laurels, and once more
    Ye myrtles brown, with ivy never sere,
I come to pluck your berries harsh and crude,
And with forced fingers rude
Shatter your leaves before the mellowing year.
Bitter constraint, and sad occasion dear
Compels me to disturb your season due:
For Lycidas is dead, dead ere his prime,
Young Lycidas, and hath not left his peer:

Who would not sing for Lycidas? he knew
Himself to sing, and build the lofty rhyme.
He must not float upon his watery bier
Unwept, and welter to the parching wind,
Without the meed of some melodious tear.

   Begin then, Sisters of the sacred well
That from beneath the seat of Jove doth spring,—
Begin, and somewhat loudly sweep the string;
Hence with denial vain and coy excuse;
So may some gentle Muse
With lucky words favour my destined urn;
And, as he passes, turn
And bid fair peace be to my sable shroud.

   For we were nursed upon the self-same hill,
Fed the same flock by fountain, shade, and rill.
Together both, ere the high lawns appear'd
Under the opening eyelids of the morn,
We drove a-field, and both together heard
What time the gray fly winds her sultry horn,
Battening our flocks with the fresh dews of night;
Oft till the star, that rose at evening bright,
Toward heaven's descent had sloped his westering wheel.
Meanwhile the rural ditties were not mute,
Temper'd to the oaten flute;
Rough Satyrs danced, and Fauns with cloven heel
From the glad sound would not be absent long;
And old Damoetas loved to hear our song.

   But, O the heavy change, now thou art gone,
Now thou art gone, and never must return!
Thee, Shepherd, thee the woods, and desert caves

With wild thyme and the gadding vine o'ergrown,
And all their echoes, mourn:
The willows and the hazel copses green
Shall now no more be seen
Fanning their joyous leaves to thy soft lays:—
As killing as the canker to the rose,
Or taint-worm to the weanling herds that graze,
Or frost to flowers, that their gay wardrobe wear
When first the white thorn blows;
Such, Lycidas, thy loss to shepherds' ear.

Where were ye, Nymphs, when the remorseless deep
Closed o'er the head of your loved Lycidas?
For neither were ye playing on the steep
Where your old bards, the famous Druids, lie,
Nor on the shaggy top of Mona high,
Nor yet where Deva spreads her wizard stream:
Ay me! I fondly dream—
Had ye been there—for what could that have done?
What could the Muse herself that Orpheus bore,
The Muse herself, for her enchanting son,
Whom universal nature did lament,
When by the rout that made the hideous roar
His gory visage down the stream was sent,
Down the swift Hebrus to the Lesbian shore?

Alas! what boots it with incessant care
To tend the homely, slighted, shepherd's trade,
And strictly meditate the thankless Muse?
Were it not better done, as others use,
To sport with Amaryllis in the shade,
Or with the tangles of Neaera's hair?

Fame is the spur that the clear spirit doth raise
(That last infirmity of noble mind)
To scorn delights, and live laborious days:
But the fair guerdon when we hope to find,
And think to burst out into sudden blaze,
Comes the blind Fury with the abhorrèd shears
And slits the thin-spun life.  "But not the praise,"
Phœbus replied, and touch'd my trembling ears;
"Fame is no plant that grows on mortal soil,
Nor in the glistering foil
Set off to the world, nor in broad rumour lies:
But lives and spreads aloft by those pure eyes
And perfect witness of all-judging Jove;
As he pronounces lastly on each deed,
Of so much fame in heaven expect thy meed."

O fountain Arethuse, and thou honour'd flood
Smooth-sliding Mincius, crown'd with vocal reeds!
That strain I heard was of a higher mood:
But now my oat proceeds,
And listens to the herald of the sea
That came in Neptune's plea;
He ask'd the waves, and ask'd the felon winds,
What hard mishap hath doom'd this gentle swain?
And question'd every gust of rugged wings
That blows from off each beakèd promontory:
They knew not of his story;
And sage Hippotadés their answer brings,
That not a blast was from his dungeon stray'd;
The air was calm, and on the level brine
Sleek Panopé with all her sisters play'd.
It was that fatal and perfidious bark

Built in the eclipse, and rigg'd with curses dark,
That sunk so low that sacred head of thine.

   Next Camus, reverend sire, went footing slow,
His mantle hairy, and his bonnet sedge
Inwrought with figures dim, and on the edge
Like to that sanguine flower inscribed with woe:
" Ah! who hath reft," quoth he, " my dearest pledge?"
Last came, and last did go
The pilot of the Galilean lake;
Two massy keys he bore of metals twain
(The golden opes, the iron shuts amain);
He shook his mitred locks, and stern bespake:
" How well could I have spared for thee, young swain,
Enow of such, as for their bellies' sake
Creep and intrude and climb into the fold!
Of other care they little reckoning make
Than how to scramble at the shearers' feast,
And shove away the worthy bidden guest;
Blind mouths! that scarce themselves know how to hold
A sheep-hook, or have learn'd aught else the least
That to the faithful herdman's art belongs!
What recks it them? What need they? They are sped;
And when they list, their lean and flashy songs
Grate on their scrannel pipes of wretched straw;
The hungry sheep look up, and are not fed,
But swoln with wind and the rank mist they draw,
Rot inwardly, and foul contagion spread:
Besides what the grim wolf with privy paw
Daily devours apace, and nothing said:
—But that two-handed engine at the door
Stands ready to smite once, and smite no more "

Return, Alphéus, the dread voice is past
That shrunk thy streams; return, Sicilian Muse,
And call the vales, and bid them hither cast
Their bells and flowerets of a thousand hues.
Ye valleys low, where the mild whispers use
Of shades, and wanton winds, and gushing brooks
On whose fresh lap the swart star sparely looks;
Throw hither all your quaint enamell'd eyes
That on the green turf suck the honey'd showers
And purple all the ground with vernal flowers.
Bring the rathe primrose that forsaken dies,
The tufted crow-toe, and pale jessamine,
The white pink, and the pansy freak'd with jet,
The glowing violet,
The musk-rose, and the well-attired woodbine,
With cowslips wan that hang the pensive head,
And every flower that sad embroidery wears:
Bid amarantus all his beauty shed,
And daffodillies fill their cups with tears
To strew the laureat hearse where Lycid lies.
For, so to interpose a little ease,
Let our frail thoughts dally with false surmise;
Ay me! whilst thee the shores and sounding seas
Wash far away,—where'er thy bones are hurl'd,
Whether beyond the stormy Hebrides,
Where thou, perhaps, under the whelming tide,
Visitest the bottom of the monstrous world;
Or whether thou, to our moist vows denied,
Sleep'st by the fable of Bellerus old,
Where the great Vision of the guarded mount
Looks towards Namancos and Bayona's hold,—
—Look homeward, Angel now, and melt with ruth:
—And, O ye dolphins, waft the hapless youth!

Weep no more, woeful shepherds, weep no more,
For Lycidas, your sorrow, is not dead,
Sunk though he be beneath the watery floor;
So sinks the day-star in the ocean-bed,
And yet anon repairs his drooping head
And tricks his beams, and with new-spangled ore
Flames in the forehead of the morning sky:
So Lycidas sunk low, but mounted high
Through the dear might of Him that walk'd the waves;
Where, other groves and other streams along,
With nectar pure his oozy locks he laves,
And hears the unexpressive nuptial song
In the blest kingdoms meek of joy and love.
There entertain him all the saints above
In solemn troops, and sweet societies,
That sing, and singing, in their glory move,
And wipe the tears forever from his eyes.
Now, Lycidas, the shepherds weep no more;
Henceforth thou art the Genius of the shore
In thy large recompense, and shalt be good
To all that wander in that perilous flood.

Thus sang the uncouth swain to the oaks and rills,
While the still morn went out with sandals gray;
He touch'd the tender stops of various quills,
With eager thought warbling his Doric lay:
And now the sun had stretch'd out all the hills,
And now was dropt into the western bay:
At last he rose, and twitch'd his mantle blue:
To-morrow to fresh woods, and pastures new.

## L'ALLÉGRO.

HENCE, loathèd Melancholy,
   Of Cerberus and blackest Midnight born
In Stygian cave forlorn
   'Mongst horrid shapes, and shrieks, and sights unholy!
Find out some uncouth cell
   Where brooding darkness spreads his jealous wings
And the night-raven sings;
   There under ebon shades, and low-brow'd rocks
As ragged as thy locks,
   In dark Cimmerian desert ever dwell.

   But come, thou Goddess fair and free,
   In heaven 'yclep'd Euphrosyne,
   And by men, heart-easing Mirth,
   Whom lovely Venus at a birth
   With two sister Graces more
   To ivy-crownèd Bacchus bore:
   Or whether (as some sages sing)
   The frolic wind that breathes the spring
   Zephyr, with Aurora playing,
   As he met her once a-Maying—
   There on beds of violets blue
   And fresh-blown roses wash'd in dew
   Fill'd her with thee, a daughter fair,
   So buxom, blithe, and debonair.
     Haste thee, Nymph, and bring with thee
   Jest, and youthful jollity,
   Quips, and cranks, and wanton wiles,
   Nods, and becks, and wreathèd smiles

Such as hang on Hebe's cheek,
And love to live in dimple sleek;
Sport that wrinkled Care derides,
And Laughter holding both his sides:—
Come, and trip it as you go
On the light fantastic toe;
And in thy right hand lead with thee
The mountain nymph, sweet Liberty;
And if I give thee honour due
Mirth, admit me of thy crew,
To live with her, and live with thee
In unreprovèd pleasures free;
To hear the lark begin his flight
And singing startle the dull night
From his watch-tower in the skies,
Till the dappled dawn doth rise;
Then to come, in spite of sorrow,
And at my window bid good-morrow
Through the sweetbriar, or the vine,
Or the twisted eglantine:
While the cock with lively din
Scatters the rear of darkness thin,
And to the stack, or the barn-door,
Stoutly struts his dames before:
Oft listening how the hounds and horn
Cheerly rouse the slumbering morn,
From the side of some hoar hill,
Through the high wood echoing shrill.
Sometime walking, not unseen,
By hedge-row elms, on hillocks green,
Right against the eastern gate
Where the great Sun begins his state

Robed in flames and amber light,
The clouds in thousand liveries dight;
While the ploughman, near at hand,
Whistles o'er the furrow'd land,
And the milkmaid singeth blithe,
And the mower whets his scythe,
And every shepherd tells his tale
Under the hawthorn in the dale.

   Straight mine eye hath caught new pleasures
Whilst the landscape round it measures;
Russet lawns, and fallows gray,
Where the nibbling flocks do stray;
Mountains, on whose barren breast
The labouring clouds do often rest;
Meadows trim with daisies pied,
Shallow brooks, and rivers wide;
Towers and battlements it sees
Bosom'd high in tufted trees,
Where perhaps some Beauty lies,
The Cynosure of neighbouring eyes.

   Hard by, a cottage chimney smokes
From betwixt two aged oaks,
Where Corydon and Thyrsis, met,
Are at their savoury dinner set
Of herbs, and other country messes
Which the neat-handed Phillis dresses;
And then in haste her bower she leaves
With Thestylis to bind the sheaves;
Or, if the earlier season lead,
To the tann'd haycock in the mead.

   Sometimes with secure delight
The upland hamlets will invite,

When the merry bells ring round,
And the jocund rebecks sound
To many a youth and many a maid,
Dancing in the chequer'd shade;
And young and old come forth to play
On a sun-shine holy-day,
Till the live-long day-light fail:
Then to the spicy nut-brown ale,
With stories told of many a feat,
How faery Mab the junkets eat;
She was pinch'd, and pull'd, she said;
And he, by friar's lantern led;
Tells how the grudging Goblin sweat
To earn his cream-bowl duly set,
When in one night, ere glimpse of morn,
His shadowy flail hath thresh'd the corn
That ten day-labourers could not end;
Then lies him down the lubber fiend,
And, stretch'd out all the chimney's length,
Basks at the fire his hairy strength;
And crop-full out of doors he flings,
Ere the first cock his matin rings.

    Thus done the tales, to bed they creep,
By whispering winds soon lull'd asleep.

    Tower'd cities please us then
And the busy hum of men,
Where throngs of knights and barons bold
In weeds of peace high triumphs hold,
With store of ladies, whose bright eyes
Rain influence, and judge the prize
Of wit or arms, while both contend
To win her grace, whom all commend.

There let Hymen oft appear
In saffron robe, with taper clear,
And pomp, and feast, and revelry,
With mask, and antique pageantry;
Such sights as youthful poets dream
On summer eves by haunted stream.
Then to the well-trod stage anon,
If Jonson's learned sock be on,
Or sweetest Shakespeare, Fancy's child,
Warble his native wood-notes wild.

   And ever against eating cares
Lap me in soft Lydian airs
Married to immortal verse,
Such as the meeting soul may pierce
In notes, with many a winding bout
Of linkèd sweetness long drawn out,
With wanton heed and giddy cunning,
The melting voice through mazes running,
Untwisting all the chains that tie
The hidden soul of harmony;
That Orpheus' self may heave his head
From golden slumber, on a bed
Of heap'd Elysian flowers, and hear
Such strains as would have won the ear
Of Pluto, to have quite set free
His half-regain'd Eurydice.

   These delights if thou canst give,
Mirth, with thee I mean to live.

## IL PENSEROSO.

HENCE, vain deluding Joys,
　　The brood of Folly without father bred!
How little you bestead
　　Or fill the fixèd mind with all your toys!
Dwell in some idle brain,
　　And fancies fond with gaudy shapes possess
As thick and numberless
　　As the gay motes that people the sunbeams,
Or likest hovering dreams
　　The fickle pensioners of Morpheus' train.

　　But hail, thou goddess sage and holy,
Hail, divinest Melancholy!
Whose saintly visage is too bright
To hit the sense of human sight,
And therefore to our weaker view
O'erlaid with black, staid Wisdom's hue;
Black, but such as in esteem
Prince Memnon's sister might beseem,
Or that starr'd Ethiop queen that strove
To set her beauty's praise above
The sea nymphs, and their powers offended:
Yet thou art higher far descended:
Thee bright-hair'd Vesta, long of yore,
To solitary Saturn bore;
His daughter she; in Saturn's reign
Such mixture was not held a stain:
Oft in glimmering bowers and glades
He met her, and in secret shades

Of woody Ida's inmost grove,
While yet there was no fear of Jove.
   Come, pensive nun, devout and pure,
Sober, steadfast, and demure,
All in a robe of darkest grain
Flowing with majestic train,
And sable stole of cypress lawn
Over thy decent shoulders drawn:
Come, but keep thy wonted state,
With even step, and musing gait,
And looks commercing with the skies,
Thy rapt soul sitting in thine eyes:
There, held in holy passion still,
Forget thyself to marble, till
With a sad leaden downward cast
Thou fix them on the earth as fast:
And join with thee calm Peace, and Quiet,
Spare Fast, that oft with gods doth diet,
And hears the Muses in a ring
Aye round about Jove's altar sing:
And add to these retired Leisure
That in trim gardens takes his pleasure:—
But first, and chiefest, with thee bring
Him that yon soars on golden wing
Guiding the fiery-wheelèd throne,
The cherub Contemplatiòn;
And the mute Silence hist along,
'Less Philomel will deign a song
In her sweetest saddest plight,
Smoothing the rugged brow of Night,
While Cynthia checks her dragon yoke
Gently o'er the accustom'd oak.

—Sweet bird, that shunn'st the noise of folly,
Most musical, most melancholy!
Thee, chauntress, oft, the woods among
I woo, to hear thy even-song;
And missing thee, I walk unseen
On the dry smooth-shaven green,
To behold the wandering Moon
Riding near her highest noon,
Like one that had been led astray
Through the heaven's wide pathless way,
And oft, as if her head she bow'd,
Stooping through a fleecy cloud.
 Oft, on a plat of rising ground
I hear the far-off curfew sound
Over some wide-water'd shore,
Swinging slow with sullen roar:
Or, if the air will not permit,
Some still removèd place will fit,
Where glowing embers through the room
Teach light to counterfeit a gloom;
Far from all resort of mirth,
Save the cricket on the hearth,
Or the belman's drowsy charm,
To bless the doors from nightly harm.
 Or let my lamp at midnight hour
Be seen in some high lonely tower,
Where I may oft out-watch the Bear
With thrice-great Hermes, or unsphere
The spirit of Plato, to unfold
What worlds or what vast regions hold
The immortal mind, that hath forsook
Her mansion in this fleshly nook:

And of those demons that are found
In fire, air, flood, or under ground,
Whose power hath a true consent
With planet, or with element.
Sometime let gorgeous Tragedy
In scepter'd pall come sweeping by,
Presenting Thebes, or Pelops' line,
Or the tale of Troy divine;
Or what (though rare) of later age
Ennobled hath the buskin'd stage.

But, O sad Virgin, that thy power
Might raise Musaeus from his bower,
Or bid the soul of Orpheus sing
Such notes as, warbled to the string,
Drew iron tears down Pluto's cheek
And made Hell grant what Love did seek!
Or call up him that left half-told
The story of Cambuscan bold,
Of Camball, and of Algarsife,
And who had Canacé to wife
That own'd the virtuous ring and glass;
And of the wondrous horse of brass
On which the Tartar king did ride:
And if aught else great bards beside
In sage and solemn tunes have sung
Of turneys, and of trophies hung,
Of forests, and enchantments drear,
Where more is meant than meets the ear.

Thus, Night, oft see me in thy pale career,
Till civil-suited Morn appear,
Not trick'd and frounced as she was wont
With the Attic Boy to hunt,

But kercheft in a comely cloud
While rocking winds are piping loud,
Or usher'd with a shower still,
When the gust hath blown his fill,
Ending on the rustling leaves
With minute drops from off the eaves.
And when the sun begins to fling
His flaring beams, me, goddess, bring
To archèd walks of twilight groves,
And shadows brown, that Sylvan loves,
Of pine, or monumental oak,
Where the rude axe, with heavèd stroke,
Was never heard the nymphs to daunt
Or fright them from their hallow'd haunt.
There in close covert by some brook
Where no profaner eye may look,
Hide me from day's garish eye,
While the bee with honey'd thigh
That at her flowery work doth sing,
And the waters murmuring,
With such concert as they keep
Entice the dewy-feather'd Sleep;
And let some strange mysterious dream
Wave at his wings in aery stream
Of lively portraiture display'd,
Softly on my eyelids laid:
And, as I wake, sweet music breathe
Above, about, or underneath,
Sent by some spirit to mortals good,
Or the unseen Genius of the wood.
  But let my due feet never fail
To walk the studious cloister's pale,

And love the high-embowèd roof,
With antique pillars massy proof,
And storied windows richly dight
Casting a dim religious light:
There let the pealing organ blow
To the full-voiced quire below
In service high and anthems clear,
As may with sweetness, through mine ear,
Dissolve me into ecstasies,
And bring all Heaven before mine eyes.

 And may at last my weary age
Find out the peaceful hermitage,
The hairy gown and mossy cell
Where I may sit and rightly spell
Of every star that heaven doth show,
And every herb that sips the dew;
Till old experience do attain
To something like prophetic strain.

 These pleasures, Melancholy, give,
And I with thee will choose to live.

## Izaak Walton.

### THE ANGLER'S WISH.

I IN these flowery meads would be:
These crystal streams should solace me;
To whose harmonious bubbling noise
I, with my angle, would rejoice,
    Sit here, and see the turtle-dove
    Court his chaste mate to acts of love:

Or, on that bank, feel the west wind
Breathe health and plenty: please my mind,
To see sweet dew-drops kiss these flowers,
And then washed off by April showers;
    Here, hear my kenna sing a song:
    There, see a blackbird feed her young,

Or a laverock build her nest:
Here, give my weary spirits rest,
And raise my low-pitched thoughts above
Earth, or what poor mortals love.
    Thus, free from lawsuits, and the noise
    Of princes' courts, I would rejoice;

Or, with my Bryan and a book,
Loiter long days near Shawford brook;
There sit by him, and eat my meat;
There see the sun both rise and set;
There bid good morning to next day;
There meditate my time away;
    And angle on; and beg to have
    A quiet passage to a welcome grave.

# John Dryden.

### ALEXANDER'S FEAST.

'TWAS at the royal feast for Persia won
    By Philip's warlike son—
Aloft in awful state
The godlike hero sate
On his imperial throne;
His valiant peers were placed around,
Their brows with roses and with myrtles bound
(So should desert in arms be crown'd);
The lovely Thais by his side
Sate like a blooming Eastern bride
In flower of youth and beauty's pride:—
Happy, happy, happy pair!
None but the brave
None but the brave
None but the brave deserves the fair!

  Timotheus placed on high
Amid the tuneful quire
With flying fingers touch'd the lyre:
The trembling notes ascend the sky
And heavenly joys inspire.
The song began from Jove
Who left his blissful seats above—
Such is the power of mighty love!
A dragon's fiery form belied the god;
Sublime on radiant spheres he rode
When he to fair Olympia prest,
And while he sought her snowy breast;

Then round her slender waist he curl'd,
And stamp'd an image of himself, a sovereign of the world.
—The listening crowd admire the lofty sound!
A present deity! they shout around:
A present deity! the vaulted roofs rebound!
With ravish'd ears
The monarch hears,
Assumes the god;
Affects to nod
And seems to shake the spheres.

The praise of Bacchus then the sweet musician sung:
Of Bacchus ever fair and ever young:
The jolly god in triumph comes!
Sound the trumpets, beat the drums!
Flush'd with a purple grace
He shows his honest face:
Now give the hautboys breath; he comes, he comes!
Bacchus, ever fair and young,
Drinking joys did first ordain;
Bacchus' blessings are a treasure,
Drinking is the soldier's pleasure:
Rich the treasure
Sweet the pleasure,
Sweet is pleasure after pain.

Soothed with the sound, the king grew vain;
Fought all his battles o'er again,
And thrice he routed all his foes, and thrice he slew the
    slain!
The master saw the madness rise,
His glowing cheeks, his ardent eyes;

And while he Heav'en and Earth defied
Changed his hand and check'd his pride.
He chose a mournful Muse
Soft pity to infuse:
He sung Darius great and good,
By too severe a fate
Fallen, fallen, fallen, fallen,
Fallen from his high estate,
And weltering in his blood;
Deserted, at his utmost need,
By those his former bounty fed;
On the bare earth exposed he lies
With not a friend to close his eyes.

—With downcast looks the joyless victor sate,
Revolving in his alter'd soul
The various turns of Chance below;
And now and then a sigh he stole,
And tears began to flow.

 The mighty master smiled to see
That love was in the next degree;
'Twas but a kindred sound to move,
For pity melts the mind to love.
Softly sweet, in Lydian measures
Soon he soothed his soul to pleasures.
War, he sung, is toil and trouble,
Honour but an empty bubble,
Never ending, still beginning;
Fighting still, and still destroying;
If the world be worth thy winning,
Think, O think, it worth enjoying:

Lovely Thais sits beside thee,
Take the good the gods provide thee!
—The many rend the skies with loud applause;
So Love was crown'd, but Music won the cause.
The prince, unable to conceal his pain,
Gazed on the fair
Who caused his care,
And sigh'd and look'd, sigh'd and look'd,
Sigh'd and look'd, and sigh'd again:
At length with love and wine at once opprest
The vanquish'd victor sunk upon her breast.

Now strike the golden lyre again:
A louder yet, and yet a louder strain!
Break his bands of sleep asunder
And rouse him like a rattling peal of thunder.
Hark! hark! the horrid sound
Has raised up his head?
As awaked from the dead
And amazed he stares around.
Revenge, revenge, Timotheus cries,
See the Furies arise!
See the snakes that they rear
How they hiss in their hair,
And the sparkles that flash from their eyes!
Behold a ghastly band
Each a torch in his hand!
Those are Grecian ghosts, that in battle were slain
And unburied remain
Inglorious on the plain:
Give the vengeance due
To the valiant crew!

Behold how they toss their torches on high,
How they point to the Persian abodes
And glittering temples of their hostile gods.
—The princes applaud with a furious joy:
And the King seized a flambeau with zeal to destroy;
Thais led the way
To light him to his prey,
And like another Helen, fired another Troy!

—Thus, long ago,
Ere heaving bellows learn'd to blow,
While organs yet were mute,
Timotheus, to his breathing flute
And sounding lyre
Could swell the soul to rage, or kindle soft desire.
At last divine Cecilia came,
Inventress of the vocal frame;
The sweet enthusiast from her sacred store
Enlarged the former narrow bounds,
And added length to solemn sounds,
With Nature's mother-wit, and arts unknown before.
—Let old Timotheus yield the prize
Or both divide the crown;
He raised a mortal to the skies;
She drew an angel down!

## ODE TO SAINT CECILIA.

FROM Harmony, from heavenly Harmony
    This universal frame began:
When Nature underneath a heap
    Of jarring atoms lay
And could not heave her head,
The tuneful voice was heard from high;
    Arise, ye more than dead!
Then cold, and hot, and moist, and dry
In order to their stations leap,
    And music's power obey.
From harmony, from heavenly harmony
    This universal frame began:
    From harmony to harmony
Through all the compass of the notes it ran,
The diapason closing full in Man.

What passion cannot music raise and quell?
    When Jubal struck the chorded shell
    His listening brethren stood around,
    And, wondering, on their faces fell
    To worship that celestial sound.
Less than a God they thought there could not dwell
    Within the hollow of that shell
    That spoke so sweetly and so well.
What passion cannot Music raise and quell?

    The trumpet's loud clangor
        Excites us to arms,
    With shrill notes of anger
        And mortal alarms.

>     The double double double beat
>         Of the thundering drum
>     Cries, "Hark! the foes come;
>     Charge, charge, 'tis too late to retreat!"
>
>     The soft complaining flute
>     In dying notes discovers
>     The woes of hopeless lovers,
>     Whose dirge is whisper'd by the warbling lute.
>
>     Sharp violins proclaim
>     Their jealous pangs and desperation,
>     Fury, frantic indignation,
>     Depth of pains, and height of passion
>         For the fair disdainful dame.
>
>     But oh! what art can teach,
>     What human voice can reach
>         The sacred organ's praise?
>     Notes inspiring holy love,
>     Notes that wing their heavenly ways
>         To mend the choirs above.
>
>     Orpheus could lead the savage race,
>     And trees uprooted left their place
>         Sequacious of the lyre:
>     But bright Cecilia raised the wonder higher:
>     When to her Organ vocal breath was given
>     An Angel heard, and straight appear'd—
>         Mistaking Earth for Heaven!

*Grand Chorus.*

As from the power of sacred lays
   The spheres began to move,
And sung the great Creator's praise
   To all the blest above;
So when the last and dreadful hour
This crumbling pageant shall devour,
The trumpet shall be heard on high,
The dead shall live, the living die,
And Music shall untune the sky.

---

## Alexander Pope.

### MESSIAH.

YE nymphs of Solyma! begin the song—
   To heavenly themes sublimer strains belong.
The mossy fountains and the sylvan shades,
The dreams of Pindus and the Aonian maids,
Delight no more—O thou my voice inspire
Who touched Isaiah's hallowed lips with fire!
   Rapt into future times the bard began:
A virgin shall conceive—a virgin bear a son!
From Jesse's root behold a branch arise
Whose sacred flower with fragrance fills the skies:
Th' ethereal spirit o'er its leaves shall move,
And on its top descends the mystic dove.
Ye heavens! from high the dewy nectar pour,
And in soft silence shed the kindly shower!

The sick and weak the healing plant shall aid—
From storm a shelter, and from heat a shade.
All crimes shall cease, and ancient frauds shall fail;
Returning Justice lift aloft her scale,
Peace o'er the world her olive wand extend,
And white-robed Innocence from heaven descend.
Swift fly the years, and rise the expected morn!
O spring to light! auspicious babe, be born!
See, nature hastes her earliest wreaths to bring,
With all the incense of the breathing spring!
See lofty Lebanon his head advance;
See nodding forests on the mountains dance;
See spicy clouds from lowly Sharon rise,
And Carmel's flowery top perfumes the skies!
Hark! a glad voice the lonely desert cheers:
Prepare the way! a God, a God appears!
A God, a God! the vocal hills reply—
The rocks proclaim the approaching Deity.
Lo, earth receives Him from the bending skies!
Sink down, ye mountains; and ye valleys, rise!
With heads declined, ye cedars, homage pay!
Be smooth, ye rocks; ye rapid floods, give way!
The Saviour comes! by ancient bards foretold—
Hear Him, ye deaf; and all ye blind, behold!
He from thick films shall purge the visual ray,
And on the sightless eyeball pour the day;
'Tis He th' obstructed paths of sound shall clear,
And bid new music charm th' unfolding ear;
The dumb shall sing; the lame his crutch forego,
And leap exulting like the bounding roe.
No sigh, no murmur, the wide world shall hear—
From every face He wipes off every tear.

In adamantine chains shall Death be bound,
And hell's grim tyrant feel th' eternal wound.
As the good shepherd tends his fleecy care,
Seeks freshest pasture, and the purest air,
Explores the lost, the wandering sheep directs,
By day o'ersees them, and by night protects;
The tender lambs He raises in His arms—
Feeds from His hand, and in His bosom warms:
Thus shall mankind His guardian care engage—
The promised father of the future age.
No more shall nation against nation rise,
Nor ardent warriors meet with hateful eyes;
Nor fields with gleaming steel be covered o'er,
The brazen trumpets kindle rage no more;
But useless lances into scythes shall bend,
And the broad falchion in a ploughshare end.
Then palaces shall rise; the joyful son
Shall finish what his short-lived sire begun;
Their vines a shadow to their race shall yield,
And the same hand that sowed shall reap the field;
The swain in barren deserts with surprise
Sees lilies spring and sudden verdure rise;
And starts, amidst the thirsty wilds, to hear
New falls of water murmuring in his ear.
On rifted rocks, the dragon's late abodes,
The green reed trembles, and the bulrush nods;
Waste sandy valleys, once perplexed with thorn,
The spiry fir and shapely box adorn;
To leafless shrubs the flowery palms succeed,
And odorous myrtle to the noisome weed;
The lambs with wolves shall graze the verdant mead,
And boys in flowery bands the tiger lead;

The steer and lion at one crib shall meet,
And harmless serpents lick the pilgrim's feet.
The smiling infant in his hand shall take
The crested basilisk and speckled snake—
Pleased, the green lustre of the scales survey,
And with their forked tongue shall innocently play.
Rise, crowned with light, imperial Salem, rise!
Exalt thy towery head, and lift thy eyes!
See a long race thy spacious courts adorn;
See future sons, and daughters yet unborn,
In crowding ranks on every side arise,
Demanding life, impatient for the skies!
See barbarous nations at thy gates attend,
Walk in thy light, and in thy temple bend;
See thy bright altars thronged with prostrate kings,
And heaped with products of Sabean springs!
For Thee Idume's spicy forests blow,
And seeds of gold in Ophir's mountains glow.
See heaven its sparkling portals wide display,
And break upon thee in a flood of day!
No more the rising sun shall gild the morn,
Nor evening Cynthia fill her silver horn;
But lost, dissolved in thy superior rays,
One tide of glory, one unclouded blaze,
O'erflow thy courts; the Light Himself shall shine
Revealed, and God's eternal day be thine!
The seas shall waste, the skies in smoke decay,
Rocks fall to dust, and mountains melt away;
But fixed His word, His saving power remains;
Thy realm forever lasts, thy own Messiah reigns!

## THE UNIVERSAL PRAYER.

FATHER of all! in every age,
    In every clime adored—
By saint, by savage, and by sage—
    Jehovah, Jove, or Lord!

Thou great First Cause, least understood,
    Who all my sense confined
To know but this: that Thou art good,
    And that myself am blind;

Yet gave me, in this dark estate,
    To see the good from ill;
And, binding nature fast in fate,
    Left free the human will.

What conscience dictates to be done,
    Or warns me not to do,
This teach me more than hell to shun,
    That more than heaven pursue.

What blessings Thy free bounty gives
    Let me not cast away—
For God is paid when man receives;
    To enjoy is to obey.

Yet not to earth's contracted span
    Thy goodness let me bound,
Or think Thee Lord alone of man,
    When thousand worlds are round.

Let not this weak, unknowing hand
   Presume Thy bolts to throw,
And deal damnation round the land
   On each I judge Thy foe.

If I am right, Thy grace impart
   Still in the right to stay;
If I am wrong, O teach my heart
   To find that better way.

Save me alike from foolish pride
   Or impious discontent,
At aught Thy wisdom has denied,
   Or aught Thy goodness lent.

Teach me to feel another's woe,
   To hide the fault I see—
That mercy I to others show,
   That mercy show to me.

Mean though I am, not wholly so,
   Since quickened by Thy breath;
O lead me, wheresoe'er I go,
   Through this day's life or death.

This day be bread and peace my lot—
   All else beneath the sun
Thou know'st if best bestowed or not,
   And let Thy will be done.

To Thee, whose temple is all space,
   Whose altar, earth, sea, skies—
One chorus let all being raise!
   All nature's incense rise!

## THE DYING CHRISTIAN TO HIS SOUL.

Vital spark of heavenly flame,
    Quit, O quit this mortal frame!
Trembling, hoping, lingering, flying—
O the pain, the bliss of dying!
Cease, fond nature, cease thy strife,
And let me languish into life!

Hark! they whisper: angels say,
Sister spirit, come away!
What is this absorbs me quite,
Steals my senses, shuts my sight,
Drowns my spirits, draws my breath?
Tell me, my soul! can this be death?

The world recedes—it disappears;
Heaven opens on my eyes; my ears
With sounds seraphic ring:
Lend, lend your wings! I mount, I fly!
O Grave! where is thy victory?
O Death! where is thy sting?

## Joseph Addison.

### A HYMN.

WHEN all thy mercies, O my God,
    My rising soul surveys,
Transported with the view, I'm lost
    In wonder, love, and praise.

O how shall words with equal warmth
    The gratitude declare,
That glows within my ravish'd heart?
    But Thou canst read it there!

Thy providence my life sustain'd,
    And all my wants redrest,
When in the silent womb I lay,
    And hung upon the breast.

To all my weak complaints and cries
    Thy mercy lent an ear,
Ere yet my feeble thoughts had learnt
    To form themselves in prayer.

Unnumbered comforts to my soul
    Thy tender care bestow'd,
Before my infant heart conceived
    From whom those comforts flow'd.

When in the slippery paths of youth
    With heedless steps I ran,
Thine arm, unseen, convey'd me safe,
    And led me up to man.

Through hidden dangers, toils, and deaths,
    It gently cleared my way,
And through the pleasing snares of vice,
    More to be fear'd than they.

When worn with sickness, oft hast Thou
    With health renew'd my face;
And, when in sins and sorrows sunk,
    Revived my soul with grace.

Thy bounteous hand with worldly bliss
    Has made my cup run o'er;
And in a kind and faithful friend
    Has doubled all my store.

Ten thousand thousand precious gifts
    My daily thanks employ;
Nor is the least a cheerful heart
    That tastes those gifts with joy.

Through every period of my life
    Thy goodness I'll pursue;
And after death, in distant worlds,
    The glorious theme renew.

When nature fails, and day and night
    Divide thy works no more,
My ever-grateful heart, O Lord,
    Thy mercy shall adore.

Through all eternity, to Thee
    A joyful song I'll raise;
But O! eternity's too short
    To utter all thy praise.

## ODE: "THE SPACIOUS FIRMAMENT."

THE spacious firmament on high,
  With all the blue ethereal sky,
The spangled heavens, a shining frame,
Their great Original proclaim.
The unwearied sun, from day to day,
Does his Creator's power display;
And publishes to every land
The work of an almighty hand.

Soon as the evening shades prevail,
The moon takes up the wond'rous tale,
And nightly, to the listening earth,
Repeats the story of her birth;
Whilst all the stars, that round her burn,
And all the planets in their turn,
Confirm the tidings as they roll,
And spread the truth from pole to pole.

What though, in solemn silence, all
Move round this dark, terrestrial ball?
What though nor real voice nor sound
Amidst their radiant orbs be found?
In reason's ear they all rejoice,
And utter forth a glorious voice,
Forever singing as they shine,
" The hand that made us is divine!"

## John Gay.

### THE POET AND THE ROSE.

I HATE the man who builds his name
   On ruins of another's fame:
Thus prudes, by characters o'erthrown,
Imagine that they raise their own;
Thus scribblers, covetous of praise,
Think slander can transplant the bays.
Beauties and bards have equal pride,
With both all rivals are decried:
Who praises Lesbia's eyes and feature,
Must call her sister "awkward creature;"
For the kind flattery's sure to charm,
When we some other nymph disarm.
   As in the cool of early day
A poet sought the sweets of May,
The garden's fragrant breath ascends,
And every stalk with odour bends;
A rose he plucked, he gazed, admired,
Thus singing, as the muse inspired—
" Go, Rose, my Chloe's bosom grace;
   How happy should I prove,
Might I supply that envied place
   With never-fading love!
There, Phœnix-like, beneath her eye,
Involved in fragrance, burn and die.
   Know, hapless flower! that thou shalt find
     More fragrant roses there:
   I see thy withering head reclined
     With envy and despair!

If chance his mate's shrill call he hear,
    And drops at once into her nest.
The noblest captain in the British fleet
Might envy William's lips those kisses sweet.

O Susan, Susan, lovely dear,
    My vows shall ever true remain;
Let me kiss off that falling tear;
    We only part to meet again.
Change, as ye list, ye winds; my heart shall be
The faithful compass that still points to thee.

Believe not what the landsmen say,
    Who tempt with doubts thy constant mind:
They'll tell thee, sailors, when away,
    In every port a mistress find:
Yes, yes, believe them when they tell thee so,
For thou art present wheresoe'er I go.

If to fair India's coast we sail,
    Thy eyes are seen in diamonds bright,
Thy breath is Afric's spicy gale,
    Thy skin is ivory so white.
Thus every beauteous object that I view,
Wakes in my soul some charm of lovely Sue.

Though battle call me from thy arms,
    Let not my pretty Susan mourn;
Though cannons roar, yet safe from harms,
    William shall to his dear return.
Love turns aside the balls that round me fly,
Lest precious tears should drop from Susan's eye.

The boatswain gave the dreadful word,
    The sails their swelling bosom spread;
No longer must she stay aboard;
    They kissed, she sighed, he hung his head.
Her lessening boat unwilling rows to land:
Adieu! she cries; and waved her lily hand.

---

## Matthew Prior.

### THE GARLAND.

THE pride of every grove I chose,
    The violet sweet and lily fair,
The dappled pink and blushing rose,
    To deck my charming Chloe's hair.

At morn the nymph vouchsafed to place
    Upon her brow the various wreath;
The flowers less blooming than her face,
    The scent less fragrant than her breath.

The flowers she wore along the day,
    And every nymph and shepherd said,
That in her hair they look'd more gay
    Than glowing in their native bed.

Undress'd at evening, when she found
    Their odours lost, their colours past,
She changed her look, and on the ground
    Her garland and her eyes she cast.

That eye dropp'd sense distinct and clear
    As any muse's tongue could speak,
When from its lid a pearly tear
    Ran trickling down her beauteous cheek.

Dissembling what I knew too well,
    My love, my life, said I, explain
This change of humour; prithee tell
    That falling tear—what does it mean?

She sigh'd, she smiled; and to the flowers
    Pointing, the lovely mor'list said,
See, friend, in some few fleeting hours,
    See yonder, what a change is made.

Ah me! the blooming pride of May
    And that of beauty are but one;
At morn both flourish bright and gay,
    Both fade at evening, pale, and gone.

---

## John Pomfret.

### THE CHOICE.

IF Heaven the grateful liberty would give
  That I might choose my method how to live;
And all those hours propitious Fate should lend,
In blissful ease and satisfaction spend;
Near some fair town I'd have a private seat,
Built uniform, not little, nor too great;
Better, if on a rising ground it stood;
On this side fields, on that a neighbouring wood.
It should within no other things contain

But what are useful, necessary, plain;
Methinks 'tis nauseous, and I'd ne'er endure
The needless pomp of gaudy furniture.
A little garden, grateful to the eye:
And a cool rivulet run murmuring by:
On whose delicious banks a stately row
Of shady limes, or sycamores, should grow.
At the end of which a silent study placed,
Should be with all the noblest authors graced:
Horace and Virgil, in whose mighty lines
Immortal wit and solid learning shines;
Sharp Juvenal, and amorous Ovid too,
Who all the turns of love's soft passion knew:
He that with judgment reads his charming lines,
In which strong art with stronger nature joins,
Must grant his fancy does the best excel;
His thoughts so tender, and express'd so well:
With all those moderns, men of steady sense,
Esteem'd for learning, and for eloquence.
In some of these, as fancy should advise,
I'd always take my morning exercise:
For sure no minutes bring us more content,
Than those in pleasing, useful studies spent.

I'd have a clear and competent estate,
That I might live genteelly, but not great:
As much as I could moderately spend;
A little more, sometimes t' oblige a friend.
Nor should the sons of poverty repine
Too much at fortune, they should taste of mine;
And all that objects of true pity were,
Should be relieved with what my wants could spare;
For that our Maker has too largely given,

Should be return'd in gratitude to Heaven;
A frugal plenty should my table spread;
With healthy, not luxurious dishes fed:
Enough to satisfy and something more,
To feed the stranger, and the neighbouring poor.
Strong meat indulges vice, and pampering food
Creates diseases, and inflames the blood.
But what's sufficient to make nature strong,
And the bright lamp of life continue long,
I'd freely take; and, as I did possess,
The bounteous Author of my plenty bless.

I'd have a little vault, but always stored
With the best wines each vintage could afford;
Wine whets the wit, improves its native force,
And gives a pleasant flavour to discourse;
By making all our spirits debonair,
Throws off the lees, the sediment of care.
But as the greatest blessing Heaven lends
May be debauch'd, and serve ignoble ends:
So, but too oft, the grape's refreshing juice
Does many mischievous effects produce.
My house should no such rude disorders know,
As from high drinking consequently flow;
Nor would I use what was so kindly given,
To the dishonour of indulgent Heaven.
If any neighbour came, he should be free,
Used with respect, and not uneasy be,
In my retreat, or to himself or me.
What freedom, prudence, and right reason give,
All men may, with impunity, receive:
But the least swerving from their rule's too much;
For what's forbidden us, 'tis death to touch.

That life may be more comfortable yet,
And all my joys refined, sincere, and great;
I'd choose two friends, whose company would be
A great advance to my felicity:
Well born, of humours suited to my own,
Discreet, and men as well as books have known:
Brave, generous, witty, and exactly free
From loose behaviour, or formality:
Airy and prudent; merry, but not light;
Quick in discerning, and in judging right:
Secret they should be, faithful to their trust;
In reasoning cool, strong, temperate, and just;
Obliging, open, without huffing, brave;
Brisk in gay talking, and in sober, grave;
Close in dispute, but not tenacious; try'd
By solid reason, and let that decide;
Not prone to lust, revenge, or envious hate;
Nor busy meddlers with intrigues of state;
Strangers to slander, and sworn foes to spite;
Not quarrelsome, but stout enough to fight;
Loyal, and pious, friends to Cæsar; true
As dying martyrs, to their Maker too.
In their society I could not miss
A permanent, sincere, substantial bliss.
   Would bounteous Heaven once more indulge, I'd choose
(For who would so much satisfaction lose
As witty nymphs, in conversation, give)
Near some obliging modest fair to live:
For there's that sweetness in a female mind,
Which in a man's we cannot hope to find!
That by a secret, but a powerful art

Winds up the spring of life, and does impart
Fresh vital heat to the transported heart.
  I'd have her reason all her passions sway:
Easy in còmpany, in private gay:
Coy to a fop, to the deserving free;
Still constant to herself, and just to me.
A soul she should have for great actions fit;
Prudence and wisdom to direct her wit:
Courage to look bold danger in the face;
No fear, but only to be proud, or base;
Quick to advise, by an emergence prest,
To give good council, or to take the best.
I'd have the expression of her thoughts be such,
She might not seem reserv'd, nor talk too much:
That shows a want of judgment and of sense;
More than enough is but impertinence.
Her conduct regular, her mirth refin'd;
Civil to strangers, to her neighbours kind:
Averse to vanity, revenge, and pride;
In all the methods of deceit untry'd:
So faithful to her friend, and good to all,
No censure might upon her actions fall:
Then would ev'n envy be compell'd to say,
She goes the least of woman-kind astray.
  To this fair creature I'd sometimes retire;
Her conversation would new joys inspire;
Give life an edge so keen, no surly care
Would venture to assault my soul, or dare,
Near my retreat, to hide one secret snare.
But so divine, so noble a repast
I'd seldom, and with moderation, taste,
For highest cordials all their virtue lose,

By a too frequent and too bold a use;
And what would cheer the spirits in distress,
Ruins our health, when taken to excess.
   I'd be concern'd in no litigious jar,
Belov'd by all, not vainly popular.
Whate'er assistance I had power to bring,
T' oblige my country, or to serve my king,
Whene'er they call'd, I'd readily afford,
My tongue, my pen, my counsel, or my sword.
Law-suits I'd shun, with as much studious care,
As I would dens where hungry lions are;
And rather put up injuries, than be
A plague to him, who'd be a plague to me.
I value quiet at a price too great,
To give for my revenge so dear a rate:
For what do we by all our bustle gain,
But counterfeit delight, for real pain?
   If Heaven a date of many years would give,
Thus I'd in pleasure, ease, and plenty live.
And as I near approach'd the verge of life,
Some kind relation (for I'd have no wife)
Should take upon him all my worldly care,
Whilst I did for a better state prepare.
Then I'd not be with any trouble vex'd,
Nor have the evening of my days perplex'd;
But by a silent and a peaceful death,
Without a sigh, resign my aged breath.
And when committed to the dust, I'd have
Few tears, but friendly, dropped into my grave;
Then would my exit so propitious be,
All men would wish to live and die like me.

## Thomas Parnell.

### THE HERMIT.

FAR in a wild, unknown to public view,
    From youth to age a reverend hermit grew;
The moss his bed, the cave his humble cell,
His food the fruits, his drink the crystal well;
Remote from men, with God he passed his days,
Prayer all his business, all his pleasure praise.
  A life so sacred, such serene repose,
Seemed heaven itself, till one suggestion rose—
That vice should triumph, virtue vice obey;
This sprung some doubt of Providence's sway;
His hopes no more a certain prospect boast,
And all the tenor of his soul is lost.
So, when a smooth expanse receives impressed
Calm nature's image on its watery breast,
Down bend the banks, the trees depending grow,
And skies beneath with answering colours glow;
But, if a stone the gentle sea divide,
Swift ruffling circles curl on every side,
And glimmering fragments of a broken sun,
Banks, trees, and skies, in thick disorder run.
To clear this doubt, to know the world by sight,
To find if books, or swains, report it right
(For yet by swains alone the world he knew,
Whose feet came wandering o'er the nightly dew),
He quits his cell; the pilgrim-staff he bore,
And fixed the scallop in his hat before;
Then, with the rising sun, a journey went,
Sedate to think, and watching each event.

The morn was wasted in the pathless grass,
And long and lonesome was the wild to pass;
But, when the southern sun had warmed the day,
A youth came posting o'er a crossing way;
His raiment decent, his complexion fair,
And soft in graceful ringlets waved his hair;
Then, near approaching, "Father, hail!" he cried,
And, "Hail, my son!" the reverend sire replied.
Words followed words, from question answer flowed,
And talk, of various kind, deceived the road;
Till each with other pleased, and loath to part,
While in their age they differ, join in heart.
Thus stands an aged elm in ivy bound,
Thus useful ivy clasps an elm around.

Now sunk the sun; the closing hour of day
Came onward, mantled o'er with sober gray;
Nature, in silence, bid the world repose,
When, near the road, a stately palace rose.
There, by the moon, through ranks of trees they pass,
Whose verdure crowned their sloping sides with grass.
It chanced the noble master of the dome
Still made his house the wandering stranger's home;
Yet still the kindness, from a thirst of praise,
Proved the vain flourish of expensive ease.
The pair arrive; the liveried servants wait;
Their lord receives them at the pompous gate;
The table groans with costly piles of food,
And all is more than hospitably good.
Then led to rest, the day's long toil they drown,
Deep sunk in sleep, and silk, and heaps of down.
At length 'tis morn, and, at the dawn of day,
Along the wide canals the zephyrs play;

Fresh o'er the gay parterres the breezes creep,
And shake the neighbouring wood to banish sleep.
Up rise the guests, obedient to the call,
An early banquet decked the splendid hall;
Rich luscious wine a golden goblet graced,
Which the kind master forced the guests to taste.
Then, pleased and thankful, from the porch they go;
And, but the landlord, none had cause of woe;
His cup was vanished; for in secret guise,
The younger guest purloined the glittering prize.

   As one who spies a serpent in his way,
Glistening and basking in the summer ray,
Disordered stops to shun the danger near,
Then walks with faintness on, and looks with fear;
So seemed the sire, when, far upon the road,
The shining spoil his wily partner showed.
He stopped with silence, walked with trembling heart,
And much he wished, but durst not ask to part;
Murmuring he lifts his eyes, and thinks it hard
That generous actions meet a base reward.
While thus they pass, the sun his glory shrouds,
The changing skies hang out their sable clouds;
A sound in air presaged approaching rain,
And beasts to covert scud across the plain.
Warned by the signs, the wandering pair retreat
To seek for shelter at a neighbouring seat.
'Twas built with turrets on a rising ground,
And strong, and large, and unimproved around;
Its owner's temper, timorous and severe,
Unkind and griping, caused a desert there.
As near the miser's heavy door they drew,
Fierce rising gusts with sudden fury blew;

The nimble lightning, mixed with showers, began,
And o'er their heads loud rolling thunders ran;
Here long they knock, but knock or call in vain,
Driven by the wind, and battered by the rain.
At length some pity warmed the master's breast
('Twas then his threshold first received a guest);
Slow creaking turns the door with jealous care,
And half he welcomes in the shivering pair;
One frugal faggot lights the naked walls,
And Nature's fervour through their limbs recalls;
Bread of the coarsest sort, with meagre wine,
(Each hardly granted), served them both to dine;
And when the tempest first appeared to cease,
A ready warning bid them part in peace.
With still remark, the pondering hermit viewed,
In one so rich, a life so poor and rude;
And why should such (within himself he cried)
Lock the lost wealth a thousand want beside?
But what new marks of wonder soon take place
In every settling feature of his face,
When, from his vest, the young companion bore
That cup, the generous landlord owned before,
And paid profusely with the precious bowl,
The stinted kindness of this churlish soul!

  But now the clouds in airy tumult fly;
The sun emerging, opes an azure sky;
A fresher green the smelling leaves display,
And, glittering as they tremble, cheer the day:
The weather courts them from their poor retreat,
And the glad master bolts the weary gate.
While hence they walk, the pilgrim's bosom wrought
With all the travail of uncertain thought:

His partner's acts without their cause appear;
'Twas there a vice, and seemed a madness here:
Detesting that, and pitying this, he goes,
Lost and confounded with the various shows.
Now night's dim shades again involve the sky;
Again the wanderers want a place to lie;
Again they search, and find a lodging nigh.
The soil improved around, the mansion neat,
And neither poorly low, nor idly great;
It seemed to speak its master's turn of mind;
Content, and not for praise, but virtue, kind.
Hither the walkers turn their weary feet,
Then bless the mansion, and the master greet.
Their greeting fair, bestowed with modest guise,
The courteous master hears, and thus replies:—

"Without a vain, without a grudging heart,
To him who gives us all, I yield a part;
From him you come, for him accept it here,
A frank and sober, more than costly cheer!"
He spoke, and bid the welcome table spread,
Then talked of virtue till the time of bed;
When the grave household round his hall repair,
Warned by a bell, and close the hours with prayer.
At length the world, renewed by calm repose,
Was strong for toil; the dappled morn arose;
Before the pilgrims part, the younger crept
Near a closed cradle, where an infant slept,
And writhed his neck: the landlord's little pride,
O strange return! grew black, and gasped, and died!
Horror of horrors! what! his only son!
How looked our hermit when the fact was done!

Not hell, though hell's black jaws in sunder part,
And breathe blue fire, could more assault his heart.
  Confused, and struck with silence at the deed,
He flies, but trembling, fails to fly with speed;
His steps the youth pursues: the country lay
Perplexed with roads; a servant showed the way;
A river crossed the path; the passage o'er
Was nice to find; the servant trod before;
Long arms of oaks an open bridge supplied,
And deep the waves beneath them bending glide.
The youth, who seemed to watch a time to sin,
Approached the careless guide, and thrust him in;
Plunging he falls, and rising, lifts his head,
Then flashing turns, and sinks among the dead.
  While sparkling rage inflames the father's eyes,
He bursts the bands of fear, and madly cries,
"Detested wretch!"—but scarce his speech began,
When the strange partner seemed no longer man!
His youthful face grew more serenely sweet;
His robe turned white, and flowed upon his feet;
Fair rounds of radiant points invest his hair;
Celestial odours breathe through purpled air;
And wings, whose colours glittered on the day,
Wide at his back their gradual plumes display.
The form ethereal bursts upon his sight,
And moves in all the majesty of light.
Though loud at first the pilgrim's passion grew,
Sudden he gazed, and wist not what to do;
Surprise, in secret chains, his words suspends,
And in a calm, his settling temper ends,
But silence here the beauteous angel broke
(The voice of Music ravish'd as he spoke):—

"Thy prayer, thy praise, thy life to vice unknown,
In sweet memorial rise before the throne:
These charms success in our bright region find,
And force an angel down to calm thy mind;
For this commissioned, I forsook the sky:
Nay, cease to kneel — thy fellow servant I.
Then know the truth of government divine,
And let these scruples be no longer thine.
The Maker justly claims that world he made;
In this the right of Providence is laid;
Its sacred majesty through all depends
On using second means to works his ends:
'Tis thus, withdrawn in state from human eye,
The power exerts his attributes on high;
Your action uses, nor controls your will,
And bids the doubting sons of men be still.
What strange events can strike with more surprise,
Than those which lately struck thy wondering eyes?
Yet, taught by these, confess the Almighty just,
And, where you can't unriddle, learn to trust.
The great vain man, who fared on costly food,
Whose life was too luxurious to be good;
Who made his ivory stands with goblets shine,
And forced his guests to morning draughts of wine;
Has, with the cup, the graceless custom lost,
And still he welcomes, but with less of cost.
The mean suspicious wretch, whose bolted door
Ne'er moved in pity to the wandering poor;
With him I left the cup, to teach his mind
That Heaven can bless, if mortals will be kind.
Conscious of wanting worth, he views the bowl,
And feels compassion touch his grateful soul.

Thus artists melt the sullen ore of lead,
With heaping coals of fire upon its head;
In the kind warmth the metal learns to glow,
And, loose from dross, the silver runs below.
Long had our pious friend in virtue trod,
But now the child half-weaned his heart from God;
(Child of his age) for him he lived in pain,
And measured back his steps to earth again.
To what excesses had his dotage run!
But God, to save the father, took the son.
To all but thee, in fits he seemed to go,
And 'twas my ministry to deal the blow.
The poor fond parent, humbled in the dust,
Now owns in tears the punishment was just.-
But how had all his fortunes felt a wrack,
Had that false servant sped in safety back?
This night his treasured heaps he meant to steal,
And what a fund of charity would fail!
Thus Heaven instructs thy mind: this trial o'er,
Depart in peace, resign, and sin no more."

  On sounding pinions here the youth withdrew,
The sage stood wondering as the seraph flew;
Thus looked Elisha, when, to mount on high,
His master took the chariot of the sky;
The fiery pomp ascending left the view;
The prophet gazed, and wished to follow too.

  The bending Hermit here a prayer begun,
"Lord, as in heaven, on earth thy will be done."
Then, gladly turning, sought his ancient place,
And passed a life of piety and peace.

## William Collins.

### ODE ON THE PASSIONS.

WHEN Music, heavenly maid, was young,
    While yet in early Greece she sung,
The Passions oft, to hear her shell,
Thronged around her magic cell—
Exulting, trembling, raging, fainting—
Possest beyond the Muse's painting;
By turns they felt the glowing mind
Disturbed, delighted, raised, refined;
Till once, 'tis said, when all were fired,
Filled with fury, rapt, inspired,
From the supporting myrtles round
They snatched her instruments of sound;
And, as they oft had heard apart
Sweet lessons of her forceful art,
Each (for Madness ruled the hour)
Would prove his own expressive power.

First Fear his hand, its skill to try,
    Amid the chords bewildered laid,
And back recoiled, he knew not why,
    E'en at the sound himself had made.

Next Anger rushed; his eyes, on fire,
    In lightnings owned his secret stings:
In one rude clash he struck the lyre,
    And swept with hurried hand the strings.

With woful measures wan Despair,
  Low, sullen sounds, his grief beguiled—
A solemn, strange, and mingled air;
  'Twas sad by fits, by starts 'twas wild.

But thou, O Hope, with eyes so fair—
  What was thy delightful measure?
Still it whispered promised pleasure,
  And bade the lovely scenes at distance hail!
Still would her touch the strain prolong;
  And from the rocks, the woods, the vale,
She called on Echo still, through all the song;
  And, where her sweetest theme she chose,
  A soft responsive voice was heard at every close;
And Hope enchanted, smiled, and waved her golden hair.

And longer had she sung—but, with a frown,
    Revenge impatient rose;
He threw his blood-stained sword in thunder down;
    And, with a withering look,
    The war-denouncing trumpet took,
And blew a blast so loud and dread,
Were ne'er prophetic sounds so full of woe!
    And, ever and anon, he beat
    The doubling drum, with furious heat;
And though sometimes, each dreary pause between,
    Dejected Pity, at his side,
    Her soul-subduing voice applied,
  Yet still he kept his wild, unaltered mien,
While each strained ball of sight seemed bursting from his head.

Thy numbers, Jealousy, to naught were fixed—
    Sad proof of thy distressful state;
Of differing themes the veering song was mixed;
And now it courted Love—now, raving, called on Hate.

With eyes upraised, as one inspired,
Pale Melancholy sate retired;
And, from her wild sequestered seat,
In notes by distance made more sweet,
Poured through the mellow horn her pensive soul;
    And, dashing soft from rocks around,
    Bubbling runnels joined the sound;
Through glades and glooms the mingled measure stole;
    Or, o'er some haunted stream, with fond delay,
        Round an holy calm diffusing,
        Love of Peace, and lonely musing,
    In hollow murmurs died away.

But O! how altered was its sprightlier tone
    When Cheerfulness, a nymph of healthiest hue,
Her bow across her shoulder flung,
    Her buskins gemmed with morning dew,
Blew an inspiring air, that dale and thicket rung—
    The hunter's call, to Faun and Dryad known!
The oak-crowned Sisters, and their chaste-eyed Queen,
    Satyrs, and sylvan boys, were seen,
    Peeping from forth their alleys green;
    Brown Exercise rejoiced to hear;
    And Sport leapt up, and seized his beechen spear.

Last came Joy's ecstatic trial:
He, with viny crown advancing,

First to the lively pipe his hand address;
But soon he saw the brisk awakening viol,
   Whose sweet entrancing voice he loved the best;
They would have thought, who heard the strain,
   They saw, in Tempe's vale, her native maids,
   Amidst the festal sounding shades,
To some unwearied minstrel dancing,
While, as his flying fingers kissed the strings,
Love framed with Mirth a gay fantastic round:
Loose were her tresses seen, her zone unbound;
   And he, amidst his frolic play,
   As if he would the charming air repay,
Shook thousand odours from his dewy wings.

   O Music! sphere-descended maid,
   Friend of Pleasure, Wisdom's aid!
   Why, goddess! why, to us denied,
   Lay'st thou thy ancient lyre aside?
   As, in that loved Athenian bower,
   You learned an all-commanding power,
   Thy mimic soul, O nymph endeared,
   Can well recall what then it heard;
   Where is thy native simple heart,
   Devote to Virtue, Fancy, Art?
   Arise, as in that elder time,
   Warm, energetic, chaste, sublime!
   Thy wonders, in that godlike age,
   Fill thy recording sister's page;
   'Tis said—and I believe the tale—
   Thy humblest reed could more prevail,
   Had more of strength, diviner rage,
   Than all which charms this laggard age—

E'en all at once together found—
Cecilia's mingled world of sound.
O bid our vain endeavours cease;
Revive the just designs of Greece!
Return in all thy simple state—
Confirm the tales her sons relate!

---

### DIRGE IN CYMBELINE,

##### SUNG BY GUIDERUS AND ARVIRAGUS OVER FIDELE, SUPPOSED TO BE DEAD.

TO fair Fidele's grassy tomb
   Soft maids and village hinds shall bring
Each opening sweet of earliest bloom,
   And rifle all the breathing Spring.

No wailing ghost shall dare appear,
   To vex with shrieks this quiet grove;
But shepherd lads assemble here,
   And melting virgins own their love.

No withered witch shall here be seen—
   No goblins lead their nightly crew;
The female fays shall haunt the green,
   And dress thy grave with pearly dew.

The redbreast oft, at evening hours,
   Shall kindly lend his little aid,
With hoary moss, and gathered flowers,
   To deck the ground where thou art laid.

When howling winds and beating rain
   In tempests shake the sylvan cell,
Or 'midst the chase, on every plain,
   The tender thought on thee shall dwell,

Each lonely scene shall thee restore,
   For thee the tear be duly shed;
Beloved till life can charm no more,
   And mourned till Pity's self be dead.

---

## "HOW SLEEP THE BRAVE."

How sleep the brave, who sink to rest
   By all their country's wishes blessed!
When Spring, with dewy fingers cold,
Returns to deck their hallowed mould,
She there shall dress a sweeter sod
Than Fancy's feet have ever trod.

By fairy hands their knell is rung;
By forms unseen their dirge is sung;
There Honour comes, a pilgrim gray,
To bless the turf that wraps their clay;
And Freedom shall awhile repair,
To dwell a weeping hermit there!

## Thomas Gray.

### ELEGY WRITTEN IN A COUNTRY CHURCHYARD.

THE curfew tolls the knell of parting day,
    The lowing herds wind slowly o'er the lea,
The ploughman homeward plods his weary way,
    And leaves the world to darkness and to me.

Now fades the glimmering landscape on the sight,
    And all the air a solemn stillness holds,
Save where the beetle wheels his drony flight,
    And drowsy tinklings lull the distant folds:—

Save that from yonder ivy-mantled tower,
    The moping owl does to the moon complain
Of such as, wand'ring near her secret bower,
    Molest her ancient solitary reign.

Beneath those rugged elms, that yew-tree's shade,
    Where heaves the turf in many a mould'ring heap,
Each in his narrow cell forever laid,
    The rude forefathers of the hamlet sleep.

The breezy call of incense-breathing morn,
    The swallow twittering from the straw-built shed,
The cock's shrill clarion, or the echoing horn,
    No more shall rouse them from their lowly bed!

For them no more the blazing hearth shall burn,
    Or busy housewife ply her evening care:
No children run to lisp their sire's return,
    Or climb his knees the envied kiss to share.

Oft did the harvest to their sickle yield,
   Their furrow oft the stubborn glebe has broke:
How jocund did they drive their team afield!
   How bow'd the woods beneath their sturdy stroke!

Let not ambition mock their useful toil,
   Their homely joys, and destiny obscure;
Nor grandeur hear with a disdainful smile
   The short and simple annals of the poor.

The boast of heraldry, the pomp of power,
   And all that beauty, all that wealth e'er gave,
Await alike th' inevitable hour,—
   The paths of glory lead—but to the grave!

Nor you, ye proud, impute to these the fault,
   If memory o'er their tombs no trophies raise,
Where through the long-drawn aisle and fretted vault,
   The pealing anthem swells the note of praise.

Can storied urn, or animated bust,
   Back to its mansion call the fleeting breath?
Can honour's voice provoke the silent dust?
   Or flattery soothe the dull, cold ear of death?

Perhaps, in this neglected spot, is laid
   Some heart once pregnant with celestial fire;—
Hands, that the rod of empire might have sway'd,
   Or waked to ecstasy the living lyre!

But knowledge to their eyes her ample page,
   Rich with the spoils of time, did ne'er unroll;
Chill penury repress'd their noble rage,
   And froze the genial current of the soul.

Full many a gem of purest ray serene,
   'The dark, unfathom'd caves of ocean bear;
Full many a flower is born to blush unseen,
   And waste its sweetness on the desert air.

Some village Hampden, that, with dauntless breast,
   The little tyrant of his fields withstood—
Some mute, inglorious Milton, here may rest—
   Some Cromwell, guiltless of his country's blood.

Th' applause of list'ning senates to command,
   The threats of pain and ruin to despise,
To scatter plenty o'er a smiling land,
   And read their history in a nation's eyes,

Their lot forbade: nor circumscribed alone
   Their growing virtues, but their crimes confined—
Forbade to wade through slaughter to a throne,
   And shut the gates of mercy on mankind;—

The struggling pangs of conscious truth to hide,
   To quench the blushes of ingenuous shame,
Or heap the shrine of luxury and pride
   With incense kindled at the Muse's flame.

Far from the madding crowd's ignoble strife,
   Their sober wishes never learn'd to stray;
Along the cool sequester'd vale of life
   They kept the noiseless tenor of their way.

Yet ev'n these bones from insult to protect,
   Some frail memorial, still erected nigh,
With uncouth rhymes and shapeless sculpture deck'd,
   Implores the passing tribute of a sigh.

Their name, their years, spell'd by th' unletter'd Muse,
    The place of fame and elegy supply;
And many a holy text around she strews,
    To teach the rustic moralist to die.

For who, to dumb forgetfulness a prey,
    This pleasing, anxious being, e'er resign'd,
Left the warm precincts of the cheerful day,
    Nor cast one longing, ling'ring look behind?

On some fond breast the parting soul relies,
    Some pious drops the closing eye requires;
Ev'n from the tomb the voice of Nature cries,
    Ev'n in our ashes live their wonted fires.

For thee, who, mindful of th' unhonour'd dead,
    Dost in these lines their artless tale relate;
If, 'chance, by lonely contemplation led,
    Some kindred spirit shall inquire thy fate,

Haply, some hoary-headed swain may say,
    "Oft have we seen him, at the peep of dawn,
Brushing with hasty steps the dew away,
    To meet the sun upon the upland lawn.

"There, at the foot of yonder nodding beech,
    That wreathes its old fantastic roots so high,
His listless length at noontide would he stretch,
    And pore upon the brook that babbles by.[1]

---

[1] Here, in his first MS., followed this stanza:—

    "Him have we seen the greenwood side along,
        While o'er the heath we hied, our labour done;
    Oft as the woodlark piped her farewell song,
        With wisful eyes pursue the setting sun."

"Hard by yon wood, now, smiling as in scorn,
   Mutt'ring his wayward fancies, he would rove;
Now drooping, woful, wan, like one forlorn,
   Or crazed with care, or cross'd in hopeless love.

"One morn, I miss'd him on th' accustom'd hill,
   Along the heath, and near his favourite tree;
Another came; nor yet beside the rill,
   Nor up the lawn, nor at the wood was he;

"The next—with dirges due, in sad array,
   Slow through the church-way path we saw him borne—
Approach, and read—for thou canst read—the lay,
   Graved on the stone beneath yon aged thorn."

### THE EPITAPH.[1]

Here rests his head upon the lap of earth,
   A youth, to fortune and to fame unknown:
Fair Science frown'd not on his humble birth,
   And Melancholy marked him for her own.

Large was his bounty, and his soul sincere;
   Heaven did a recompense as largely send:
He gave to Misery all he had,—a tear;
   He gained from Heaven—'twas all he wish'd—a friend.

---

[1] In the poem, as originally printed, the following beautiful stanza preceded the epitaph:—

   "There scattered oft, the earliest of the year,
      By hands unseen are showers of violets found:
   The redbreast loves to build and warble there,
      And little footsteps lightly print the ground."

It was afterwards omitted, because he thought it too long a parenthesis.

No farther seek his merits to disclose,
  Or draw his frailties from their dread abode—
(There they alike in trembling hope repose!)—
  The bosom of his Father and his God!

---

### HYMN TO ADVERSITY.

DAUGHTER of Jove, relentless power,
  Thou tamer of the human breast,
Whose iron scourge and torturing hour
  The bad affright, afflict the best!
Bound in thy adamantine chain
The proud are taught to taste of pain,
And purple tyrants vainly groan
With pangs unfelt before, unpitied and alone.

When first thy Sire to send on earth
  Virtue, his darling child, design'd,
To thee he gave the heavenly birth,
  And bade to form her infant mind.
Stern rugged Nurse! thy rigid lore
With patience many a year she bore:
What sorrow was, thou bad'st her know,
And from her own she learn'd to melt at others' woe.

Scared at thy frown terrific, fly
  Self-pleasing Folly's idle brood,
Wild Laughter, Noise, and thoughtless Joy,
  And leave us leisure to be good.

Light they disperse, and with them go
The summer Friend, the flattering Foe;
By vain Prosperity received
To her they vow their truth, and are again believed.

Wisdom in sable garb array'd
    Immersed in rapturous thought profound,
And Melancholy, silent maid,
    With leaden eye, that loves the ground,
Still on thy solemn steps attend:
Warm Charity, the general friend,
With Justice, to herself severe,
And Pity dropping soft the sadly-pleasing tear.

O, gently on thy suppliant's head
    Dread Goddess, lay thy chastening hand!
Not in thy Gorgon terrors clad,
    Not circled with the vengeful band
(As by the impious thou art seen)
With thundering voice, and threatening mien,
With screaming Horror's funeral cry,
Despair, and fell Disease, and ghastly Poverty:

Thy form benign, O Goddess, wear,
    Thy milder influence impart,
Thy philosophic train be there
    To soften, not to wound my heart.
The generous spark extinct revive,
Teach me to love and to forgive,
Exact my own defects to scan,
What others are to feel, and know myself a Man.

## Allan Ramsay.

### LOCHABER NO MORE.

FAREWELL to Lochaber! and farewell, my Jean,
  Where heartsome with thee I hae mony day been!
For Lochaber no more, Lochaber no more,
We'll maybe return to Lochaber no more!
These tears that I shed they are a' for my dear,
And no for the dangers attending on war,
Though borne on rough seas to a far bloody shore,
Maybe to return to Lochaber no more.

Though hurricanes rise, and rise every wind,
They'll ne'er make a tempest like that in my mind;
Though loudest of thunder on louder waves roar,
That's naething like leaving my love on the shore.
To leave thee behind me my heart is sair pained;
By ease that's inglorious no fame can be gained;
And beauty and love's the reward of the brave,
And I must deserve it before I can crave.

Then glory, my Jeany, maun plead my excuse;
Since honour commands me, how can I refuse?
Without it I ne'er can have merit for thee,
And without thy favour I'd better not be.
I gae then, my lass, to win honour and fame,
And if I should luck to come gloriously hame,
I'll bring a heart to thee with love running o'er,
And then I'll leave thee and Lochaber no more.

## James Thomson.

#### UNIVERSAL HYMN TO THE SEASONS.

THESE, as they change, Almighty Father, these
    Are but the varied God. The rolling year
Is full of Thee. Forth in the pleasing Spring
Thy beauty walks, Thy tenderness and love.
Wide flush the fields; the softening air is balm;
Echo the mountains round; the forest smiles;
And every sense, and every heart is joy.
Then comes Thy glory in the Summer-months,
With light and heat refulgent. Then Thy sun
Shoots full perfection through the swelling year:
And oft Thy voice in dreadful thunder speaks:
And oft at dawn, deep noon, or falling eve,
By brooks and groves, in hollow-whispering gales
Thy bounty shines in Autumn unconfin'd,
And spreads a common feast for all that lives.
In Winter, awful Thou! with clouds and storms
Around Thee thrown, tempest o'er tempest roll'd,
Majestic darkness! on the whirlwind's wing,
Riding sublime, Thou bidd'st the world adore,
And humblest Nature with Thy northern blast.

  Mysterious round! what skill, what force divine,
Deep felt, in these appear! a simple train,
Yet so delightful mix'd, with such kind art,
Such beauty and beneficence combin'd;
Shade, unperceiv'd, so softening into shade;
And all so forming an harmonious whole;
That, as they still succeed, they ravish still.

But wandering oft, with brute unconscious gaze,
Man marks not Thee, marks not the mighty hand,
That, ever busy, wheels the silent spheres;
Works in the secret deep; shoots, steaming, thence
The fair profusion that o'erspreads the Spring;
Flings from the sun direct the flaming day;
Feeds every creature; hurls the tempest forth;
And, as on earth this grateful change revolves,
With transport touches all the springs of life.

   Nature, attend! join, every living soul,
Beneath the spacious temple of the sky;
In adoration join; and, ardent, raise
One general song! To Him, ye vocal gales,
Breathe soft, whose Spirit in your freshness breathes;
Oh, talk of Him in solitary glooms,
Where, o'er the rock, the scarcely-waving pine
Fills the brown shade with a religious awe.
And ye, whose bolder note is heard afar,
Who shake th' astonish'd world, lift high to heaven
Th' impetuous song, and say from whom you rage.
His praise, ye brooks, attune, ye trembling rills;
And let me catch it as I muse along.
Ye headlong torrents, rapid, and profound;
Ye softer floods, that lead the humid maze
Along the vale; and thou, majestic main,
A secret world of wonders in thyself,
Sound his stupendous praise; whose greater voice
Or bids you roar, or bids your roarings fall.
Soft roll your incense, herbs, and fruits, and flowers,
In mingled clouds to Him; whose sun exalts,
Whose breath perfumes you, and whose pencil paints.
Ye forests bend, ye harvests wave, to Him;

Breathe your still song into the reaper's heart,
As home he goes beneath the joyous moon.
Ye that keep watch in heaven, as earth asleep
Unconscious lies, effuse your mildest beams,
Ye constellations, while your angels strike,
Amid the spangled sky, the silver lyre.
Great source of day! best image here below
Of thy Creator, ever pouring wide,
From world to world, the vital ocean round,
On Nature write with every beam His praise.
The thunder rolls! be hush'd the prostrate world!
While cloud to cloud returns the solemn hymn.
Bleat out afresh, ye hills: ye mossy rocks,
Retain the sound: the broad responsive low,
Ye valleys, raise; for the Great Shepherd reigns;
And his unsuffering kingdom yet will come.
Ye woodlands all, awake: a boundless song
Burst from the groves! and when the restless day,
Expiring, lays the warbling world asleep,
Sweetest of birds! sweet Philomela, charm
The listening shades, and teach the night His praise.
Ye chief, for whom the whole creation smiles,
At once the head, the heart, and tongue of all,
Crown the great hymn! in swarming cities vast,
Assembled men, to the deep organ join
The long-resounding voice, oft breaking clear,
At solemn pauses, through the swelling bass;
And, as each mingling flame increases each,
In one united ardour rise to heaven.
Or if you rather choose the rural shade,
And find a fane in every sacred grove;
There let the shepherd's flute, the virgin's lay,

The prompting seraph, and the poet's lyre,
Still sing the God of Seasons, as they roll.
For me, when I forget the darling theme,
Whether the blossom blows, the summer-ray
Russets the plain, inspiring Autumn gleams,
Or Winter rises in the blackening east;
Be my tongue mute, my fancy paint no more,
And, dead to joy, forget my heart to beat!
    Should fate command me to the furthest verge
Of the green earth, to distant barbarous climes,
Rivers unknown to song; where first the sun
Gilds Indian mountains, or his setting beam
Flames on th' Atlantic isles; 'tis naught to me:
Since God is ever present, ever felt,
In the void waste as in the city full;
And where He vital breathes there must be joy.
When even at last the solemn hour shall come,
And wing my mystic flight to future worlds,
I cheerful will obey; there, with new powers,
Will rising wonders sing: I cannot go
Where Universal Love not smiles around,
Sustaining all yon orbs, and all their suns;
From seeming evil still educing good,
And better thence again, and better still,
In infinite progression. But I lose
Myself in Him, in Light ineffable!
Come then, expressive Silence, muse His praise.
    6*

## LAVINIA.

THE lovely young Lavinia once had friends;
    And fortune smil'd, deceitful, on her birth.
For, in her helpless years depriv'd of all,
Of every stay, save innocence and Heaven,
She, with her widow'd mother, feeble, old,
And poor, liv'd in a cottage, far retir'd
Among the windings of a woody vale;
By solitude and deep surrounding shades,
But more by bashful modesty, conceal'd.
Together thus they shunn'd the cruel scorn
Which virtue, sunk to poverty, would meet
From giddy passion and low-minded pride:
Almost on Nature's common bounty fed;
Like the gay birds that sung them to repose,
Content, and careless of to-morrow's fare.
Her form was fresher than the morning-rose,
When the dew wets its leaves; unstain'd and pure,
As is the lily, or the mountain snow.
The modest virtues mingled in her eyes,
Still on the ground dejected, darting all
Their humid beams into the blooming flowers:
Or when the mournful tale her mother told,
Of what her faithless fortune promis'd once,
Thrill'd in her thought, they, like the dewy star
Of evening, shone in tears. A native grace
Sat fair-proportion'd on her polish'd limbs,
Veil'd in a simple robe, their best attire,
Beyond the pomp of dress; for loveliness
Needs not the foreign aid of ornament,

But is, when unadorn'd, adorn'd the most.
Thoughtless of beauty, she was beauty's self,
Recluse amid the close-embowering woods.
As in the hollow breast of Appenine,
Beneath the shelter of encircling hills,
A myrtle rises, far from human eye,
And breathes its balmy fragrance o'er the wild;
So flourish'd blooming, and unseen by all,
The sweet Lavinia; till, at length, compell'd
By strong Necessity's supreme command,
With smiling patience in her looks, she went
To glean Palemon's fields. The pride of swains
Palemon was, the generous, and the rich;
Who led the rural life in all its joy
And elegance, such as Arcadian song
Transmits from ancient uncorrupted times;
When tyrant custom had not shackled man,
But free to follow Nature was the mode.
He then, his fancy with autumnal scenes
Amusing, chanc'd beside his reaper train
To walk, when poor Lavinia drew his eye:
Unconscious of her power, and turning quick
With unaffected blushes from his gaze:
He saw her charming, but he saw not half
The charms her downcast modesty conceal'd.
That very moment love and chaste desire
Sprung in his bosom, to himself unknown;
For still the world prevail'd, and its dread laugh,
Which scarce the firm philosopher can scorn,
Should his heart own a gleaner in the field:
And thus in secret to his soul he sigh'd:—

"What pity! that so delicate a form,

By beauty kindled, where enlivening sense,
And more than vulgar goodness seem to dwell,
Should be devoted to the rude embrace
Of some indecent clown! She looks, methinks,
Of old Acasto's line: and to my mind
Recalls that patron of my happy life,
From whom my liberal fortune took its rise;
Now to the dust gone down; his houses, lands,
And once fair-spreading family, dissolv'd.
'Tis said that in some lone, obscure retreat,
Urg'd by remembrance sad, and decent pride,
Far from those scenes which knew their better days,
His aged widow and his daughter live,
Whom yet my fruitless search could never find.
Romantic wish! would this the daughter were!"

 When, strict inquiring, from herself he found
She was the same, the daughter of his friend,
Of bountiful Acasto; who can speak
The mingled passions that surpris'd his heart,
And through his nerves in shivering transport ran?
Then blaz'd his smother'd flame, avow'd, and bold;
And as he view'd her, ardent, o'er and o'er,
Love, gratitude, and pity, wept at once.
Confus'd, and frighten'd, at his sudden tears,
Her rising beauties flush'd a higher bloom,
As thus Palemon, passionate and just,
Pour'd out the pious rapture of his soul:

 "And art thou then Acasto's dear remains?
She whom my restless gratitude has sought
So long in vain? O heavens! the very same,
The soften'd image of my noble friend;
Alive his every look, his every feature,

More elegantly touch'd. Sweeter than Spring!
Thou sole surviving blossom from the root
That nourish'd up my fortune! say, ah where,
In what sequester'd desert, hast thou drawn
The kindest aspect of delighted Heaven?
Into such beauty spread, and blown so fair;
Though Poverty's cold wind, and crushing rain,
Beat keen and heavy on thy tender years?
O let me now, into a richer soil,
Transplant thee safe! where vernal sun and showers
Diffuse their warmest, largest influence;
And of my garden be the pride and joy!
Ill it befits thee, oh it ill befits
Acasto's daughter, his, whose open stores,
Though vast, were little to his ampler heart,
The father of a country, thus to pick
The very refuse of those harvest fields
Which from his bounteous friendship I enjoy.
Then throw that shameful pittance from thy hand,
But ill applied to such a rugged task!
The fields, the master, all, my fair, are thine;
If, to the various blessings which thy house
Has on me lavish'd, thou wilt add that bliss,
That dearest bliss, the power of blessing thee!"
   Here ceas'd the youth; yet still his speaking eye
Express'd the sacred triumph of his soul,
With conscious virtue, gratitude, and love,
Above the vulgar joy divinely rais'd.
Nor waited he reply. Won by the charm
Of goodness irresistible, and all
In sweet disorder lost, she blush'd consent.
The news immediate to her mother brought,

While, pierc'd with anxious thought, she pin'd away
The lonely moments for Lavinia's fate;
Amaz'd, and scarce believing what she heard,
Joy seiz'd her wither'd veins, and one bright gleam
Of setting life shone on her evening hours:
Not less enraptur'd than the happy pair:
Who flourish'd long in tender bliss, and rear'd
A numerous offspring, lovely like themselves,
And good, the grace of all the country round.

---

## David Mallet.

### WILLIAM AND MARGARET.

'TWAS at the silent solemn hour
    When night and morning meet;
In glided Margaret's grimly ghost,
    And stood at William's feet.

Her face was like an April morn
    Clad in a wintry cloud;
And clay-cold was her lily hand
    That held her sable shroud.

So shall the fairest face appear
    When youth and years are flown:
Such is the robe that kings must wear,
    When death has reft their crown.

Her bloom was like the springing flower,
    That sips the silver dew;
The rose was budded in her cheek,
    Just opening to the view.

But love had, like the canker-worm,
    Consumed her early prime;
The rose grew pale, and left her cheek—
    She died before her time.

Awake! she cried, thy true love calls,
    Come from her midnight grave:
Now let thy pity hear the maid
    Thy love refused to save.

This is the dark and dreary hour
    When injured ghosts complain;
When yawning graves give up their dead,
    To haunt the faithless swain.

Bethink thee, William, of thy fault,
    Thy pledge and broken oath!
And give me back my maiden-vow,
    And give me back my troth.

Why did you promise love to me,
    And not that promise keep?
Why did you swear my eyes were bright,
    Yet leave those eyes to weep?

How could you say my face was fair,
    And yet that face forsake?
How could you win my virgin heart,
    Yet leave that heart to break?

Why did you say my lip was sweet,
    And made the scarlet pale?
And why did I, young witless maid!
    Believe the flattering tale?

That face, alas! no more is fair,
    Those lips no longer red:
Dark are my eyes, now closed in death,
    And every charm is fled.

The hungry worm my sister is;
    This winding-sheet I wear:
And cold and weary lasts our night,
    Till that last morn appear.

But hark! the cock has warned me hence;
    A long and last adieu!
Come see, false man, how low she lies,
    Who died for love of you.

The lark sung loud; the morning smiled
    With beams of rosy red:
Pale William quaked in every limb,
    And raving left his bed.

He hied him to the fatal place
    Where Margaret's body lay;
And stretched him on the green-grass turf
    That wrapt her breathless clay.

And thrice he called on Margaret's name,
    And thrice he wept full sore;
Then laid his cheek to her cold grave,
    And word spake never more!

# John Logan.

### TO THE CUCKOO.

Hail, beauteous stranger of the grove!
    Thou messenger of Spring!
Now heaven repairs thy rural seat,
    And woods thy welcome sing.

Soon as the daisy decks the green,
    Thy certain voice we hear.
Hast thou a star to guide thy path,
    Or mark the rolling year?

Delightful visitant! with thee
    I hail the time of flowers,
And hear the sound of music sweet
    From birds among the bowers.

The schoolboy, wandering through the wood
    To pull the primrose gay,
Starts, thy most curious voice to hear,
    And imitates thy lay.

What time the pea puts on the bloom,
    Thou fliest thy vocal vale,
An annual guest in other lands,
    Another Spring to hail.

Sweet bird! thy bower is ever green,
    Thy sky is ever clear;
Thou hast no sorrow in thy song,
    No Winter in thy year.

Oh, could I fly, I'd fly with thee!
We'd make, with joyful wing,
Our annual visit o'er the globe,
Attendants on the Spring.

---

## Oliver Goldsmith.

EXTRACTS FROM "THE DESERTED VILLAGE."

SWEET Auburn! loveliest village of the plain,
Where health and plenty cheered the labouring swain,
Where smiling Spring its earliest visit paid,
And parting Summer's lingering blooms delayed!
Dear lovely bowers of innocence and ease—
Seats of my youth, when every sport could please!
How often have I loitered o'er thy green,
Where humble happiness endeared each scene!
How often have I paused on every charm—
The sheltered cot, the cultivated farm,
The never-failing brook, the busy mill,
The decent church that topt the neighbouring hill,
The hawthorn bush, with seats beneath the shade—
For talking age and whispering lovers made!
How often have I blessed the coming day,
When toil, remitting, lent its turn to play,
And all the village train, from labour free,
Led up their sports beneath the spreading tree;
While many a pastime circled in the shade,
The young contending as the old surveyed;
And many a gambol frolicked o'er the ground,
And sleights of art and feats of strength went round;

And still, as each repeated pleasure tired,
Succeeding sports the mirthful band inspired:
The dancing pair, that simply sought renown
By holding out, to tire each other down;
The swain, mistrustless of his smutted face,
While secret laughter tittered round the place;
The bashful virgin's sidelong looks of love,
The matron's glance that would those looks reprove:
These were thy charms, sweet village! sports like these,
With sweet succession, taught e'en toil to please;
These round thy bowers their cheerful influence shed;
These were thy charms—but all these charms are fled.

   Sweet-smiling village, loveliest of the lawn!
Thy sports are fled, and all thy charms withdrawn;
Amidst thy bowers the tyrant's hand is seen,
And desolation saddens all thy green;
One only master grasps the whole domain,
And half a tillage stints thy smiling plain;
No more thy glassy brook reflects the day,
But, choked with sedges, works its weedy way;
Along thy glades, a solitary guest,
The hollow-sounding bittern guards its nest;
Amidst thy desert walks the lapwing flies,
And tires their echoes with unvaried cries;
Sunk are thy bowers in shapeless ruin all,
And the long grass o'ertops the mouldering wall;
And, trembling, shrinking from the spoiler's hand,
Far, far away thy children leave the land.

   Ill fares the land, to hastening ills a prey,
Where wealth accumulates, and men decay;

Princes and lords may flourish, or may fade—
A breath can make them, as a breath has made;
But a bold peasantry, their country's pride,
When once destroyed, can never be supplied.

\* \* \* \*

Sweet Auburn! parent of the blissful hour,
Thy glades forlorn confess the tyrant's power.
Here, as I take my solitary rounds
Amidst thy tangling walks and ruined grounds,
And, many a year elapsed, return to view
Where once the cottage stood, the hawthorn grew,
Remembrance wakes with all her busy train,
Swells at my breast, and turns the past to pain.

\* \* \* \*

Sweet was the sound, when oft at evening's close
Up yonder hill the village murmur rose;
There, as I passed with careless steps and slow,
The mingling notes came softened from below:
The swain responsive as the milkmaid sung,
The sober herd that lowed to meet their young,
The noisy geese that gabbled o'er the pool,
The playful children just let loose from school,
The watch-dog's voice that bayed the whispering wind,
And the loud laugh that spoke the vacant mind.
These all in sweet confusion sought the shade,
And filled each pause the nightingale had made.
But now the sounds of population fail;
No cheerful murmurs fluctuate in the gale;
No busy steps the grass-grown footway tread—
But all the bloomy blush of life is fled.
All but one widowed, solitary thing,

That feebly bends beside the plashy spring;
She, wretched matron, forced in age, for bread,
To strip the brook with mantling cresses spread,
To pick her wintry fagot from the thorn,
To seek her nightly shed, and weep till morn—
She only left of all the harmless train,
The sad historian of the pensive plain.

   Ne'er yonder copse, where once the garden smiled,
And still where many a garden-flower grows wild,
There, where a few torn shrubs the place disclose,
The village preacher's modest mansion rose.
A man he was to all the country dear,
And passing rich with forty pounds a year;
Remote from towns he ran his godly race,
Nor e'er had changed, nor wished to change, his place;
Unskilful he to fawn, or seek for power
By doctrines fashioned to the varying hour;
Far other aims his heart had learned to prize—
More bent to raise the wretched than to rise.
His house was known to all the vagrant train;
He chid their wanderings, but relieved their pain.
The long-remembered beggar was his guest,
Whose beard, descending, swept his aged breast;
The ruined spendthrift, now no longer proud,
Claimed kindred there, and had his claims allowed;
The broken soldier, kindly bade to stay,
Sate by his fire, and talked the night away—
Wept o'er his wounds, or, tales of sorrow done,
Shouldered his crutch, and showed how fields were won.
Pleased with his guests, the good man learned to glow,
And quite forgot their vices in their woe;

Careless their merits or their faults to scan,
His pity gave ere charity began.

Thus to relieve the wretched was his pride,
And e'en his failings leaned to virtue's side;
But in his duty prompt at every call,
He watched and wept, he prayed and felt for all;
And, as a bird each fond endearment tries
To tempt its new-fledged offspring to the skies,
He tried each art, reproved each dull delay,
Allured to brighter worlds, and led the way.

Beside the bed where parting life was laid,
And sorrow, guilt, and pain, by turns dismayed,
The reverend champion stood.  At his control
Despair and anguish fled the struggling soul;
Comfort came down the trembling wretch to raise,
And his last faltering accents whispered praise.

At church, with meek and unaffected grace,
His looks adorned the venerable place;
Truth from his lips prevailed with double sway,
And fools, who came to scoff, remained to pray.
The service past, around the pious man,
With ready zeal, each honest rustic ran;
E'en children followed, with endearing wile,
And plucked his gown, to share the good man's smile.
His ready smile a parent's warmth expressed;
Their welfare pleased him, and their cares distressed;
To them his heart, his love, his griefs were given—
But all his serious thoughts had rest in heaven.
As some tall cliff that lifts its awful form,
Swells from the vale, and midway leaves the storm,

Though round its breast the rolling clouds are spread,
Eternal sunshine settles on its head.

   Beside yon straggling fence that skirts the way,
With blossomed furze unprofitably gay,
There, in his noisy mansion, skilled to rule,
The village master taught his little school.
A man severe he was, and stern to view—
I knew him well, and every truant knew;
Well had the boding tremblers learned to trace
The day's disasters in his morning face;
Full well they laughed, with counterfeited glee,
At all his jokes, for many a joke had he;
Full well the busy whisper, circling round,
Conveyed the dismal tidings when he frowned;
Yet he was kind—or, if severe in aught,
The love he bore to learning was in fault.
The village all declared how much he knew;
'Twas certain he could write, and cipher too;
Lands he could measure, terms and tides presage,
And e'en the story ran that he could gauge.
In arguing, too, the parson owned his skill,
For, e'en though vanquished, he could argue still;
While words of learned length and thundering sound
Amazed the gazing rustics ranged around;
And still they gazed, and still the wonder grew,
That one small head could carry all he knew.
But past is all his fame; the very spot,
Where many a time he triumphed, is forgot.

   Near yonder thorn, that lifts its head on high,
Where once the sign-post caught the passing eye,

Low lies that house where nut-brown draughts inspired,
Where graybeard mirth and smiling toil retired,
Where village statesmen talked with looks profound,
And news much older than their ale went round.
Imagination fondly stoops to trace
The parlour splendours of that festive place:
The whitewashed wall, the nicely-sanded floor,
The varnished clock that clicked behind the door,
The chest contrived a double debt to pay—
A bed by night, a chest of drawers by day,
The pictures placed for ornament and use,
The twelve good rules, the royal game of goose;
The hearth, except when winter chilled the day,
With aspen boughs, and flowers and fennel gay;
While broken tea-cups, wisely kept for show,
Ranged o'er the chimney, glistened in a row.

Vain, transitory splendour! could not all
Reprieve the tottering mansion from its fall?
Obscure it sinks, nor shall it more impart
An hour's importance to the poor man's heart;
Thither no more the peasant shall repair
To sweet oblivion of his daily care;
No more the farmer's news, the barber's tale,
No more the woodman's ballad shall prevail;
No more the smith his dusky brow shall clear,
Relax his ponderous strength, and lean to hear;
The host himself no longer shall be found
Careful to see the mantling bliss go round;
Nor the coy maid, half willing to be prest,
Shall kiss the cup to pass it to the rest.

Yes! let the rich deride, the proud disdain,
These simple blessings of the lowly train;
To me more dear, congenial to my heart,
One native charm than all the gloss of art:
Spontaneous joys, where nature has its play,
The soul adopts, and owns their first-born sway;
Lightly they frolic o'er the vacant mind,
Unenvied, unmolested, unconfined;
But the long pomp, the midnight masquerade,
With all the freaks of wanton wealth arrayed—
In these, ere triflers half their wish obtain,
The toiling pleasure sickens into pain;
And, e'en while fashion's brightest arts decoy,
The heart, distrusting, asks if this be joy.

Ye friends to truth, ye statesmen, who survey
The rich man's joys increase, the poor's decay!
'Tis yours to judge how wide the limits stand
Between a splendid and a happy land.
Proud swells the tide with loads of freighted ore,
And shouting Folly hails them from her shore;
Hoards, e'en beyond the miser's wish, abound,
And rich men flock from all the world around.
Yet count our gains: this wealth is but a name,
That leaves our useful products still the same.
Not so the loss: the man of wealth and pride
Takes up a space that many poor supplied—
Space for his lake, his park's extended bounds—
Space for his horses, equipage, and hounds;
The robe that wraps his limbs in silken sloth
Has robbed the neighbouring fields of half their growth;
His seat, where solitary sports are seen,

Indignant spurns the cottage from the green;
Around the world each needful product flies,
For all the luxuries the world supplies;
While thus the land, adorned for pleasure all,
In barren splendour, feebly waits the fall.

---

### RETALIATION.

OF old, when Scarron his companions invited,
Each guest brought his dish, and the feast was united;
If our ¹landlord supplies us with beef and with fish,
Let each guest bring himself, and he brings the best dish:
Our ²dean shall be venison, just fresh from the plains;
Our ³Burke shall be tongue, with the garnish of brains;
Our ⁴Will shall be wildfowl, of excellent flavour,
And ⁵Dick with his pepper shall heighten their savour:
Our ⁶Cumberland's sweetbread its place shall obtain,
And ⁷Douglas is pudding, substantial and plain;

---

¹ The master of the St. James's Coffee-house, where the Doctor, and the friends he has characterized in this poem, occasionally dined.

² Doctor Bernard, Dean of Derry, in Ireland.

³ Mr. Edmund Burke.

⁴ Mr. William Burke, late secretary to General Conway, and member for Bedwin.

⁵ Mr. Richard Burke, collector of Grenada.

⁶ Mr. Richard Cumberland, author of "The West Indian," "Fashionable Lover," "The Brothers," and other dramatic pieces.

⁷ Doctor Douglas, canon of Windsor, an ingenious Scotch gentleman, who has no less distinguished himself as a citizen of the world, than a sound critic, in detecting several literary mistakes (or rather forgeries) of his countrymen; particularly Lauder on Milton, and Power's "History of the Popes."

Our ⁸Garrick's a salad; for in him we see
Oil, vinegar, sugar, and saltness agree;
To make out the dinner, full certain I am
That ⁹Ridge is anchovy, and ¹⁰Reynolds is lamb.
That ¹¹Hickey's a capon, and, by the same rule,
Magnanimous Goldsmith a gooseberry fool.
At a dinner so various, at such a repast,
Who'd not be a glutton, and stick to the last?
Here, waiter, more wine! let me sit while I'm able,
Till all my companions sink under the table;
Then, with chaos and blunders encircling my head,
Let me ponder, and tell what I think of the dead.

¹²Here lies the good dean,¹³ reunited to earth,
Who mixt reason with pleasure, and wisdom with mirth:
If he had any faults, he has left us in doubt,
At least in six weeks I could not find 'em out;
Yet some have declared, and it can't be denied 'em,
That slyboots was cursedly cunning to hide 'em.

Here lies our good ¹⁴Edmund, whose genius was such,
We scarcely can praise it or blame it too much;
Who, born for the universe, narrow'd his mind,
And to party gave up what was meant for mankind.

---

⁸ David Garrick, Esq.
⁹ Counsellor John Ridge, a gentleman belonging to the Irish Bar.
¹⁰ Sir Joshua Reynolds.
¹¹ An eminent attorney, whose hospitality and good humour acquired him in his club the title of "Honest Tom Hickey."
¹² *Here lies the good dean.*] See a poem by Dean Bernard to Sir J. Reynolds, in Northcote's Life of Reynolds, p. 130.
¹³ Vide page 128.
¹⁴ Vide page 128.

Though fraught with all learning, yet straining his throat
To persuade [15]Tommy Townshend to lend him a vote;
Who, too deep for his hearers, still went on refining,
And thought of convincing, while they thought of dining:
Though equal to all things, for all things unfit;
Too nice for a statesman, too proud for a wit;
For a patriot too cool; for a drudge disobedient;
And too fond of the *right* to pursue the *expedient*.
In short, 'twas his fate, unemployed or in place, sir,
To eat mutton cold, and cut blocks with a razor.

Here lies honest [16]William, whose heart was a mint,
While the owner ne'er knew half the good that was in't;
The pupil of impulse, it forced him along,
His conduct still right, with his argument wrong;
Still aiming at honour, yet fearing to roam,
The coachman was tipsy, the chariot drove home:
Would you ask for his merits? alas! he had none;
What was good was spontaneous, his faults were his own.

Here lies honest Richard, whose fate I must sigh at;
Alas that such frolic should now be so quiet!
What spirits were his! what wit and what whim!
[17]Now breaking a jest, and now breaking a limb;
Now wrangling and grumbling to keep up the ball,
Now teasing and vexing, yet laughing at all!

---

[15] M. T. Townshend, member for Whitchurch.—See *H. Walpole's Letter to Lord Hertford*, p. 6

[16] Vide page 128.

[17] Mr. Richard Burke; vide page 128. This gentleman having slightly fractured one of his arms and legs, at different times, the Doctor has rallied him on those accidents, as a kind of retributive justice, for breaking his jests upon other people.

In short, so provoking a devil was Dick,
That we wished him full ten times a day at Old Nick;
But, missing his mirth and agreeable vein,
As often we wished to have Dick back again.

    Here [18] Cumberland lies, having acted his parts,
The Terence of England, the mender of hearts;
A flattering painter, who made it his care
To draw men as they ought to be, not as they are.
His gallants are all faultless, his women divine,
And comedy wonders at being so fine;
Like a tragedy queen he has dizened her out,
Or rather like tragedy giving a rout.
His fools have their follies so lost in a crowd
Of virtues and feelings, that folly grows proud;
And coxcombs, alike in their failings alone,
Adopting his portraits, are pleased with their own.
Say, where has our poet this malady caught,
Or wherefore his characters thus without fault?
Say, was it that vainly directing his view
To find out men's virtues, and finding them few,
Quite sick of pursuing each troublesome elf,
He grew lazy at last, and drew from himself?

    Here [19] Douglas retires from his toils to relax,
The scourge of impostors, the terror of quacks:
Come, all ye quack bards, and ye quacking divines,
Come, and dance on the spot where your tyrant reclines:
When satire and censure encircled his throne,
I feared for your safety, I feared for my own;

---

[18] Vide page 128.      [19] Vide page 128.

But now he is gone, and we want a detector,
Our [20] Dodds shall be pious, our [21] Kenricks shall lecture;
[22] Macpherson write bombast, and call it a style;
Our [23] Townshend make speeches, and I shall compile;
New [24] Lauders and Bowers the Tweed shall cross over,
No countryman living their tricks to discover;
Detection her taper shall quench to a spark,
[25] And Scotchman meet Scotchman, and cheat in the dark.

Here lies [26] David Garrick, describe me who can,
An abridgment of all that was pleasant in man;
As an actor, confest without rival to shine;
As a wit, if not first, in the very first line:
Yet, with talents like these, and an excellent heart,
The man had his failings, a dupe to his art.
Like an ill-judging beauty, his colours he spread,
And beplastered with rouge his own natural red.
On the stage he was natural, simple, affecting;
'Twas only that, when he was off, he was acting.
With no reason on earth to go out of his way,
He turned and he varied full ten times a day:
Though secure of our hearts, yet confoundedly sick
If they were not his own by finessing and trick.
He cast off his friends, as a huntsman his pack;
For he knew, when he pleased, he could whistle them back.

---

[20] The Rev. Dr. Dodd.

[21] Dr. Kenrick, who read lectures at the Devil Tavern, under the title of "The School of Shakespeare."

[22] James Macpherson, Esq., who lately, from the mere force of his style, wrote down the first poet of all antiquity.

[23] Vide page 130.   [24] Vide page 128.   [25] Vide page 129.

[26] "And gods meet gods, and jostle in the dark."
    See *Farquhar's Love in a Bottle*, vol. i. p. 150.

Of praise a mere glutton, he swallowed what came,
And the puff of a dunce he mistook it for fame;
Till his relish grown callous, almost to disease,
Who peppered the highest was surest to please.
But let us be candid, and speak out our mind,
If dunces applauded, he paid them in kind.
Ye [27] Kenricks, ye [28] Kellys, and [29] Woodfalls so grave,
What a commerce was yours, while you got and you gave!
How did Grub-street re-echo the shouts that you raised,
While he was be-Rosciused and you were bepraised!
But peace to his spirit, wherever it flies,
To act as an angel, and mix with the skies.
Those poets who owe their best fame to his skill,
Shall still be his flatterers, go where he will;
Old Shakespeare receive him with praise and with love,
And Beaumonts and Bens be his Kellys above.[30]

---

[27] Vide page 132.

[28] Mr. Hugh Kelly, author of "False Delicacy," "Word to the Wise," "Clementina," "School for Wives," &c., &c.

[29] Mr. William Woodfall, printer of the Morning Chronicle.

[30] The following poems, by Mr. Garrick, may in some measure account for the severity exercised by Dr. Goldsmith in respect to that gentleman:—

JUPITER AND MERCURY.

A FABLE.

Here, Hermes, says Jove, who with nectar was mellow,
Go fetch me some clay,—I will make an odd fellow.
Right and wrong shall be jumbled, much gold and some dross;
Without cause be he pleased, without cause be he cross:
Be sure, as I work, to throw in contradictions;
A great love of truth, yet a mind turned to fictions.
Now mix these ingredients, which, warmed in the baking,
Turn to learning and gaming, religion and raking.

Here [31] Hickey reclines, a most blunt, pleasant creature,
And slander itself must allow him good nature;
He cherished his friend, and he relished a bumper;
Yet one fault he had, and that one was a thumper.
Perhaps you may ask if the man was a miser:
I answer, No, no, for he always was wiser.
Too courteous, perhaps, or obligingly flat?
His very worst foe can't accuse him of that.
Perhaps he confided in men as they go,
And so was too foolishly honest?  Ah, no!
Then what was his failing? come, tell it, and burn ye:
He was — could he help it? — a special attorney.

Here [32] Reynolds is laid, and, to tell you my mind,
He has not left a wiser or better behind.

---

With the love of a wench, let his writings be chaste;
Tip his tongue with strange matter, his pen with fine taste.
   \*    \*    \*    \*    \*    \*
For the joy of each sex, on the world I'll bestow it,
This scholar, rake, Christian, dupe, gamester, and poet.
Though a mixture so odd, he shall merit great fame,
And among brother mortals be Goldsmith his name.
When on earth this strange meteor no more shall appear,
You, Hermes, shall fetch him to make us sport here.

---

### ON DR. GOLDSMITH'S CHARACTERISTICAL COOKERY.

#### A JEU D'ESPRIT.

Are these the choice dishes the Doctor has sent us?
Is this the great poet whose works so content us?
This Goldsmith's fine feast who has written fine books?
Heaven sends us good meat, but the devil sends cooks.

---

[3] Vide page 129.      [32] Vide page 129.

His pencil was striking, resistless, and grand;
His manners were gentle, complying, and bland:
Still born to improve us in every part,
His pencil our faces, his manners our heart.
To coxcombs averse, yet most civilly steering;
When they judged without skill, he was still hard of hearing;
When they talked of their Raphaels, Correggios, and stuff,
He shifted his [33] trumpet, and only took snuff.

### POSTSCRIPT.

AFTER the fourth edition of this poem was printed, the publisher received the following epitaph on Mr. Whitefoord,[34] from a friend of the late Dr. Goldsmith :—

HERE Whitefoord reclines, and deny it who can,
Though he merrily lived, he is now a [35] grave man;
Rare compound of oddity, frolic, and fun!
Who relished a joke, and rejoiced in a pun;
Whose temper was generous, open, sincere;
A stranger to flattery, a stranger to fear;
Who scattered around wit and humour at will;
Whose daily *bon mots* half a column might fill;
A Scotchman, from pride and from prejudice free;
A scholar, yet surely no pedant was he.

What pity, alas! that so liberal a mind
Should so long be to newspaper esssays confined!

---

[33] Sir Joshua Reynolds was so remarkably deaf as to be under the necessity of using an ear-trumpet in company.

[34] Mr. Caleb Whitefoord, author of many humorous essays.

[35] Mr. W. was so notorious a punster, that Dr. Goldsmith used to say it was impossible to keep him company, without being infected with the itch of punning.

Who perhaps to the summit of science could soar,
Yet content "if the table he set in a roar;"
Whose talents to fill any station were fit,
Yet happy if [26] Woodfall confessed him a wit.

Ye newspaper witlings! ye pert scribbling folks!
Who copied his squibs, and re-echoed his jokes;
Ye tame imitators, ye servile herd, come,
Still follow your master, and visit his tomb:
To deck it, bring with you festoons of the vine,
And copious libations bestow on his shrine;
Then strew all around it (you can do no less)
[27] *Cross readings, ship news, and mistakes of the press.*

Merry Whitefoord, farewell! for thy sake I admit
That a Scot may have humour, I had almost said wit:
This debt to thy memory I cannot refuse,
[28] "Thou best humoured man with the worst humoured muse."

---

[26] Mr. H. S. Woodfall, printer of the Public Advertiser.

[27] Mr. Whitefoord has frequently indulged the town with humorous pieces under those titles in the Public Advertiser. On C. Whitefoord, see *Smith's Life of Nollekens*, vol. i. p. 338–340. See his poem to Sir Joshua Reynolds, "Admire not, dear knight," in Northcote's Life of Reynolds, p. 128.

[28] "When you and Southern, Moyle, and Congreve meet,
      The best good men, with the best natured wit."
                C. *Hopkins.*  *v. Nicholls' Col. Poems,* ii. p. 207.

## Tobias Smollett.

### ODE TO LEVEN-WATER.

ON Leven's banks, while free to rove,
    And tune the rural pipe to love,
I envied not the happiest swain
That ever trod the Arcadian plain.
    Pure stream, in whose transparent wave
My youthful limbs I wont to lave;
No torrents stain thy limpid source,
No rocks impede thy dimpling course,
That sweetly warbles o'er its bed,
With white, round, polished pebbles spread;
While, lightly poised, the scaly brood
In myriads cleave thy crystal flood;
The springing trout in speckled pride,
The salmon, monarch of the tide;
The ruthless pike, intent on war,
The silver eel, and mottled par.
Devolving from thy parent lake,
A charming maze thy waters make,
By bowers of birch, and groves of pine,
And edges flowered with eglantine.
    Still on thy banks so gayly green,
May numerous herds and flocks be seen:
And lasses chanting o'er the pail,
And shepherds piping in the dale;
And ancient faith that knows no guile,
And industry embrowned with toil;
And hearts resolved, and hands prepared,
The blessings they enjoy to guard!

## Bishop Percy.

### "O, NANNY, WILT THOU GANG WI' ME."

O NANNY, wilt thou gang wi' me,
    Nor sigh to leave the flaunting town?
Can silent glens have charms for thee,
    The lowly cot and russet gown?
Nae langer drest in silken sheen,
    Nae langer decked wi' jewels rare,
Say, canst thou quit each courtly scene,
    Where thou wert fairest of the fair?

O, Nanny, when thou'rt far awa,
    Wilt thou not cast a look behind?
Say, canst thou face the flaky snaw,
    Nor shrink before the winter wind?
O can that soft and gentle mien
    Severest hardships learn to bear,
Nor, sad, regret each courtly scene,
    Where thou wert fairest of the fair?

O, Nanny, canst thou love so true,
    Through perils keen wi' me to gae?
Or, when thy swain mishap shall rue,
    To share with him the pang of wae?
Say, should disease or pain befall,
    Wilt thou assume the nurse's care,
Nor, wishful, those gay scenes recall,
    Where thou wert fairest of the fair?

And when at last thy love shall die,
  Wilt thou receive his parting breath?
Wilt thou repress each struggling sigh,
  And cheer with smiles the bed of death!
And wilt thou o'er his much-loved clay
  Strew flowers, and drop the tender tear?
Nor then regret those scenes so gay,
  Where thou wert fairest of the fair?

---

## THE FRIAR OF ORDERS GRAY.

IT was a friar of orders gray
  Walked forth to tell his beads,
And he met with a lady fair,
  Clad in a pilgrim's weeds.

"Now Christ thee save, thou reverend friar!
  I pray thee tell to me,
If ever at yon holy shrine
  My true love thou didst see."

"And how should I know your true love
  From many another one?"
"Oh! by his cockle hat and staff,
  And by his sandal shoon:

"But chiefly by his face and mien,
  That were so fair to view,
His flaxen locks that sweetly curled,
  And eyes of lovely blue."

"O lady, he is dead and gone!
　　Lady, he's dead and gone!
At his head a green grass turf,
　　And at his heels a stone.

"Within these holy cloisters long
　　He languished, and he died,
Lamenting of a lady's love,
　　And 'plaining of her pride.

"Here bore him barefaced on his bier
　　Six proper youths and tall;
And many a tear bedewed his grave
　　Within yon kirkyard wall."

"And art thou dead, thou gentle youth—
　　And art thou dead and gone?
And didst thou die for love of me?
　　Break, cruel heart of stone!"

"O weep not, lady, weep not so,
　　Some ghostly comfort seek:
Let not vain sorrow rive thy heart,
　　Nor tears bedew thy cheek."

"O do not, do not, holy friar,
　　My sorrow now reprove;
For I have lost the sweetest youth
　　That e'er won lady's love.

"And now, alas! for thy sad loss
　　I'll evermore weep and sigh;
For thee I only wished to live,
　　For thee I wish to die."

"Weep no more, lady, weep no more;
    Thy sorrow is in vain:
For violets plucked, the sweetest shower
    Will ne'er make grow again.

"Our joys as wingèd dreams do fly;
    Why, then, should sorrow last?
Since grief but aggravates thy loss,
    Grieve not for what is past."

"O say not so, thou holy friar!
    I pray thee, say not so;
For since my true love died for me,
    'Tis meet my tears should flow.

"And will he never come again—
    Will he ne'er come again?
Ah, no! he is dead, and laid in his grave,
    Forever to remain.

"His cheek was redder than the rose—
    The comeliest youth was he;
But he is dead and laid in his grave,
    Alas! and woe is me."

"Sigh no more, lady, sigh no more,
    Men were deceivers ever;
One foot on sea, and one on land,
    To one thing constant never.

"Hadst thou been fond, he had been false,
    And left thee sad and heavy;
For young men ever were fickle found,
    Since summer trees were leafy."

"Now say not so, thou holy friar,
   I pray thee say not so;
My love he had the truest heart—
   O, he was ever true:

"And art thou dead, thou much-loved youth?
   And didst thou die for me?
Then farewell home; for evermore
   A pilgrim I will be.

"But first upon my true love's grave
   My weary limbs I'll lay,
And thrice I'll kiss the green grass turf
   That wraps his breathless clay."

"Yet stay, fair lady; rest awhile
   Beneath this cloister wall;
The cold wind through the hawthorn blows,
   And drizzly rain doth fall."

"O stay me not, thou holy friar;
   O stay me not, I pray;
No drizzly rain that falls on me
   Can wash my fault away."

"Yet stay, fair lady; turn again,
   And dry those pearly tears;
For see, beneath this gown of gray,
   Thy own true love appears.

"Here, forced by grief and hopeless love,
   These holy weeds I sought;
And here, amid these lonely walls,
   To end my days I thought.

"But haply, for my year of grace
   Is not yet passed away,
Might I still hope to win thy love,
   No longer would I stay."

"Now farewell grief, and welcome joy
   Once more unto my heart;
For since I've found thee, lovely youth,
   We never more will part."

---

## James Beattie.

### DESCRIPTION OF EDWIN, THE MINSTREL BOY.

AND yet poor Edwin was no vulgar boy.
   Deep thought oft seemed to fix his infant eye.
Dainties he heeded not, nor gaude, nor toy,
Save one short pipe of rudest minstrelsy;
Silent when glad; affectionate, though shy;
And now his look was most demurely sad,
And now he laughed aloud, yet none knew why.
The neighbours stared and sighed, yet blessed the lad;
Some deemed him wondrous wise, and some believed him
   mad.

But why should I his childish feats display?
Concourse, and noise, and toil, he ever fled;
Nor cared to mingle in the clamorous fray
Of squabbling imps; but to the forest sped,
Or roamed at large the lonely mountain's head,

Or where the maze of some bewildered stream
To deep untrodden groves his footsteps led,
There would he wander wild, till Phœbus' beam,
Shot from the western cliff, released the weary team.

The exploit of strength, dexterity, or speed,
To him nor vanity nor joy could bring:
His heart, from cruel sport estranged, would bleed
To work the woe of any living thing,
By trap or net, by arrow or by sling;
These he detested; those he scorned to wield;
He wished to be the guardian, not the king,
Tyrant far less, or traitor of the field,
And sure the sylvan reign unbloody joy might yield.

Lo! where the stripling, wrapt in wonder, roves
Beneath the precipice o'erhung with pine;
And sees on high, amidst the encircling groves,
From cliff to cliff the foaming torrents shine;
While waters, woods, and winds, in concert join,
And echo swells the chorus to the skies.
Would Edwin this majestic scene resign
For aught the huntsman's puny craft supplies?
Ah, no! he better knows great Nature's charms to prize.

And oft he traced the uplands to survey,
When o'er the sky advanced the kindling dawn,
The crimson cloud, blue main, and mountain gray,
And lake, dim-gleaming on the smoky lawn:
Far to the west the long, long vale withdrawn,
Where twilight loves to linger for a while;
And now he faintly kens the bounding fawn

And villager abroad at early toil:
But, lo! the sun appears! and heaven, earth, ocean, smile.

And oft the craggy cliff he loved to climb,
When all in mist the world below was lost—
What dreadful pleasure! there to stand sublime,
Like shipwrecked mariner on desert coast,
And view the enormous waste of vapour, tost
In billows, lengthening to the horizon round,
Now scooped in gulfs, with mountains now embossed!
And hear the voice of mirth and song rebound,
Flocks, herds, and waterfalls, along the hoar profound!

In truth he was a strange and wayward wight,
Fond of each gentle and each dreadful scene.
In darkness and in storm he found delight;
Nor less than when on ocean-wave serene,
The southern sun diffused his dazzling shene.
Even sad vicissitude amused his soul;
And if a sigh would sometimes intervene,
And down his cheek a tear of pity roll,
A sigh, a tear, so sweet, he wished not to control.

\*   \*   \*   \*

Oft when the winter storm had ceased to rave,
He roamed the snowy waste at even, to view
The cloud stupendous, from the Atlantic wave
High-towering, sail along the horizon blue;
Where, 'midst the changeful scenery, ever new,
Fancy a thousand wondrous forms descries,
More wildly great than ever pencil drew;
Rocks, torrents, gulfs, and shapes of giant size,
And glittering cliffs on cliffs, and fiery ramparts rise.

Thence musing onward to the sounding shore,
The lone enthusiast oft would take his way,
Listening, with pleasing dread, to the deep roar
Of the wide-weltering waves. In black array
When sulphurous clouds rolled on the autumnal day,
Even then he hastened from the haunt of man,
Along the trembling wilderness to stray,
What time the lightning's fierce career began,
And o'er heaven's rending arch the rattling thunder ran.

Responsive to the sprightly pipe, when all
In sprightly dance the village youth were joined,
Edwin, of melody aye held in thrall,
From the rude gambol far remote reclined,
Soothed with the soft notes warbling in the wind.
Ah then, all jollity seemed noise and folly!
To the pure soul by Fancy's fire refined,
Ah, what is mirth but turbulence unholy,
When with the charm compared of heavenly melancholy!

Is there a heart that music cannot melt?
Alas! how is that rugged heart forlorn!
Is there, who ne'er those mystic transports felt
Of solitude and melancholy born?
He needs not woo the Muse; he is her scorn.
The sophist's rope of cobweb he shall twine;
Mope o'er the schoolman's peevish rage; or mourn,
And delve for life in Mammon's dirty mine;
Sneak with the scoundrel fox, or grunt with glutton swine.

For Edwin, Fate a nobler doom had planned;
Song was his favourite and first pursuit.

The wild harp rang to his adventurous hand,
And languished to his breath the plaintive flute.
His infant muse, though artless, was not mute.
Of elegance as yet he took no care;
For this of time and culture is the fruit;
And Edwin gained at last this fruit so rare:
As in some future verse I purpose to declare.

Meanwhile, whate'er of beautiful or new,
Sublime, or dreadful, in earth, sea, or sky,
By chance, or search, was offered to his view,
He scanned with curious and romantic eye.
Whate'er of lore tradition could supply
From Gothic tale, or song, or fable old,
Roused him, still keen to listen and to pry.
At last, though long by penury controlled,
And solitude, his soul her graces 'gan unfold.

Thus on the chill Lapponian's dreary land,
For many a long month lost in snow profound,
When Sol from Cancer sends the season bland,
And in their northern cave the storms are bound;
From silent mountains, straight, with startling sound,
Torrents are hurled; green hills emerge; and lo!
The trees with foliage, cliffs with flowers are crowned;
Pure rills through vales of verdure warbling go;
And wonder, love, and joy, the peasant's heart o'erflow.

## Sir William Jones.

#### A PERSIAN SONG OF HAFIZ.

SWEET maid, if thou wouldst charm my sight,
    And bid these arms thy neck enfold;
That rosy cheek, that lily hand,
Would give thy poet more delight
Than all Bocara's vaunted gold,
Than all the gems of Samarcand.

Boy, let yon liquid ruby flow,
And bid thy pensive heart be glad,
Whate'er the frowning zealots say:
Tell them, their Eden cannot show
A stream so clear as Rocnabad,
A bower so sweet as Mosellay.

O! when these fair perfidious maids,
Whose eyes our secret haunts infest,
Their dear destructive charms display,
Each glance my tender breast invades,
And robs my wounded soul of rest,
As Tartars seize their destined prey.

In vain with love our bosoms glow:
Can all our tears, can all our sighs,
New lustre to those charms impart?
Can cheeks, where living roses blow,
Where nature spreads her richest dyes,
Require the borrowed gloss of art?

Speak not of fate: ah! change the theme,
And talk of odours, talk of wine,
Talk of the flowers that round us bloom:
'Tis all a cloud, 'tis all a dream;
To love and joy thy thoughts confine,
Nor hope to pierce the sacred gloom.

Beauty has such resistless power,
That even the chaste Egyptian dame
Sighed for the blooming Hebrew boy:
For her how fatal was the hour,
When to the banks of Nilus came
A youth so lovely and so coy!

But ah! sweet maid, my counsel hear
(Youth should attend when those advise
Whom long experience renders sage):
While music charms the ravished ear;
While sparkling cups delight our eyes,
Be gay, and scorn the frowns of age.

What cruel answer have I heard?
And yet, by Heaven, I love thee still:
Can aught be cruel from thy lip?
Yet say, how fell that bitter word
From lips which streams of sweetness fill,
Which naught but drops of honey sip?

Go boldly forth, my simple lay,
Whose accents flow with artless ease,
Like orient pearls at random strung:
Thy notes are sweet, the damsels say;
But oh! far sweeter, if they please
The nymph for whom these notes are sung!

## James Merrick.

### THE CHAMELEON.

Oft has it been my lot to mark
   A proud, conceited, talking spark,
With eyes that hardly served at most
To guard their master 'gainst a post;
Yet round the world the blade has been,
To see whatever could be seen.
Returning from his finished tour,
Grown ten times perter than before;
Whatever word you chance to drop,
The travelled fool your mouth will stop:
" Sir, if my judgment you'll allow—
I've seen—and sure I ought to know."—
So begs you'd pay a due submission,
And acquiesce in his decision.

  Two travellers of such a cast,
As o'er Arabia's wilds they passed,
And on their way, in friendly chat,
Now talked of this, and then of that;
Discoursed awhile, 'mongst other matter,
Of the Chameleon's form and nature.
" A stranger animal," cries one,
" Sure never lived beneath the sun:
A lizard's body lean and long,
A fish's head, a serpent's tongue,
Its foot with triple claw disjoined;
And what a length of tail behind!

How slow its pace! and then its hue —
Who ever saw so fine a blue?"
  "Hold there," the other quick replies,
"'Tis green, I saw it with these eyes,
As late with open mouth it lay,
And warmed it in the sunny ray;
Stretched at its ease the beast I viewed,
And saw it eat the air for food."
  "I've seen it, sir, as well as you,
And must again affirm it blue;
At leisure I the beast surveyed
Extended in the cooling shade."
  "'Tis green, 'tis green, sir, I assure ye."
"Green!" cries the other in a fury:
"Why, sir, d'ye think I've lost my eyes?"
"'Twere no great loss," the friend replies;
"For if they always serve you thus,
You'll find them but of little use."
  So high at last the contest rose,
From words they almost came to blows:
When luckily came by a third;
To him the question they referred:
And begged he'd tell them, if he knew,
Whether the thing was green or blue.
  "Sirs," cries the umpire, "cease your pother;
The creature's neither one nor t'other.
I caught the animal last night,
And viewed it o'er by candle-light:
I marked it well, 'twas black as jet —
You stare — but sirs, I've got it yet,
And can produce it." — "Pray, sir, do;
I'll lay my life the thing is blue."

"And I'll be sworn, that when you've seen
The reptile, you'll pronounce him green."
    "Well, then, at once to ease the doubt,"
Replies the man, "I'll turn him out:
And when before your eyes I've set him,
If you don't find him black, I'll eat him."
    He said; and full before their sight
Produced the beast, and lo!—'twas white.
Both stared, the man looked wondrous wise—
"My children," the Chameleon cries,
(Then first the creature found a tongue)
"You all are right, and all are wrong:
When next you talk of what you view,
Think others see as well as you:
Nor wonder if you find that none
Prefers your eye-sight to his own."

---

## Lady Anne Lindsay.

### AULD ROBIN GRAY.

WHEN the sheep are in the fauld, when the cows come hame,
When a' the weary warld to quiet rest are gane;
The woes of my heart fa' in showers frae my ee,
Unkenned by my gudeman, who soundly sleeps by me.

Young Jamie loo'd me weel, and sought me for his bride;
But, saving ae crown piece, he'd naething else beside.
To make the crown a pound, my Jamie gaed to sea;
And the crown and the pound, O they were baith for me!

Before he had been gane a twelvemonth and a day,
My father brak his arm, our cow was stown away;
My mother she fell sick—my Jamie was at sea—
And Auld Robin Gray, O! he came a-courting me.

My father cou'dna work—my mother cou'dna spin;
I toiled day and night, but their bread I cou'dna win;
Auld Rob maintained them baith, and, wi' tears in his ee,
Said, "Jenny, O! for their sakes, will you marry me?"

My heart it said na, and I looked for Jamie back;
But hard blew the winds, and his ship was a wrack;
His ship it was a wrack! Why didna Jamie dee?
Or, wherefore am I spared to cry out, Woe is me!

My father argued sair—my mother didna speak,
But she looked in my face till my heart was like to break;
They gied him my hand, but my heart was in the sea;
And so Auld Robin Gray he was gudeman to me.

I hadna been his wife a week but only four,
When, mournfu' as I sat on the stane at my door,
I saw my Jamie's ghaist—I cou'dna think it he,
Till he said, "I'm come hame, my love, to marry thee!"

O sair, sair did we greet, and mickle say of a';
Ae kiss we took, nae mair—I bade him gang awa.
I wish that I were dead, but I'm no like to dee;
For O, I am but young to cry out, Woe is me!

I gang like a ghaist, and I carena much to spin,
I darena think o' Jamie, for that wad be a sin;
But I will do my best a gude wife aye to be,
For Auld Robin Gray, O! he is sae kind to me.

## Henry Carey.

### SALLY IN OUR ALLEY.

OF all the girls that are so smart
    There's none like pretty Sally;
She is the darling of my heart,
    And she lives in our alley.
There is no lady in the land
    Is half so sweet as Sally;
She is the darling of my heart,
    And she lives in our alley.

Her father he makes cabbage-nets
    And through the streets does cry 'em;
Her mother she sells laces long
    To such as please to buy 'em:
But sure such folks could ne'er beget
    So sweet a girl as Sally!
She is the darling of my heart,
    And she lives in our alley.

When she is by, I leave my work,
    I love her so sincerely;
My master comes like any Turk,
    And bangs me most severely—
But let him bang his bellyful,
    I'll bear it all for Sally;
She is the darling of my heart,
    And she lives in our alley.

Of all the days that's in the week
    I dearly love but one day—
And that's the day that comes betwixt
    A Saturday and Monday;
For then I'm drest all in my best
    To walk abroad with Sally;
She is the darling of my heart,
    And she lives in our alley.

My master carries me to church,
    And often am I blamed
Because I leave him in the lurch
    As soon as text is named;
I leave the church in sermon-time
    And slink away to Sally;
She is the darling of my heart,
    And she lives in our alley.

When Christmas comes about again,
    O then I shall have money;
I'll hoard it up, and box it all,
    I'll give it to my honey:
I would it were ten thousand pound,
    I'd give it all to Sally;
She is the darling of my heart,
    And she lives in our alley.

My master and the neighbours all
    Make game of me and Sally,
And, but for her, I'd better be
    A slave and row a galley;

>   But when my seven long years are out
>     O then I'll marry Sally,—
>   O then we'll wed, and then we'll bed,
>     But not in our alley!

---

## Thomas Chatterton.

### THE BRISTOW TRAGEDY.[1]

THE feathered songster chanticleer
  Had wound his bugle-horn,
And told the early villager
  The coming of the morn:

King Edward saw the ruddy streaks
  Of light eclipse the gray,
And heard the raven's croaking throat
  Proclaim the fated day.

"Thou'rt right," quoth he; "for by the God
  That sits enthroned on high!
Charles Bawdin, and his fellows twain,
  To-day shall surely die."

Then with a jug of nappy ale
  His knights did on him wait;
"Go tell the traitor, that to-day
  He leaves this mortal state."

---

[1] Chatterton's antiquated orthography is not followed in this specimen.

Sir Canterlone then bended low,
  With heart brimful of woe;
He journied to the castle-gate,
  And to Sir Charles did go.

But when he came, his children twain,
  And eke his loving wife,
With briny tears did wet the floor,
  For good Sir Charles's life.

"Oh, good Sir Charles!" said Canterlone,
  "Bad tidings I do bring."
"Speak boldly, man," said brave Sir Charles;
  "What says the traitor king?"

"I grieve to tell: before yon sun
  Does from the welkin fly,
He hath upon his honour sworn,
  That thou shalt surely die."

"We all must die," said brave Sir Charles;
  "Of that I'm not afraid;
What boots to live a little space?
  Thank Jesus, I'm prepared.

"But tell thy king, for mine he's not,
  I'd sooner die to-day,
Than live his slave, as many are,
  Though I should live for aye."

Then Canterlone he did go out,
  To tell the mayor straight
To get all things in readiness
  For good Sir Charles's fate.

Then Mr. Canynge sought the king,
   And fell down on his knee;
"I'm come," quoth he, "unto your grace,
   To move your clemency."

"Then," quoth the king, "your tale speak out,
   You have been much our friend;
Whatever your request may be,
   We will to it attend."

"My noble liege! all my request
   Is for a noble knight,
Who, though mayhap he has done wrong,
   He thought it still was right.

"He has a spouse and children twain;
   All ruined are for aye,
If that you are resolved to let
   Charles Bawdin die to-day."

"Speak not of such a traitor vile,"
   The king in fury said;
"Before the evening star doth shine,
   Bawdin shall lose his head:

"Justice does loudly for him call,
   And he shall have his meed:
Speak, Mr. Canynge! what thing else
   At present do you need?"

"My noble liege!" good Canynge said,
   "Leave justice to our God,
And lay the iron rule aside;
   Be thine the olive rod.

" Was God to search our hearts and reins,
　　The best were sinners great;
Christ's vicar only knows no sin,
　　In all this mortal state.

" Let mercy rule thine infant reign,
　　'Twill fix thy crown full sure;
From race to race thy family
　　All sovereigns shall endure:

" But if with blood and slaughter thou
　　Begin thy infant reign,
Thy crown upon thy children's brows
　　Will never long remain."

" Canynge, away! this traitor vile
　　Has scorned my power and me;
How canst thou, then, for such a man
　　Intreat my clemency?"

" My noble liege! the truly brave
　　Will valorous actions prize;
Respect a brave and noble mind,
　　Although in enemies."

" Canynge, away! By God in heaven
　　That did me being give,
I will not taste a bit of bread
　　Whilst this Sir Charles doth live!

" By Mary, and all saints in heaven,
　　This sun shall be his last!"
Then Canynge dropped a briny tear,
　　And from the presence passed.

With heart brimful of gnawing grief,
   He to Sir Charles did go,
And sat him down upon a stool,
   And tears began to flow.

"We all must die," said brave Sir Charles;
   "What boots it how or when?
Death is the sure, the certain fate,
   Of all we mortal men.

"Say why, my friend, thy honest soul
   Runs over at thine eye;
Is it for my most welcome doom
   That thou dost child-like cry?"

Saith godly Canynge, "I do weep,
   That thou so soon must die,
And leave thy sons and helpless wife;
   'Tis this that wets mine eye."

"Then dry the tears that out thine eye
   From godly fountains spring;
Death I despise, and all the power
   Of Edward, traitor king.

"When through the tyrant's welcome means
   I shall resign my life,
The God I serve will soon provide
   For both my sons and wife.

"Before I saw the lightsome sun,
   This was appointed me;
Shall mortal man repine or grudge
   What God ordains to be?

' How oft in battle have I stood,
    When thousands died around;
When smoking streams of crimson blood
    Imbrued the fattened ground:

" How did I know that every dart
    That cut the airy way,
Might not find passage to my heart,
    And close mine eyes for aye?

" And shall I now, for fear of death,
    Look wan and be dismayed?
No! from my heart fly childish fear;
    Be all the man displayed."

" Ah, godlike Henry! God forefend,
    And guard thee and thy son,
If 'tis His will; but if 'tis not,
    Why, then, His will be done."

" My honest friend, my fault has been
    To serve God and my prince;
And that I no time-server am,
    My death will soon convince.

" In London city was I born,
    Of parents of great note;
My father did a noble arms
    Emblazon on his coat:

" I make no doubt but he is gone
    Where soon I hope to go,
Where we forever shall be blest,
    From out the reach of woe.

"He taught me justice and the laws
   With pity to unite;
And eke he taught me how to know
   The wrong cause from the right:

"He taught me with a prudent hand
   To feed the hungry poor,
Nor let my servants drive away
   The hungry from my door:

"And none can say but all my life
   I have his wordis kept;
And summed the actions of the day
   Each night before I slept.

"I have a spouse; go ask of her
   If I defiled her bed?
I have a king, and none can lay
   Black treason on my head.

"In Lent, and on the holy eve,
   From flesh I did refrain;
Why should I then appear dismayed
   To leave this world of pain?

"No, hapless Henry! I rejoice
   I shall not see thy death;
Most willingly in thy just cause
   Do I resign my breath.

"Oh, fickle people! ruined land!
   Thou wilt ken peace no moe;
While Richard's sons exalt themselves,
   Thy brooks with blood will flow.

"Say, were ye tired of godly peace,
    And godly Henry's reign,
That you did chop¹ your easy days
    For those of blood and pain?

"What though I on a sledge be drawn,
    And mangled by a hind,
I do defy the traitor's power,
    He cannot harm my mind:

"What though, uphoisted on a pole,
    My limbs shall rot in air,
And no rich monument of brass
    Charles Bawdin's name shall bear;

"Yet in the holy book above,
    Which time can't eat away,
There with the servants of the Lord
    My name shall live for aye.

"Then welcome death! for life eterne
    I leave this mortal life:
Farewell, vain world, and all that's dear,
    My sons and loving wife!

"Now death as welcome to me comes
    As e'er the month of May;
Nor would I even wish to live,
    With my dear wife to stay."

Saith Canynge, "'Tis a goodly thing
    To be prepared to die;
And from this world of pain and grief
    To God in heaven to fly."

---

¹ Exchange.

And now the bell began to toll,
   And clarions to sound;
Sir Charles he heard the horses' feet
   A-prancing on the ground.

And just before the officers
   His loving wife came in,
Weeping unfeignèd tears of woe
   With loud and dismal din.

"Sweet Florence! now I pray forbear,
   In quiet let me die;
Pray God that every Christian soul
   May look on death as I.

"Sweet Florence! why these briny tears?
   They wash my soul away,
And almost make me wish for life,
   With thee, sweet dame, to stay.

"'Tis but a journey I shall go
   Unto the land of bliss;
Now, as a proof of husband's love,
   Receive this holy kiss."

Then Florence, faltering in her say,
   Trembling, these wordis spoke:
"Ah, cruel Edward! bloody king!
   My heart is well-nigh broke.

"Ah, sweet Sir Charles! why wilt thou go
   Without thy loving wife?
The cruel axe that cuts thy neck,
   It eke shall end my life."

And now the officers came in
  To bring Sir Charles away,
Who turnèd to his loving wife,
  And thus to her did say:

" I go to life, and not to death;
  Trust thou in God above,
And teach thy sons to fear the Lord,
  And in their hearts Him love.

" 'Teach them to run the noble race
  That I their father run:
Florence! should death thee take—adieu!
  Ye officers, lead on."

Then Florence raved as any mad,
  And did her tresses tear;
" Oh stay, my husband, lord, and life!"
  Sir Charles then dropped a tear.

'Till tirèd out with raving loud,
  She fell upon the floor;
Sir Charles exerted all his might,
  And marched from out the door.

Upon a sledge he mounted then,
  With looks full brave and sweet;
Looks that enshone no more concern
  Than any in the street.

Before him went the council-men,
  In scarlet robes and gold,
And tassels spangling in the sun,
  Much glorious to behold:

The friars of Saint Augustine next
    Appearèd to the sight,
All clad in homely russet weeds,
    Of godly monkish plight:

In different parts a godly Psalm
    Most sweetly they did chant;
Behind their back six minstrels came,
    Who tuned the strange bataunt.

Then five-and-twenty archers came;
    Each one the bow did bend,
From rescue of King Henry's friends
    Sir Charles for to defend.

Bold as a lion came Sir Charles,
    Drawn on a cloth-laid sledde,
By two black steeds in trappings white,
    With plumes upon their head.

Behind him five-and-twenty more
    Of archers strong and stout,
With bended bow each one in hand,
    Marchèd in goodly rout.

Saint James's friars marchèd next,
    Each one his part did chant;
Behind their backs six minstrels came,
    Who tuned the strange bataunt.

Then came the mayor and aldermen,
    In cloth of scarlet decked;
And their attending men each one,
    Like eastern princes tricked.

And after them a multitude
  Of citizens did throng;
The windows were all full of heads,
  As he did pass along.

And when he came to the high cross,
  Sir Charles did turn and say:
"O Thou that savest man from sin,
  Wash my soul clean this day."

At the great minster window sat
  The king in mickle state,
To see Charles Bawdin go along
  To his most welcome fate.

Soon as the sledde drew nigh enough,
  That Edward he might hear,
The brave Sir Charles he did stand up,
  And thus his words declare:

"Thou seest me, Edward! traitor vile!
  Exposed to infamy;
But be assured, disloyal man,
  I'm greater now than thee.

"By foul proceedings, murder, blood,
  Thou wearest now a crown;
And hast appointed me to die
  By power not thine own.

"Thou thinkest I shall die to-day;
  I have been dead till now,
And soon shall live to wear a crown
  For aye upon my brow;

"Whilst thou, perhaps, for some few years,
  Shalt rule this fickle land,
To let them know how wide the rule
  'Twixt king and tyrant hand.

"Thy power unjust, thou traitor slave!
  Shall fall on thy own head"—
From out of hearing of the king
  Departed then the sledde.

King Edward's soul rushed to his face,
  He turned his head away,
And to his brother Gloucester
  He thus did speak and say:

"To him that so-much-dreaded death
  No ghastly terrors bring;
Behold the man! he spake the truth;
  He's greater than a king!"

"So let him die!" Duke Richard said;
  "And may each one our foes
Bend down their necks to bloody axe,
  And feed the carrion crows."

And now the horses gently drew
  Sir Charles up the high hill;
The axe did glister in the sun,
  His precious blood to spill.

Sir Charles did up the scaffold go,
  As up a gilded car
Of victory, by valorous chiefs
  Gained in the bloody war.

And to the people he did say:
  "Behold you see me die,
For serving loyally my king,
  My king most rightfully.

"As long as Edward rules this land,
  No quiet you will know;
Your sons and husbands shall be slain,
  And brooks with blood shall flow.

"You leave your good and lawful king,
  When in adversity;
Like me, unto the true cause stick,
  And for the true cause die."

Then he, with priests, upon his knees,
  A prayer to God did make,
Beseeching Him unto Himself
  His parting soul to take.

Then, kneeling down, he laid his head
  Most seemly on the block;
Which from his body fair at once
  The able headsman stroke:

And out the blood began to flow,
  And round the scaffold twine;
And tears, enough to wash't away,
  Did flow from each man's eyne.

The bloody axe his body fair
  Into four partis cut;
And every part, and eke his head,
  Upon a pole was put.

One part did rot on Kinwulph-hill,
  One on the minster-tower,
And one from off the castle-gate
  The crowen did devour.

The other on Saint Paul's good gate,
  A dreary spectacle;
His head was placed on the high cross,
  In high street most noble.

Thus was the end of Bawdin's fate:
  God prosper long our king,
And grant he may, with Bawdin's soul,
  In heaven God's mercy sing!

---

## William Cowper.

### VERSES SUPPOSED TO BE WRITTEN BY ALEXANDER SELKIRK, DURING HIS SOLITARY ABODE IN THE ISLAND OF JUAN FERNANDEZ.

I AM monarch of all I survey—
  My right there is none to dispute;
From the centre all round to the sea,
  I am lord of the fowl and the brute.
O Solitude! where are the charms
  That sages have seen in thy face?
Better dwell in the midst of alarms
  Than reign in this horrible place.

I am out of humanity's reach;
  I must finish my journey alone,

Never hear the sweet music of speech—
    I start at the sound of my own.
The beasts that roam over the plain
    My form with indifference see;
They are so unacquainted with man,
    Their tameness is shocking to me.

Society, friendship, and love,
    Divinely bestowed upon man!
O, had I the wings of a dove,
    How soon would I taste you again!
My sorrows I then might assuage
    In the ways of religion and truth—
Might learn from the wisdom of age,
    And be cheered by the sallies of youth.

Religion! What treasure untold
    Resides in that heavenly word!—
More precious than silver and gold,
    Or all that this earth can afford;
But the sound of the church-going bell
    These valleys and rocks never heard,
Never sighed at the sound of a knell,
    Or smiled when a sabbath appeared.

Ye winds that have made me your sport,
    Convey to this desolate shore
Some cordial endearing report
    Of a land I shall visit no more!
My friends—do they now and then send
    A wish or a thought after me?
O tell me I yet have a friend,
    Though a friend I am never to see.

How fleet is a glance of the mind!
    Compared with the speed of its flight,
The tempest itself lags behind,
    And the swift-winged arrows of light.
When I think of my own native land,
    In a moment I seem to be there;
But, alas! recollection at hand
    Soon hurries me back to despair.

But the sea-fowl is gone to her nest,
    The beast is laid down in his lair;
Even here is a season of rest,
    And I to my cabin repair.
There's mercy in every place,
    And mercy—encouraging thought!—
Gives even affliction a grace,
    And reconciles man to his lot.

---

## THE PULPIT.

THE pulpit, therefore (and I name it filled
    With solemn awe, that bids me well beware
With what intent I touch that holy thing)—
The pulpit (when the satirist has at last,
Strutting and vapouring in an empty school,
Spent all his force, and made no proselyte)—
I say the pulpit (in the sober use
Of its legitimate, peculiar powers)
Must stand acknowledged, while the world shall stand,
The most important and effectual guard,
Support, and ornament of Virtue's cause.

There stands the messenger of truth : there stands
The legate of the skies !—His theme divine,
His office sacred, his credentials clear.
By him the violated law speaks out
Its thunders; and by him, in strains as sweet
As angels use, the Gospel whispers peace.
He 'stablishes the strong, restores the weak,
Reclaims the wanderer, binds the broken heart,
And, armed himself in panoply complete
Of heavenly temper, furnishes with arms
Bright as his own, and trains, by every rule
Of holy discipline, to glorious war,
The sacramental host of God's elect !
Are all such teachers — would to Heaven all were !

## THE POPLAR FIELD.

THE poplars are felled, farewell to the shade
    And the whispering sound of the cool colonnade ;
The winds play no longer and sing in the leaves,
Nor Ouse on his bosom their image receives.

Twelve years have elapsed since I last took a view
Of my favourite field, and the bank where they grew :
And now in the grass behold they are laid,
And the tree is my seat that once lent me a shade.

The blackbird has fled to another retreat
Where the hazels afford him a screen from the heat ;
And the scene where his melody charmed me before
Resounds with his sweet-flowing ditty no more.

My fugitive years are all hasting away,
And I must ere long lie as lowly as they,
With a turf on my breast and a stone at my head,
Ere another such grove shall arise in its stead.

'Tis a sight to engage me, if any thing can,
To muse on the perishing pleasures of man;
Short-lived as we are, our enjoyments, I see
Have a still shorter date, and die sooner than we.

---

### TO MARY UNWIN.

THE twentieth year is well nigh past
  Since first our sky was overcast;
Ah, would that this might be the last!
   My Mary!

Thy spirits have a fainter flow,
I see thee daily weaker grow—
'Twas my distress that brought thee low,
   My Mary!

Thy needles, once a shining store,
For my sake restless heretofore,
Now rust disused, and shine no more;
   My Mary!

For though thou gladly wouldst fulfil
The same kind office for me still,
Thy sight now seconds not thy will,
   My Mary!

But well thou playd'st the housewife's part
And all thy threads with magic art
Have wound themselves about this heart,
  My Mary!

Thy indistinct expressions seem
Like language uttered in a dream;
Yet me they charm, whate'er the theme,
  My Mary!

Thy silver locks, once auburn bright,
Are still more lovely in my sight
Than golden beams of orient light,
  My Mary!

For could I view nor them nor thee,
What sight worth seeing could I see?
The sun would rise in vain for me,
  My Mary!

Partakers of thy sad decline,
Thy hands their little force resign,
Yet gently pressed, press gently mine,
  My Mary!

Such feebleness of limbs thou prov'st
That now at every step thou mov'st
Upheld by two; yet still thou lov'st,
  My Mary!

And still to love, though pressed with ill,
In wintry age to feel no chill,
With me is to be lovely still,
  My Mary!

But ah! by constant heed I know
How oft the sadness that I show
Transforms thy smiles to looks of woe,
    My Mary!

And should my future lot be cast
With much resemblance of the past,
Thy worn-out heart will break at last—
    My Mary!

---

## Anna Letitia Barbauld.

### HYMN TO CONTENT.

O THOU, the nymph with placid eye!
  O seldom found, yet ever nigh!
    Receive my temperate vow:
Not all the storms that shake the pole
Can e'er disturb thy halcyon soul,
    And smooth the unaltered brow.

O come, in simple vest arrayed,
With all thy sober cheer displayed,
    To bless my longing sight;
Thy mien composed, thy even pace,
Thy meek regard, thy matron grace,
    And chaste subdued delight.

No more by varying passions beat,
O gently guide my pilgrim feet
    To find thy hermit cell;

Where in some pure and equal sky,
Beneath thy soft indulgent eye,
    The modest virtues dwell.

Simplicity in Attic vest,
And Innocence with candid breast,
    And clear, undaunted eye;
And Hope, who points to distant years,
Fair opening through this vale of tears,
    A vista to the sky.

There Health, through whose calm bosom glide
The temperate joys in even tide,
    That rarely ebb or flow;
And Patience there, thy sister meek,
Presents her mild, unvarying cheek
    To meet the offered blow.

Her influence taught the Phrygian sage
A tyrant master's wanton rage
    With settled smiles to wait:
Inured to toil and bitter bread,
He bowed his meek, submissive head,
    And kissed thy sainted feet.

But thou, O nymph retired and coy!
In what brown hamlet dost thou joy
    To tell thy tender tale?
The lowliest children of the ground,
Moss-rose and violet, blossom round,
    And lily of the vale.

O say what soft propitious hour
I best may choose to hail thy power,
   And court thy gentle sway?
When autumn, friendly to the Muse,
Shall thy own modest tints diffuse,
   And shed thy milder day.

When eve, her dewy star beneath,
Thy balmy spirit loves to breathe,
   And every storm is laid;
If such an hour was e'er thy choice,
Oft let me hear thy soothing voice
   Low whispering through the shade.

---

## Matthew Gregory Lewis.

### THE MANIAC.

STAY, jailor, stay, and hear my woe!
   She is not mad who kneels to thee:
For what I'm now, too well I know,
   And what I was, and what should be.
I'll rave no more in proud despair;
   My language shall be mild, though sad:
But yet I firmly, truly swear,
   I am not mad, I am not mad.

My tyrant husband forged the tale,
   Which chains me in this dismal cell;
My fate unknown my friends bewail—
   O jailor, haste that fate to tell:

Oh! haste my father's heart to cheer:
    His heart at once 'twill grieve and glad
To know, though kept a captive here,
    I am not mad, I am not mad.


He smiles in scorn, and turns the key;
    He quits the grate; I knelt in vain;
His glimmering lamp, still, still I see—
    'Tis gone! and all is gloom again.
Cold, bitter cold!—No warmth! no light!—
    Life, all thy comforts once I had;
Yet here I'm chained, this freezing night,
    Although not mad; no, no, not mad.


'Tis sure some dream, some vision vain;
    What! I,—the child of rank and wealth,—
Am I the wretch who clanks this chain,
    Bereft of freedom, friends, and health?
Ah! while I dwell on blessings fled,
    Which never more my heart must glad,
How aches my heart, how burns my head!
    But 'tis not mad; no, 'tis not mad.


Hast thou, my child, forgot, ere this,
    A mother's face, a mother's tongue?
She'll ne'er forget your parting kiss,
    Nor round her neck how fast you clung;
Nor how with her you sued to stay,
    Nor how that suit your sire forbade;
Nor how—I'll drive such thoughts away;
    They'll make me mad, they'll make me mad.

His rosy lips, how sweet they smiled!
    His mild blue eyes, how bright they shone!
None ever bore a lovelier child:
    And art thou now forever gone?
And must I never see thee more,
    My pretty, pretty, pretty lad?
I will be free! unbar the door!
    I am not mad; I am not mad.

Oh, hark! what mean those yells and cries?
    His chain some furious madman breaks;
He comes,—I see his glaring eyes;
    Now, now, my dungeon-grate he shakes.
Help! help!—He's gone!—Oh! fearful woe,
    Such screams to hear, such sights to see!
My brain, my brain,—I know, I know
    I am not mad, but soon shall be.

Yes, soon;—for lo! you—while I speak—
    Mark how yon demon's eyeballs glare!
He sees me; now, with dreadful shriek,
    He whirls a serpent high in air.
Horror!—the reptile strikes his tooth
    Deep in my heart, so crushed and sad;
Ay, laugh, ye fiends;—I feel the truth;
    Your task is done—I'm mad! I'm mad!

# Henry Kirke White.

### THE STAR OF BETHLEHEM.

WHEN marshalled on the nightly plain,
    The glittering host bestud the sky;
One star alone, of all the train,
    Can fix the sinner's wandering eye.

Hark! hark! to God the chorus breaks,
    From every host, from every gem;
But one alone the Saviour speaks,
    It is the Star of Bethlehem.

Once on the raging seas I rode,
    The storm was loud—the night was dark;
The ocean yawned—and rudely blowed
    The wind that tossed my foundering bark.

Deep horror then my vitals froze,
    Death-struck, I ceased the tide to stem;
When suddenly a star arose,
    It was the Star of Bethlehem.

It was my guide, my light, my all,
    It bade my dark forebodings cease;
And through the storm and dangers' thrall,
    It led me to the port of peace.

Now safely moored—my perils o'er,
    I'll sing, first in night's diadem,
For ever and for evermore,
    The Star—the Star of Bethlehem!

## TO AN EARLY PRIMROSE.

MILD offspring of a dark and sullen sire!
    Whose modest form, so delicately fine,
        Was nursed in whirling storms,
        And cradled in the winds.

Thee, when young Spring first questioned Winter's sway,
And dared the sturdy blusterer to the fight,
        Thee on this bank he threw
        To mark his victory.

In this low vale, the promise of the year,
Serene, thou openest to the nipping gale,
        Unnoticed and alone,
        Thy tender elegance.

So Virtue blooms, brought forth amid the storms
Of chill Adversity.; in some lone walk
        Of life she rears her head,
        Obscure and unobserved;

While every bleaching breeze that on her blows,
Chastens her spotless purity of breast,
        And hardens her to bear
        Serene the ills of life.

## Robert Burns.

### THE COTTER'S SATURDAY NIGHT.

> " Let not ambition mock their useful toil,
>   Their homely joys and destiny obscure;
> Nor grandeur hear, with a disdainful smile,
>   The short and simple annals of the poor."
>
> GRAY.

MY loved, my honoured, much-respected friend!
  No mercenary bard his homage pays;
With honest pride I scorn each selfish end,
  My dearest meed a friend's esteem and praise.
To you I sing, in simple Scottish lays,
  The lowly train in life's sequestered scene;
The native feelings strong, the guileless ways—
  What Aiken in a cottage would have been;
Ah! tho' his worth unknown, far happier there, I ween.

November chill blaws loud wi' angry sugh;
  The short'ning winter day is near a close;
The miry beasts retreating frae the pleugh,
  The black'ning trains o' craws to their repose.
The toil-worn cotter frae his labour goes—
  This night his weekly moil is at an end—
Collects his spades, his mattocks, and his hoes,
  Hoping the morn in ease and rest to spend;
And weary, o'er the moor, his course does hameward bend.

At length his lonely cot appears in view,
  Beneath the shelter of an aged tree;
Th' expectant wee things, todlin, stacher thro'
    To meet their dad wi' flichterin noise and glee.

His wee bit ingle blinkin' bonnilie,
　　His clean hearth-stane, his thriftie wifie's smile,
The lisping infant prattling on his knee,
　　Does a' his weary, carking cares beguile,
An' makes him quite forget his labour and his toil.

Belyve the elder bairns come drappin' in—
　　At service out, amang the farmers roun';
Some ca' the pleugh, some herd, some tentie rin
　　A cannie errand to a neebour town.
Their eldest hope, their Jenny, woman grown,
　　In youthfu' bloom, love sparkling in her e'e,
Comes hame, perhaps, to shew a braw new gown,
　　Or deposite her sair-won penny fee,
To help her parents dear, if they in hardship be.

Wi' joy unfeigned, brothers and sisters meet,
　　An' each for other's weelfare kindly spiers;
The social hours, swift-winged, unnoticed fleet;
　　Each tells the uncos that he sees or hears;
The parents, partial, eye their hopeful years—
　　Anticipation forward points the view.
The mother, wi' her needle an' her sheers,
　　Gars auld claes look amaist as weel's the new;
The father mixes a' wi' admonition due:

Their masters' and their mistresses' command
　　The younkers a' are warned to obey,
An' mind their labours wi' an eydent hand,
　　An' ne'er, tho' out o' sight, to jauk or play;
An' O! be sure to fear the Lord alway!
　　An' mind your duty, duly, morn an' night!
Lest in temptation's path ye gang astray,

Implore His counsel and assisting might:
They never sought in vain that sought the Lord aright!


But hark! a rap comes gently to the door;
   Jenny, wha kens the meaning o' the same,
Tells how a neebour lad cam o'er the moor
   To do some errands, and convoy her hame.
The wily mother sees the conscious flame
   Sparkle in Jenny's e'e, and flush her cheek;
Wi' heart-struck, anxious care, inquires his name,
   While Jenny hafflins is afraid to speak;
Weel pleased the mother hears it's nae wild, worthless rake.


Wi' kindly welcome, Jenny brings him ben—
   A strappan youth, he taks the mother's eye;
Blythe Jenny sees the visit's no ill ta'en;
   The father cracks of horses, pleughs, and kye;
The youngster's artless heart o'erflows wi' joy,
   But blate and laithfu', scarce can weel behave;
The mother, wi' a woman's wiles, can spy
   What makes the youth sae bashfu' and sae grave—
Weel pleased to think her bairn's respected like the lave.


O happy love! where love like this is found!
   O heart-felt raptures! bliss beyond compare!
I've pacèd much this weary mortal round,
   And sage experience bids me this declare—
If Heaven a draught of heavenly pleasure spare,
   One cordial in this melancholy vale,
'Tis when a youthful, loving, modest pair,
   In other's arms breathe out the tender tale,
Beneath the milk-white thorn that scents the evening gale.

Is there, in human form that bears a heart,
  A wretch, a villain, lost to love and truth,
That can, with studied, sly, ensnaring art,
  Betray sweet Jenny's unsuspecting youth?
Curse on his perjured arts! dissembling smooth!
  Are honour, virtue, conscience, all exiled?
Is there no pity, no relenting ruth,
  Points to the parents fondling o'er their child—
Then paints the ruined maid, and their distraction wild?

But now the supper crowns their simple board:
  The halesome parritch, chief o' Scotia's food;
The soup their only hawkie does afford,
  That 'yont the hallan snugly chows her cud;
The dame brings forth, in complimental mood,
  To grace the lad, her weel-hained kebbuck fell,
An' aft he's pressed, and aft he ca's it good;
  The frugal wifie, garrulous, will tell
How 'twas a towmond auld, sin' lint was i' the bell.

The cheerfu' supper done, wi' serious face
  They, round the ingle, form a circle wide;
The sire turns o'er, wi' patriarchal grace,
  The big Ha'-Bible, ance his father's pride:
His bonnet rev'rently is laid aside,
  His lyart haffets wearin' thin and bare;
Those strains that once did sweet in Zion glide
  He wales a portion with judicious care;
And "Let us worship God!" he says with solemn air.

They chant their artless notes in simple guise;
  They tune their hearts, by far the noblest aim;

Perhaps *Dundee's* wild, warbling measures rise,
   Or plaintive *Martyrs*, worthy o' the name;
Or noble *Elgin* beets the heavenward flame—
   The sweetest far o' Scotia's holy lays;
Compared with these, Italian trills are tame;
   The tickled ears no heartfelt raptures raise—
Nae unison hae they with our Creator's praise.

The priest-like father reads the sacred page:
   How Abraham was the friend of God on high;
Or Moses bade eternal warfare wage
   With Amalek's ungracious progeny;
Or how the royal bard did groaning lie
   Beneath the stroke of Heaven's avenging ire;
Or Job's pathetic plaint, and wailing cry;
   Or rapt Isaiah's wild, seraphic fire;
Or other holy seers that tune the sacred lyre.

Perhaps the Christian volume is the theme:
   How guiltless blood for guilty man was shed;
How He, who bore in Heaven the second name,
   Had not on earth whereon to lay His head;
How His first followers and servants sped—
   The precepts sage they wrote to many a land;
How he, who lone in Patmos banished,
   Saw in the sun a mighty angel stand,
And heard great Bab'lon's doom pronounced by Heaven's command.

Then kneeling down to Heaven's eternal King,
   The saint, the father, and the husband prays:
Hope "springs exulting on triumphant wing"
   That thus they all shall meet in future days;

There ever bask in uncreated rays,
    No more to sigh, or shed the bitter tear—
Together hymning their Creator's praise,
    In such society, yet still more dear,
While circling time moves round in an eternal sphere.

Compared with this, how poor religion's pride,
    In all the pomp of method and of art,
When men display to congregations wide
    Devotion's every grace except the heart!
The Power, incensed, the pageant will desert,
    The pompous strain, the sacerdotal stole;
But haply, in some cottage far apart,
    May hear, well pleased, the language of the soul,
And in His book of life the inmates poor enroll.

Then homeward all take off their sev'ral way;
    The youngling cottagers retire to rest;
The parent-pair their secret homage pay,
    And proffer up to Heaven the warm request
That He who stills the raven's clam'rous nest,
    And decks the lily fair in flowery pride,
Would, in the way His wisdom sees the best,
    For them and for their little ones provide—
But chiefly in their hearts with grace divine preside.

From scenes like these old Scotia's grandeur springs,
    That makes her loved at home, revered abroad.
Princes and lords are but the breath of kings—
    "An honest man's the noblest work of God;"
And, certes, in fair virtue's heavenly road,
    The cottage leaves the palace far behind.

What is a lordling's pomp? a cumbrous load,
  Disguising oft the wretch of human kind,
Studied in arts of hell, in wickedness refined!

O Scotia! my dear, my native soil!
  For whom my warmest wish to Heaven is sent!
Long may thy hardy sons of rustic toil
  Be blest with health, and peace, and sweet content!
And, O! may Heaven their simple lives prevent
  From luxury's contagion weak and vile!
Then, howe'er crowns and coronets be rent,
  A virtuous populace may rise the while,
And stand a wall of fire around their much-loved isle.

O Thou! who poured the patriotic tide
  That streamed through Wallace's undaunted heart—
Who dared to nobly stem tyrannic pride,
  Or nobly die, the second glorious part—
(The patriot's God peculiarly Thou art—
  His friend, inspirer, guardian, and reward!)
O never, never Scotia's realm desert;
  But still the patriot and the patriot bard
In bright succession raise, her ornament and guard!

## TAM O' SHANTER.

### A TALE.

"Of Brownyis and of Bogilis full is this Buke."
GAWIN DOUGLASS.

WHEN chapman billies leave the street,
And drouthy neebours neebours meet,
As market-days are wearing late,
An' folk begin to tak the gate;
While we sit bousing at the nappy,
An' getting fou and unco happy,
We think na on the lang Scots miles,
The mosses, waters, slaps, and styles,
That lie between us and our hame,
Whare sits our sulky, sullen dame,
Gathering her brows like gathering storm,
Nursing her wrath to keep it warm.

This truth fand honest Tam o' Shanter,
As he, frae Ayr, ae night did canter
(Auld Ayr, wham ne'er a town surpasses,
For honest men and bonnie lasses).

O Tam! hadst thou but been sae wise
As taen thy ain wife Kate's advice!
She tauld thee weel thou was a skellum,
A bleth'ring, blust'ring, drunken blellum;
That frae November till October,
Ae market-day thou was na sober;
That ilka melder, wi' the miller,
Thou sat as lang as thou had siller;
That every naig was ca'd a shoe on,
The smith and thee gat roaring fou on;

That at the L—d's house, ev'n on Sunday,
Thou drank wi' Kirton Jean till Monday.
She prophesy'd that, late or soon,
Thou would be found deep drown'd in Doon;
Or catch'd wi' warlocks in the mirk,
By Alloway's auld haunted kirk.

  Ah, gentle dames! it gars me greet
To think how monie counsels sweet,
How monie lengthened sage advices,
The husband frae the wife despises!

  But to our tale: Ae market night
Tam had got planted unco right,
Fast by an ingle, bleezing finely,
Wi' reaming swats, that drank divinely;
And at his elbow souter Johnny,
His ancient, trusty, drouthy crony—
Tam lo'ed him like a vera brither—
They had been fou for weeks thegither.
The night drave on wi' sangs and clatter;
And ay the ale was growing better.
The landlady and Tam grew gracious,
Wi' favours secret, sweet, and precious;
The souter tauld his queerest stories;
The landlord's laugh was ready chorus;
The storm without might rair and rustle,
Tam did na mind the storm a whistle.

  Care, mad to see a man sae happy,
E'en drowned himself amang the nappy;
As bees flee hame wi' lades o' treasure,
The minutes winged their way wi' pleasure;
Kings may be blest, but Tam was glorious,
O'er a' the ills o' life victorious.

But pleasures are like poppies spread—
You seize the flower, its bloom is shed;
Or like the snow-fall in the river,
A moment white—then melts forever;
Or like the borealis race,
That flit ere you can point their place;
Or like the rainbow's lovely form,
Evanishing amid the storm.
Nae man can tether time or tide;
The hour approaches Tam maun ride—
That hour o' night's black arch the key-stane,
That dreary hour he mounts his beast in;
And sic a night he takes the road in
As ne'er poor sinner was abroad in.

 The wind blew as 'twad blawn its last;
The rattling showers rose on the blast;
The speedy gleams the darkness swallowed;
Loud, deep, and lang the thunder bellowed;
That night a child might understand
The Deil had business on his hand.

 Weel mounted on his gray mare, Meg
(A better never lifted leg),
Tam skelpit on thro' dub and mire,
Despising wind, and rain, and fire—
Whyles holding fast his guid blue bonnet,
Whyles crooning o'er some auld Scots sonnet,
Whyles glow'ring round wi' prudent cares,
Lest bogles catch him unawares;
Kirk-Alloway was drawing nigh,
Where ghaists and houlets nightly cry.

 By this time he was 'cross the ford,
Whare in the snaw the chapman smoored;

And past the birks and meikle stane,
Whare drunken Charlie brak 's neck-bane;
And thro' the whins, and by the cairn,
Where hunters fand the murdered bairn;
And near the thorn, aboon the well,
Whare Mungo's mither hanged hersel.
Before him Doon pours all his floods:
The doubling storm roars thro' the woods;
The lightnings flash from pole to pole;
Near and more near the thunders roll;
When, glimmering thro' the groaning trees,
Kirk-Alloway seemed in a bleeze;
Thro' ilka bore the beams were glancing,
And loud resounded mirth and dancing.

   Inspiring bold John Barleycorn!
What dangers thou canst make us scorn!
Wi' tippenny we fear nae evil;
Wi' usquabae we'll face the Devil!—
The swats sae ream'd in Tammie's noddle,
Fair play, he cared na Deils a bodle.
But Maggie stood right sair astonished,
Till, by the heel and hand admonished,
She ventured forward on the light;
And, wow! Tam saw an unco sight—
Warlocks and witches in a dance:
Nae cotillion brent new frae France,
But hornpipes, jigs, strathspeys, and reels
Put life and mettle in their heels.
A winnock-bunker in the east,
There sat auld Nick, in shape o' beast—
A towzie tyke, black, grim, and large—
To gie them music was his charge;

He screwed the pipes and gart them skirl,
Till roof an' rafters a' did dirl.
Coffins stood round like open presses,
That shaw'd the dead in their last dresses;
And by some devilish cantrips sleight,
Each in its cauld hand held a light—
By which heroic Tam was able
To note upon the haly table,
A murderer's banes in gibbet airns;
Twa span-lang, wee, unchristen'd bairns;
A thief, new cutted fra a rape,
Wi' his last gasp his gab did gape;
Five tomahawks, wi' bluid red rusted;
Five scymitars, wi' murder crusted;
A garter which a babe had strangled;
A knife a father's throat had mangled,
Whom his ain son o' life bereft—
The gray hairs yet stack to the heft;
Three lawyers' tongues turned inside out,
Wi' lies seamed like a beggar's clout;
And priests' hearts, rotten, black as muck,
Lay stinking, vile, in every neuk:
Wi' mair o' horrible and awfu',
Which ev'n to name wad be unlawfu'.

    As Tammie glowr'd, amazed, and curious,
The mirth and fun grew fast and furious;
The piper loud and louder blew;
The dancers quick and quicker flew;
They reeled, they set, they crossed, they cleckit,
Till ilka carlin swat and reekit,
And coost her duddies to the wark,
And linket at it in her sark.

Now, Tam, O Tam! had they been queans
A' plump and strapping in their teens:
Their sarks, instead o' creeshie flannen,
Been snaw-white seventeen-hunder linen;
Thir breeks o' mine, my only pair,
That ance were plush, o' guid blue hair,
I wad hae gi'en them aff my hurdies
For ae blink o' the bonnie burdies!

But withered beldams, auld and droll,
Rigwoodie hags wad spean a foal,
Lowping an' flinging on a crummock—
I wonder did na turn thy stomach.

But Tam kenn'd what was what fu' brawlie.
There was ae winsome wench and walie,
That night inlisted in the core
(Lang after kenn'd on Carrick shore!
For monie a beast to dead she shot,
And perished monie a bonnie boat,
And shook baith meikle corn and bear,
And kept the country-side in fear),
Her cutty-sark o' Paisley harn,
That while a lassie she had worn—
In longitude though sorely scanty,
It was her best, and she was vauntie.
Ah! little kenn'd thy reverend grannie
That sark she coft for her wee Nannie,
Wi' twa pund Scots (twas a' her riches)—
Wad ever graced a dance o' witches!

But here my Muse her wing maun cower—
Sic flights are far beyond her power—
To sing how Nannie lap and flang
(A souple jad she was and strang);

And how Tam stood, like ane bewitched,
And thought his very een enriched.
Ev'n Satan glowr'd, and fidged fu' fain,
And hotched and blew wi' might and main;
Till first ae caper, syne anither—
Tam tint his reason a'thegither,
And roars out, *Weel done, Cutty-sark!*
And in an instant a' was dark;
And scarcely had he Maggie rallied,
When out the hellish legion sallied.

 As bees bizz out wi' angry fyke,
When plundering herds assail their byke;
As open pussie's mortal foes,
When pop! she starts before their nose;
As eager runs the market-crowd,
When *Catch the thief!* resounds aloud;
So Maggie runs—the witches follow,
Wi' monie an eldritch skreech and hollow.

 Ah, Tam! ah, Tam! thou'll get thy fairin'!
In hell they'll roast thee like a herrin'!
In vain thy Kate awaits thy comin'—
Kate soon will be a waefu' woman!
Now, do thy speedy utmost, Meg,
And win the key-stane o' the brig;
There at them thou thy tail may toss—
A running stream they dare na cross.
But ere the key-stane she could make,
The fient a tale she had to shake;
For Nannie, far before the rest,
Hard upon noble Maggie prest,
And flew at Tam wi' furious ettle;
But little wist she Maggie's mettle—

Ae spring brought aff her master hale,
But left behind her ain gray tail:
The carlin claught her by the rump,
And left poor Maggie scarce a stump.
   Now, wha this tale o' truth shall read,
Ilk man and mother's son take heed;
Whene'er to drink you are inclined,
Or cutty-sarks run in your mind,
Think, ye may buy the joys o'er dear—
Remember Tam o' Shanter's mare.

---

## MY LUVE IS LIKE A RED, RED ROSE.

O MY Luve's like a red, red rose
   That's newly sprung in June:
O my Luve's like the melodie
   That's sweetly played in tune.
As fair art thou, my bonnie lass,
   So deep in luve am I:
And I will luve thee still, my dear,
   Till a' the seas gang dry:

Till a' the seas gang dry, my dear,
   And the rocks melt wi' the sun;
I will luve thee still, my dear,
   While the sands o' life shall run.
And fare thee weel, my only Luve!
   And fare thee weel awhile!
And I will come again, my Luve,
   Tho' it were ten thousand mile.

## JOHN ANDERSON.

JOHN Anderson my jo, John,
    When we were first acquent,
Your locks were like the raven,
    Your bonnie brow was brent;
But now your brow is bald, John,
    Your locks are like the snow;
But blessings on your frosty pow,
    John Anderson my jo.

John Anderson my jo, John,
    We clamb the hill thegither,
And mony a canty day, John,
    We've had wi' ane anither:
Now we maun totter down, John,
    But hand in hand we'll go,
And sleep thegither at the foot,
    John Anderson my jo.

---

## HIGHLAND MARY.

YE banks and braes and streams around
    The castle o' Montgomery,
Green be your woods, and fair your flowers,
    Your waters never drumlie.
There simmer first unfauld her robes,
    And there the langest tarry;
For there I took the last fareweel
    O' my sweet Highland Mary.

How sweetly bloom'd the gay green birk,
   How rich the hawthorn's blossom,
As underneath their fragrant shade
   I clasp'd her to my bosom!
The golden hours on angel wings
   Flew o'er me and my dearie;
For dear to me as light and life
   Was my sweet Highland Mary.

Wi' mony a vow and lock'd embrace
   Our parting was fu' tender;
And pledging aft to meet again,
   We tore oursels asunder;
But, O! fell Death's untimely frost,
   That nipt my flower sae early!
Now green's the sod, and cauld's the clay,
   That wraps my Highland Mary!

O pale, pale now, those rosy lips,
   I aft hae kiss'd sae fondly!
And closed for aye the sparkling glance
   That dwelt on me sae kindly:
And mouldering now in silent dust
   That heart that lo'ed me dearly!
But still within my bosom's core
   Shall live my Highland Mary.

## TO MARY IN HEAVEN.

THOU lingering star, with less'ning ray,
   That lov'st to greet the early morn,
Again thou usherest in the day
   My Mary from my soul was torn.
O Mary! dear, departed shade!
   Where is thy place of blissful rest?
Seest thou thy lover lowly laid?
   Hear'st thou the groans that rend his breast?

That sacred hour can I forget,
   Can I forget the hallowed grove,
Where by the winding Ayr we met,
   To live one day of parting love?
Eternity will not efface
   Those records dear of transports past—
Thy image at our last embrace!
   Ah! little thought we 'twas our last!

Ayr, gurgling, kissed his pebbled shore,
   O'erhung with wild woods, thickening, green;
The fragrant birch, and hawthorn hoar,
   Twined amorous round the raptured scene.
The flowers sprang wanton to be prest,
   The birds sang love on every spray,
Till too, too soon, the glowing west
   Proclaimed the speed of wingèd day.

Still o'er these scenes my memory wakes,
   And fondly broods with miser care;

Time but th' impression deeper makes,
   As streams their channels deeper wear.
My Mary! dear, departed shade!
   Where is thy place of blissful rest?
Seest thou thy lover lowly laid?
   Hear'st thou the groans that rend his breast?

---

### A MAN'S A MAN FOR A' THAT.

IS there for honest poverty,
   Wha hangs his head, and a' that?
The coward-slave, we pass him by;
   We dare be poor for a' that.
      For a' that, and a' that,
         Our toils obscure, and a' that;
        The rank is but the guinea's stamp—
         The man's the gowd for a' that.

What tho' on hamely fare we dine,
   Wear hodden gray, and a' that;
Gie fools their silks, and knaves their wine—
   A man's a man for a' that.
      For a' that, and a' that,
         Their tinsel show, and a' that;
        The honest man, though e'er sae poor,
         Is king o' men for a' that.

You see yon birkie ca'd a lord,
   Wha struts, and stares, and a' that—

Tho' hundreds worship at his word,
  He's but a coof for a' that;
    For a' that, and a' that,
      His riband, star, and a' that;
    The man of independent mind,
      He looks and laughs at a' that.

A prince can mak a belted knight,
  A marquis, duke, and a' that;
But an honest man's aboon his might—
  Guid faith, he mauna fa' that!
    For a' that, and a' that,
      Their dignities, and a' that;
    The pith o' sense, and pride o' worth,
      Are higher ranks than a' that.

Then let us pray that come it may,
  As come it will for a' that,
That sense and worth, o'er a' the earth,
  May bear the gree, and a' that.
    For a' that, and a' that,
      It's coming yet, for a' that—
    When man to man, the warld o'er,
      Shall brothers be for a' that.

# Mrs Piozzi.

### THE THREE WARNINGS.

The tree of deepest root is found
  Least willing still to quit the ground;
'Twas therefore said by ancient sages,
  That love of life increased with years
So much, that in our latter stages,
When pains grow sharp, and sickness rages,
  The greatest love of life appears.
This strong affection to believe
Which all confess, but few perceive,
If old assertions can't prevail,
Be pleased to hear a modern tale.

When sports went round, and all were gay,
On neighbour Dobson's wedding-day,
Death called aside the jocund groom,
With him into another room,
And, looking grave, "You must," says he,
"Quit your sweet bride, and come with me."
"With you! and quit my Susan's side?
With you!" the hapless husband cried:
"Young as I am! 'tis monstrous hard!
Besides, in truth, I'm not prepared:
My thoughts on other matters go;
This is my wedding-night, you know."
  What more he urged I have not heard;
His reasons could not well be stronger;
  So Death the poor delinquent spared,
And left to live a little longer.

Yet calling up a serious look,
His hour-glass trembled while he spoke:
"Neighbour," he said, "farewell; no more
Shall Death disturb your mirthful hour;
And farther, to avoid all blame
Of cruelty upon my name,
To give you time for preparation,
And fit you for your future station,
Three several warnings you shall have,
Before you're summoned to the grave:
Willing, for once, I'll quit my prey,
   And grant a kind reprieve;
In hopes you'll have no more to say,
But when I call again this way,
   Well pleased the world will leave."
To these conditions both consented,
And parted perfectly contented.

What next the hero of our tale befell,
How long he lived, how wisely well;
How roundly he pursued his course,
And smoked his pipe, and stroked his horse,
   The willing muse shall tell:
He chaffered, then he bought, he sold,
Nor once perceived his growing old,
   Nor thought of Death as near;
His friends not false, his wife no shrew,
Many his gains, his children few,
He passed his smiling hours in peace;
And still he viewed his wealth increase.
While thus along life's dusty road
The beaten track content he trod,

Old Time, whose haste no mortal spares,
Uncalled, unheeded, unawares,
   Brought on his eightieth year.

When lo! one night, in musing mood,
   As all alone he sate,
The unwelcome messenger of fate
   Once more before him stood.

Half-killed with anger and surprise,
  "So soon returned?" old Dobson cries.
"So soon, d'ye call it?" Death replies:
"Surely, my friend, you're but in jest;
   Since I was here before,
'Tis six-and-thirty years at least,
   And you are now fourscore."
"So much the worse," the clown rejoined;
"To spare the aged would be kind:
Besides, you promised me Three Warnings,
Which I have looked for nights and mornings:
And for that loss of time and ease,
I can recover damages."

"I know," says Death, "that, at the best,
I seldom am a welcome guest;
But don't be captious, friend, at least;
I little thought you'd still be able
To stump about your farm and stable;
Your years have run to a great length—
I wish you joy, though, of your strength."

"Hold," says the farmer; "not so fast;
I have been lame these four years past."

"And no great wonder," Death replies;
"However, you still keep your eyes;
And sure to see one's loves and friends,
For legs and arms may make amends."

"Perhaps," says Dobson, "so it might,
But latterly I've lost my sight."

"This is a shocking tale, in truth;
Yet there's some comfort still," says Death;
"Each strives your sadness to amuse;
I warrant you hear all the news."
"There's none," he cries; "and, if there were,
I'm grown so deaf I could not hear."

"Nay then," the spectre stern rejoined,
  "These are unjustifiable yearnings;
If you are lame, and deaf, and blind,
  You've had your *three* sufficient warnings;
So come along, no more we'll part:"
He said, and touched him with his dart.
And now old Dobson, turning pale,
Yields to his fate—so ends my tale.

## William Wordsworth.

### LAODAMIA.

"With sacrifice before the rising morn
   Vows have I made by fruitless hope inspired;
And from th' infernal gods, 'mid shades forlorn
   Of night, my slaughtered lord have I required:
Celestial pity I again implore;—
Restore him to my sight—great Jove, restore!"

So speaking, and by fervent love endowed
   With faith, the suppliant heavenward lifts her hands;
While, like the sun emerging from a cloud,
   Her count'nance brightens and her eye expands;
Her bosom heaves and spreads, her stature grows;
And she expects the issue in repose.

O terror! what hath she perceived?—O joy!
   What doth she look on?—whom doth she behold?
Her hero slain upon the beach of Troy?
   His vital presence? his corporeal mould?
It is—if sense deceive her not—'tis he!
And a god leads him—winged Mercury!

Mild Hermes spake—and touched her with his wand
   That calms all fear: "Such grace hath crowned thy prayer,
Laodamia! that at Jove's command
   Thy husband walks the paths of upper air;
He comes to tarry with thee three hours' space;
Accept the gift, behold him face to face!"

Forth sprang the impassioned queen her lord to clasp;
    Again that consummation she essayed;
But unsubstantial form eludes her grasp
    As often as that eager grasp was made.
The phantom parts—but parts to reunite,
And reassume his place before her sight.

" Protesilaus, lo! thy guide is gone!
    Confirm, I pray, the vision with thy voice:
This is our palace,—yonder is thy throne;
    Speak! and the floor thou tread'st on will rejoice.
Not to appal me have the gods bestowed
This precious boon, and blest a sad abode."

" Great Jove, Laodamia, doth not leave
    His gifts imperfect:—spectre though I be,
I am not sent to scare thee or deceive;
    But in reward of thy fidelity.
And something also did my worth obtain;
For fearless virtue bringeth boundless gain.

" Thou know'st, the Delphic oracle foretold
    That the first Greek who touched the Trojan strand
Should die; but me the threat could not withhold—
    A generous cause a victim did demand;
And forth I leapt upon the sandy plain—
A self-devoted chief, by Hector slain."

" Supreme of heroes! bravest, noblest, best!
    Thy matchless courage I bewail no more,
Which then, when tens of thousands were deprest
    By doubt, propelled thee to the fatal shore;
Thou found'st—and I forgive thee—here thou art—
A nobler counsellor than my poor heart.

"But thou, though capable of sternest deed,
   Wert kind as resolute, and good as brave;
And he whose power restores thee hath decreed
   Thou shouldst elude the malice of the grave;
Redundant are thy locks, thy lips as fair
As when their breath enriched Thessalian air.

"No spectre greets me,—no vain shadow this;
   Come, blooming hero, place thee by my side!
Give, on this well-known couch, one nuptial kiss
   To me, this day a second time thy bride!"
Jove frowned in heaven; the conscious Parcæ threw
Upon those roseate lips a Stygian hue.

"This visage tells thee that my doom is past;
   Nor should the change be mourned, even if the joys
Of sense were able to return as fast
   And surely as they vanish. Earth destroys
Those raptures duly—Erebus disdains;
Calm pleasures there abide—majestic pains.

"Be taught, O faithful consort, to control
   Rebellious passion: for the gods approve
The depth, and not the tumult, of the soul;
   A fervent, not ungovernable, love.
Thy transports moderate; and meekly mourn
When I depart, for brief is my sojourn—"

"Ah, wherefore?—Did not Hercules by force
   Wrest from the guardian monster of the tomb
Alcestis, a reanimated corse,
   Given back to dwell on earth in vernal bloom?
Medea's spells dispersed the weight of years,
And Æson stood a youth 'mid youthful peers.

" The gods to us are merciful, and they
    Yet further may relent; for mightier far
Than strength of nerve and sinew, or the sway
    Of magic potent over sun and star,
Is love, though oft to agony distrest,
And though his favourite seat be feeble woman's breast.

" But if thou goest, I follow—" " Peace !" he said ;—
    She looked upon him and was calmed and cheered;
The ghastly colour from his lips had fled;
    In his deportment, shape, and mien appeared
Elysian beauty, melancholy grace,
Brought from a pensive, though a happy place.

He spake of love, such love as spirits feel
    In worlds whose course is equable and pure;
No fears to beat away—no strife to heal—
    The past unsighed for, and the future sure;
Spake of heroic arts in graver mood
Revived, with finer harmony pursued;

Of all that is most beauteous, imaged there
    In happier beauty; more pellucid streams,
An ampler ether, a diviner air,
    And fields invested with purpureal gleams;
Climes which the sun, who sheds the brightest day
Earth knows, is all unworthy to survey.

Yet there the soul shall enter which hath earned
    That privilege by virtue.—" Ill," said he,
" The end of man's existence I discerned,
    Who from ignoble games and revelry
Could draw, when we had parted, vain delight,
While tears were thy best pastime, day and night;

"And while my youthful peers before my eyes
　(Each hero following his peculiar bent)
Prepared themselves for glorious enterprise
　By martial sports,—or, seated in the tent,
Chieftains and kings in council were detained,
What time the fleet at Aulis lay enchained.

"The wished-for wind was given;—I then revolved
　The oracle, upon the silent sea;
And, if no worthier led the way, resolved
　That, of a thousand vessels, mine should be
The foremost prow in pressing to the strand—
Mine the first blood that tinged the Trojan sand.

"Yet bitter, ofttimes bitter, was the pang
　When of thy loss I thought, beloved wife!
On thee too fondly did my memory hang,
　And on the joys we shared in mortal life—
The paths which we had trod—these fountains, flowers—
My new-planned cities, and unfinished towers.

"But should suspense permit the foe to cry,
　'Behold they tremble!—haughty their array,
Yet of their number no one dares to die?'
　In soul I swept th' indignity away.
Old frailties then recurred;—but lofty thought,
In act embodied, my deliverance wrought.

"And thou, though strong in love, art all too weak
　In reason, in self-government too slow;
I counsel thee by fortitude to seek
　Our blest reunion in the shades below.
Th' invisible world with thee hath sympathized:
Be thy affections raised and solemnized.

"Learn, by a mortal yearning, to ascend,—
   Seeking a higher object.   Love was given,
Encouraged, sanctioned, chiefly for that end;
   For this the passion to excess was driven,—
That self might be annulled—her bondage prove
The fetters of a dream, opposed to love."

Aloud she shrieked! for Hermes reappears!
   Round the dear shade she would have clung,—'tis vain;
The hours are past,—too brief had they been years;
   And him no mortal effort can detain.
Swift, toward the realms that know not earthly day,
He through the portal takes his silent way,
And on the palace floor a lifeless corse she lay.

Thus, all in vain exhorted and reproved,
   She perished; and, as for a wilful crime,
By the just gods, whom no weak pity moved,
   Was doomed to wear out her appointed time,
Apart from happy ghosts, that gather flowers
Of blissful quiet 'mid unfading bowers.

—Yet tears to human suffering are due;
And mortal hopes defeated and o'erthrown
Are mourned by man, and not by man alone,
As fondly he believes.—Upon the side
Of Hellespont (such faith was entertained)
   A knot of spiry trees for ages grew
From out the tomb of him for whom she died;
And ever, when such stature they had gained
   That Ilium's walls were subject to their view,
The trees' tall summits withered at the sight;
A constant interchange of growth and blight.

## TO THE DAISY.

WITH little here to do or see
    Of things that in the great world be,
Sweet Daisy! oft I talk to thee,
    For thou art worthy,
Thou unassuming commonplace
Of Nature, with that homely face,
And yet with something of a grace
    Which love makes for thee!

Oft on the dappled turf at ease
I sit and play with similes,
Loose types of things through all degrees,
    Thoughts of thy raising;
And many a fond and idle name
I give to thee, for praise or blame
As is the humour of the game,
    While I am gazing.

A nun demure, of lowly port;
Or sprightly maiden, of Love's court,
In thy simplicity the sport
    Of all temptations;
A queen in crown of rubies drest;
A starveling in a scanty vest;
Are all, as seems to suit thee best,
    Thy appellations.

A little Cyclops, with one eye
Staring to threaten and defy,
That thought comes next—and instantly
    The freak is over,

The shape will vanish, and behold!
A silver shield with boss of gold
That spreads itself, some fairy bold
    In fight to cover.

I see thee glittering from afar—
And then thou art a pretty star,
Not quite so fair as many are
    In heaven above thee!
Yet like a star, with glittering crest,
Self-poised in air thou seem'st to rest;—
May peace come never to his nest
    Who shall reprove thee!

Sweet Flower! for by that name at last
When all my reveries are past
I call thee, and to that cleave fast,
    Sweet silent Creature!
That breath'st with me in sun and air,
Do thou, as thou art wont, repair
My heart with gladness, and a share
    Of thy meek nature!

---

## TO THE SKYLARK.

ETHEREAL minstrel! pilgrim of the sky!
  Dost thou despise the earth where cares abound?
Or while the wings aspire, are heart and eye
  Both with thy nest upon the dewy ground?
Thy nest which thou canst drop into at will,
Those quivering wings composed, that music still!

To the last point of vision, and beyond,
   Mount, daring warbler!—that love-prompted strain
—'Twixt thee and thine a never-failing bond—
   Thrills not the less the bosom of the plain:
Yet mightst thou seem, proud privilege! to sing
All independent of the leafy Spring.

Leave to the nightingale her shady wood;
   A privacy of glorious light is thine,
Whence thou dost pour upon the world a flood
   Of harmony, with instinct more divine;
Type of the wise, who soar, but never roam—
True to the kindred points of Heaven and Home!

---

### THE DAFFODILS.

I WANDERED lonely as a cloud
   That floats on high o'er vales and hills,
When all at once I saw a crowd,
   A host of golden daffodils,
Beside the lake, beneath the trees
Fluttering and dancing in the breeze.

Continuous as the stars that shine
   And twinkle on the milky way,
They stretched in never-ending line
   Along the margin of a bay:
Ten thousand saw I at a glance
Tossing their heads in sprightly dance.

The waves beside them danced, but they
    Outdid the sparkling waves in glee :—
A Poet could not but be gay
    In such a jocund company !
I gazed—and gazed—but little thought
What wealth the show to me had brought;

For oft, when on my couch I lie
    In vacant or in pensive mood,
They flash upon that inward eye
    Which is the bliss of solitude;
And then my heart with pleasure fills,
And dances with the daffodils.

---

## THE EDUCATION OF NATURE.

THREE years she grew in sun and shower;
    Then Nature said, " A lovelier flower
    On earth was never sown :
This child I to myself will take;
She shall be mine, and I will make
    A lady of my own.

" Myself will to my darling be
Both law and impulse : and with me
    The girl, in rock and plain,
In earth and heaven, in glade and bower,
Shall feel an overseeing power
    To kindle or restrain.

" She shall be sportive as the fawn
That wild with glee across the lawn
   Or up the mountain springs;
And hers shall be the breathing balm,
And hers the silence and the calm
   Of mute insensate things.

" The floating clouds their state shall lend
To her; for her the willow bend;
   Nor shall she fail to see
E'en in the motions of the storm
Grace that shall mould the maiden's form
   By silent sympathy.

" The stars of midnight shall be dear
To her; and she shall lean her ear
   In many a secret place
Where rivulets dance their wayward round,
And beauty born of murmuring sound
   Shall pass into her face.

" And vital feelings of delight
Shall rear her form to stately height,
   Her virgin bosom swell;
Such thoughts to Lucy I will give
While she and I together live
   Here in this happy dell."

Thus Nature spake—The work was done—
How soon my Lucy's race was run!
   She died, and left to me
This heath, this calm and quiet scene;
The memory of what has been,
   And never more will be.

## THE LOST LOVE.

SHE dwelt among the untrodden ways
   Beside the springs of Dove;
A maid whom there were none to praise,
   And very few to love.

A violet by a mossy stone
   Half-hidden from the eye!
—Fair as a star, when only one
   Is shining in the sky.

She lived unknown, and few could know
   When Lucy ceased to be;
But she is in her grave, and O!
   The difference to me!

---

## A PORTRAIT.

SHE was a phantom of delight
   When first she gleamed upon my sight;
A lovely apparition, sent
To be a moment's ornament;
Her eyes as stars of twilight fair;
Like Twilight's, too, her dusky hair;
But all things else about her drawn
From May-time and the cheerful dawn;
A dancing shape, an image gay,
To haunt, to startle, and waylay.

I saw her upon nearer view,
A spirit, yet a woman too!
Her household motions light and free,
And steps of virgin-liberty;
A countenance in which did meet
Sweet records, promises as sweet;
A creature not too bright or good
For human nature's daily food,
For transient sorrows, simple wiles,
Praise, blame, love, kisses, tears, and smiles.

And now I see with eye serene
The very pulse of the machine;
A being breathing thoughtful breath,
A traveller between life and death:
The reason firm, the temperate will,
Endurance, foresight, strength, and skill;
A perfect woman, nobly planned
To warn, to comfort, and command;
And yet a Spirit still, and bright
With something of an angel-light.

## BY THE SEA.

IT is a beauteous evening, calm and free;
    The holy time is quiet as a nun
Breathless with adoration; the broad sun
Is sinking down in its tranquillity;
The gentleness of heaven is on the Sea;
Listen! the mighty being is awake,
And doth with his eternal motion make
A sound like thunder—everlastingly.

## Samuel Taylor Coleridge.

### RIME OF THE ANCIENT MARINER.

#### IN SEVEN PARTS.

##### PART I.

*An Ancient Mariner meeteth three gallants bidden to a wedding-feast, and detaineth one.*

IT is an Ancient Mariner,
  And he stoppeth one of three:
"By thy long gray beard and glittering eye,
Now wherefore stopp'st thou me?

"The Bridegroom's doors are opened wide,
And I am next of kin;
The guests are met, the feast is set—
Mayst hear the merry din."

He holds him with his skinny hand:
"There was a ship," quoth he.
"Hold off! unhand me, gray-beard loon!"
Eftsoons his hand dropt he.

*The Wedding-Guest is spellbound by the eye of the old seafaring man, and constrained to hear his tale.*

He holds him with his glittering eye—
The Wedding-Guest stood still;
He listens like a three years' child:
The Mariner hath his will.

The Wedding-Guest sat on a stone—
He cannot choose but hear;
And thus spake on that ancient man,
The bright-eyed Mariner:

"The ship was cheered, the harbour cleared;
Merrily did we drop
Below the kirk, below the hill,
Below the light-house top.

"The sun came up upon the left, *The Mariner tells how the ship sailed southward with a good wind and fair weather, till it reached the Line.*
Out of the sea came he;
And he shone bright, and on the right
Went down into the sea;

"Higher and higher every day,
Till over the mast at noon—"
The Wedding-Guest here beat his breast,
For he heard the loud bassoon.

The bride hath paced into the hall— *The Wedding-Guest heareth the bridal music; but the Mariner continueth his tale.*
Red as a rose is she;
Nodding their heads before her goes
The merry minstrelsy.

The Wedding-Guest he beat his breast,
Yet he cannot choose but hear;
And thus spake on that ancient man,
The bright-eyed Mariner:

"And now the Storm-blast came, and he *The ship drawn by a storm toward the south pole.*
Was tyrannous and strong;
He struck with his o'ertaking wings,
And chased us south along.

"With sloping masts and dipping prow—
As who pursued with yell and blow
Still treads the shadow of his foe,

And forward bends his head—
The ship drove fast; loud roared the blast,
And southward aye we fled.

"And now there came both mist and snow,
And it grew wondrous cold;
And ice, mast-high, came floating by,
As green as emerald.

*The land of ice, and of fearful sounds, where no living thing was to be seen.*

"And through the drifts the snowy cliffs
Did send a dismal sheen;
Nor shapes of men nor beasts we ken—
The ice was all between.

"The ice was here, the ice was there,
The ice was all around;
It cracked and growled, and roared and howled,
Like noises in a swound!

*Till a great sea-bird, called the Albatross, came through the snow-fog, and was received with great joy and hospitality.*

"At length did cross an Albatross—
Thorough the fog it came;
As if it had been a Christian soul,
We hailed it in God's name.

"It ate the food it ne'er had eat,
And round and round it flew:

*And lo! the Albatross proveth a bird of good omen, and followeth the ship as it returned northward through fog and floating ice.*

The ice did split with a thunder-fit—
The helmsman steered us through!

"And a good south wind sprang up behind;
The Albatross did follow,
And every day, for food or play,
Came to the mariners' hollo!

"In mist or cloud, on mast or shroud,
It perched for vespers nine;
Whiles all the night, through fog-smoke white,
Glimmered the white moon-shine."

"God save thee, Ancient Mariner!  *The Ancient*
From the fiends that plague thee thus!— *Mariner inhospi-*
Why look'st thou so?"—"With my cross- *tably killeth the*
    bow *pious bird of good*
I shot the Albatross!" *omen.*

## PART II.

"The sun now rose upon the right—
Out of the sea came he,
Still hid in mist, and on the left
Went down into the sea.

"And the good south wind still blew behind;
But no sweet bird did follow,
Nor any day for food or play
Came to the mariners' hollo.

"And I had done a hellish thing,  *His ship-mates*
And it would work 'em woe; *cry out against*
For all averred I had killed the bird *the Ancient Mar-*
That made the breeze to blow: *iner, for killing*
'Ah, wretch!' said they, 'the bird to slay, *the bird of good*
That made the breeze to blow!' *luck.*

"Nor dim nor red, like God's own head *But when the fog*
The glorious sun uprist; *cleared off, they*
Then all averred I had killed the bird *justify the same,*
    *and thus make*
    *themselves ac-*
    *complices in the*
    *crime.*

That brought the fog and mist:
'"Twas right,' said they, 'such birds to slay,
That bring the fog and mist.'

*The fair breeze continues; the ship enters the Pacific Ocean, and sails northward, even till it reached the Line.*

"The fair breeze blew, the white foam flew,
The furrow followed free;
We were the first that ever burst
Into that silent sea.

*The ship hath been suddenly becalmed;*

"Down dropt the breeze, the sails dropt down—
'Twas sad as sad could be;
And we did speak only to break
The silence of the sea.

"All in a hot and copper sky
The bloody sun, at noon,
Right up above the mast did stand,
No bigger than the moon.

"Day after day, day after day,
We stuck—nor breath nor motion;
As idle as a painted ship
Upon a painted ocean.

*And the Albatross begins to be avenged.*

"Water, water everywhere,
And all the boards did shrink;
Water, water everywhere,
Nor any drop to drink!

"The very deep did rot; O Christ!
That ever this should be!
Yea, slimy things did crawl with legs
Upon the slimy sea!

"About, about, in reel and rout,
The death-fires danced at night;
The water, like a witch's oils,
Burnt green, and blue, and white.

"And some in dreams assurèd were
Of the Spirit that plagued us so;
Nine fathom deep he had followed us
From the land of mist and snow.

"And every tongue, through utter drought,
Was withered at the root;
We could not speak, no more than if
We had been choked with soot.

"Ah! well-a-day! what evil looks
Had I from old and young!
Instead of the cross, the Albatross
About my neck was hung.

*A Spirit had followed them— one of the invisible inhabitants of this planet, neither departed souls nor angels; concerning whom the learned Jew, Josephus, and the Platonic Constantinopolitan, Michael Psellus, may be consulted. They are very numerous, and there is no climate or element without one or more.*

*The ship-mates, in their sore distress, would fain throw the whole guilt on the Ancient Mariner: in sign whereof they hang the dead sea-bird round his neck.*

### PART III.

"There passed a weary time. Each throat
Was parched, and glazed each eye—
A weary time! a weary time!
How glazed each weary eye!—
When, looking westward, I beheld
A something in the sky.

"At first it seemed a little speck,
And then it seemed a mist;
It moved and moved, and took at last
A certain shape, I wist—

*The Ancient Mariner beholdeth a sign in the element afar off.*

"A speck, a mist, a shape, I wist!
And still it neared and neared;
As if it dodged a water-sprite,
It plunged and tacked and veered.

*At its nearer approach, it seemeth him to be a ship: and at a dear ransom he freeth his speech from the bonds of thirst.*

"With throats unslaked, with black lips baked,
We could nor laugh nor wail;
Through utter drought all dumb we stood!
I bit my arm, I sucked the blood,
And cried, 'A sail! a sail!'

*A flash of joy.*

"With throats unslaked, with black lips [baked,
Agape they heard me call;
Gramercy! they for joy did grin,
And all at once their breath drew in,
As they were drinking all.

*And horror follows. For can it be a ship that comes onward without wind or tide?*

"'See! see!' I cried, 'she tacks no more!
Hither to work us weal—
Without a breeze, without a tide,
She steadies with upright keel!'

"The western wave was all a-flame;
The day was well nigh done;
Almost upon the western wave
Rested the broad, bright sun,
When that strange shape drove suddenly
Betwixt us and the sun.

*It seemeth him but the skeleton of a ship.*

"And straight the sun was flecked with bars,
(Heaven's mother send us grace!)
As if through a dungeon-grate he peered
With broad and burning face.

"'Alas!' thought I—and my heart beat loud—
'How fast she nears and nears!
Are those her sails that glance in the sun,
Like restless gossameres?

"'Are those her ribs through which the sun
Did peer as through a grate?
And is that woman all her crew?
Is that a death? and are there two?
Is Death that woman's mate?'

"Her lips were red, her looks were free,
Her locks were yellow as gold;
Her skin was as white as leprosy:
The night-mare, Life-in-Death, was she,
Who thicks man's blood with cold.

"The naked hulk alongside came,
And the twain were casting dice:
'The game is done! I've won! I've won!'
Quoth she, and whistles thrice.

"The sun's rim dips, the stars rush out,
At one stride comes the dark;
With far-heard whisper, o'er the sea,
Off shot the spectre bark.

"We listened, and looked sideways up;
Fear at my heart, as at a cup,
My life-blood seemed to sip;
The stars were dim, and thick the night—
The steersman's face by his lamp gleamed white;

*And its ribs are seen as bars on the face of the setting sun. The spectre-woman and her death-mate, and no other on board the skeleton ship.*

*Like vessel, like crew!*

*Death and Life-in-Death have diced for the ship's crew, and she (the latter) winneth the Ancient Mariner.*

*No twilight within the courts of the Sun.*

*At the rising of the moon.*

>    From the sails the dew did drip—
>    Till clomb above the eastern bar
>    The hornèd moon, with one bright star
>    Within the nether tip.

*One after another.*

>    "One after one, by the star-dogged moon,
>    Too quick for groan or sigh,
>    Each turned his face with a ghastly pang,
>    And cursed me with his eye.

*His ship-mates drop down dead.*

>    "Four times fifty living men,
>    (And I heard nor sigh nor groan!)
>    With heavy thump, a lifeless lump,
>    They dropped down one by one.

*But Life-in-Death begins her work on the Ancient Mariner.*

>    "The souls did from their bodies fly,—
>    They fled to bliss or woe!
>    And every soul it passed me by,
>    Like the whizz of my cross-bow!"

## PART IV.

*The Wedding-Guest feareth that a Spirit is talking to him.*

>    "I FEAR thee, Ancient Mariner!
>    I fear thy skinny hand!
>    And thou art long, and lank, and brown,
>    As is the ribbed sea-sand.

*But the Ancient Mariner assureth him of his bodily life, and proceedeth to relate his horrible penance.*

>    "I fear thee and thy glittering eye,
>    And thy skinny hand so brown"—
>    "Fear not, fear not, thou Wedding-Guest!
>    This body dropped not down.

"Alone, alone, all, all alone,
Alone on a wide, wide sea!
And never a saint took pity on
My soul in agony.

"The many men, so beautiful! *He despiseth the*
And they all dead did lie; *creatures of the*
And a thousand thousand slimy things *calm.*
Lived on—and so did I.

"I looked upon the rotting sea, *And envied that*
And drew my eyes away; *they should live,*
I looked upon the rotting deck, *and so many lie*
And there the dead men lay. *dead.*

"I looked to heaven, and tried to pray;
But or ever a prayer had gusht,
A wicked whisper came, and made
My heart as dry as dust.

"I closed my lids, and kept them close,
And the balls like pulses beat;
For the sky and the sea and the sea and the
    sky
Lay like a load on my weary eye,
And the dead were at my feet.

"The cold sweat melted from their limbs— *But the curse*
Nor rot nor reek did they; *liveth for him in*
The look with which they looked on me *the eye of the*
Had never passed away. *dead men.*

"An orphan's curse would drag to hell
A spirit from on high;

| | |
|---|---|
| In his loneliness and fixedness he yearneth towards the journeying moon, and the stars that still sojourn, yet still move onward; and everywhere the blue sky belongs to them, and is their appointed rest, and their native country, and their own natural homes, which they enter unannounced, as lords that are certainly expected; and yet there is a silent joy at their arrival.<br><br>By the light of the moon he beholdeth God's creatures of the great calm. | But O! more horrible than that<br>Is the curse in a dead man's eye!<br>Seven days, seven nights, I saw that curse—<br>And yet I could not die.<br><br>" The moving moon went up the sky,<br>And nowhere did abide;<br>Softly she was going up,<br>And a star or two beside—<br><br>" Her beams bemocked the sultry main,<br>Like April hoar-frost spread;<br>But where the ship's huge shadow lay<br>The charmèd water burnt alway,<br>A still and awful red.<br><br>" Beyond the shadow of the ship<br>I watched the water-snakes;<br>They movēd in tracks of shining white;<br>And when they reared, the elfish light<br>Fell off in hoary flakes.<br><br>" Within the shadow of the ship<br>I watched their rich attire—<br>Blue, glossy green, and velvet black,<br>They coiled and swam; and every track<br>Was a flash of golden fire. |
| Their beauty and their happiness.<br><br>He blesseth them in his heart. | " O happy living things! no tongue<br>Their beauty might declare;<br>A spring of love gushed from my heart,<br>And I blessed them unaware—<br>Sure my kind saint took pity on me,<br>And I blessed them unaware. |

"The self-same moment I could pray;
And from my neck so free
The Albatross fell off, and sank
Like lead into the sea."

*The spell begins to break.*

### PART V.

"O sleep! it is a gentle thing,
Beloved from pole to pole!
To Mary Queen the praise be given!
She sent the gentle sleep from Heaven
That slid into my soul.

"The silly buckets on the deck,
That had so long remained,
I dreamt that they were filled with dew;
And when I awoke, it rained.

*By grace of the holy Mother, the Ancient Mariner is refreshed with rain.*

"My lips were wet, my throat was cold,
My garments all were dank;
Sure I had drunken in my dreams,
And still my body drank.

"I moved, and could not feel my limbs;
I was so light—almost
I thought that I had died in sleep,
And was a blessed ghost.

"And soon I heard a roaring wind—
It did not come anear;
But with its sound it shook the sails,
That were so thin and sere.

*He heareth sounds and seeth strange sights and commotions in the sky and the element.*

"The upper air burst into life;
And a hundred fire-flags sheen,

To and fro they were hurried about;
And to and fro, and in and out,
The wan stars danced between.

"And the coming wind did roar more loud,
And the sails did sigh like sedge;
And the rain poured down from one black
    cloud—
The moon was at its edge.

" The thick black cloud was cleft, and still
The moon was at its side;
Like waters shot from some high crag,
The lightning fell with never a jag—
A river steep and wide.

<small>The bodies of the ship's crew are inspired, and the ship moves on;</small>

" The loud wind never reached the ship,
Yet now the ship moved on!
Beneath the lightning and the moon
The dead men gave a groan.

" They groaned, they stirred, they all up-
    rose—
Nor spake, nor moved their eyes;
It had been strange, even in a dream,
To have seen those dead men rise.

" The helmsman steered, the ship moved
    on;
Yet never a breeze up blew;
The mariners all 'gan work the ropes,
Where they were wont to do;
They raised their limbs like lifeless tools—
We were a ghastly crew.

"The Body of my brother's son
Stood by me, knee to knee;
The body and I pulled at one rope,
But he said naught to me."

"I fear thee, Ancient Mariner!"
"Be calm, thou Wedding-Guest!
'Twas not those souls that fled in pain,
Which to their corses came again,
But a troop of spirits blest;
For when it dawned they dropped their arms,
And clustered round the mast;
Sweet sounds rose slowly through their mouths,
And from their bodies passed.

*But not by the souls of the men, nor by demons of earth or middle air, but by a blessed troop of angelic spirits, sent down by the invocation of the guardian saint.*

"Around, around flew each sweet sound,
Then darted to the sun;
Slowly the sounds came back again—
Now mixed, now one by one.

"Sometimes, a-dropping from the sky,
I heard the sky-lark sing;
Sometimes all little birds that are—
How they seemed to fill the sea and air
With their sweet jargoning!

"And now 'twas like all instruments,
Now like a lonely flute;
And now it is an angel's song,
That makes the heavens be mute.

"It ceased; yet still the sails made on
A pleasant noise till noon—
A noise like of a hidden brook
In the leafy month of June,
That to the sleeping woods all night
Singeth a quiet tune.

"Till noon we quietly sailed on,
Yet never a breeze did breathe;
Slowly and smoothly went the ship,
Moved onward from beneath.

*The lonesome spirit from the south-pole carries on the ship as far as the Line in obedience to the angelic troop; but still requireth vengeance.*

"Under the keel, nine fathom deep,
From the land of mist and snow
The spirit slid; and it was he
That made the ship to go.
The sails at noon left off their tune,
And the ship stood still also.

"The sun, right up above the mast,
Had fixed her to the ocean;
But in a minute she 'gan stir,
With a short uneasy motion—
Backwards and forwards half her length,
With a short uneasy motion.

"Then like a pawing horse let go,
She made a sudden bound—
It flung the blood into my head,
And I fell down in a swound.

*The polar spirit's fellow-demons,*

"How long in that same fit I lay
I have not to declare;

But ere my living life returned
I heard, and in my soul discerned,
Two voices in the air:

" 'Is it he?' quoth one, 'Is this the man?
By Him who died on cross,
With his cruel bow he laid full low
The harmless Albatross!

" 'The spirit who bideth by himself
In the land of mist and snow,
He loved the bird that loved the man
Who shot him with his bow.'

" The other was a softer voice,
As soft as honey-dew:
Quoth he, 'The man hath penance done,
And penance more will do.'

*the invisible inhabitants of the element, take part in his wrong; and two of them relate, one to the other, that penance, long and heavy for the Ancient Mariner, hath been accorded to the polar spirit, who returneth southward.*

### PART VI.

#### FIRST VOICE.

" 'But tell me, tell me! speak again,
Thy soft response renewing—
What makes that ship drive on so fast?
What is the ocean doing?'

#### SECOND VOICE.

" 'Still as a slave before his lord,
The ocean hath no blast;
His great bright eye most silently
Up to the moon is cast—

" 'If he may know which way to go;
For she guides him smooth or grim.
See, brother, see! how graciously
She looketh down on him.'

**FIRST VOICE.**

<small>The Mariner hath been cast into a trance; for the angelic power causeth the vessel to drive northward faster than human life could endure.</small>

" 'But why drives on that ship so fast,
Without or wave or wind?'

**SECOND VOICE.**

" 'The air is cut away before,
And closes from behind.

" 'Fly, brother, fly! more high, more high!
Or we shall be belated;
For slow and slow that ship will go,
When the Mariner's trance is abated.'

<small>The supernatural motion is retarded; the Mariner awakes, and his penance begins anew.</small>

" I woke, and we were sailing on
As in a gentle weather;
'Twas night, calm night—the moon was high;
The dead men stood together.

" All stood together on the deck,
For a charnel-dungeon fitter;
All fixed on me their stony eyes,
That in the moon did glitter.

" The pang, the curse, with which they died,
Had never passed away;
I could not draw my eyes from theirs,
Nor turn them up to pray.

"And now this spell was snapt; once more    The curse is
I viewed the ocean green,                    finally ex-
And looked far forth, yet little saw         piated.
Of what had else been seen—

"Like one that on a lonesome road
Doth walk in fear and dread,
And, having once turned round, walks on,
And turns no more his head;
Because he knows a frightful fiend
Doth close behind him tread.

"But soon there breathed a wind on me,
Nor sound nor motion made;
Its path was not upon the sea,
In ripple or in shade.

"It raised my hair, it fanned my cheek,
Like a meadow-gale of Spring—
It mingled strangely with my fears,
Yet it felt like a welcoming.

"Swiftly, swiftly flew the ship,
Yet she sailed softly too;
Sweetly, sweetly blew the breeze—
On me alone it blew.

"Oh! dream of joy! is this indeed         And the An-
The light-house top I see?                cient Mariner
Is this the hill? is this the kirk?       beholdeth his
Is this mine own countree?                native country.

"We drifted o'er the harbour-bar,
And I with sobs did pray—
'O let me be awake, my God!
Or let me sleep alway.'

"The harbour-bay was clear as glass,
So smoothly it was strewn!
And on the bay the moonlight lay,
And the shadow of the moon.

"The rock shone bright, the kirk no less
That stands above the rock;
The moonlight steeped in silentness
The steady weathercock.

*The angelic spirits leave the dead bodies,*

"And the bay was white with silent light
Till, rising from the same,
Full many shapes, that shadows were,
In crimson colours came.

*And appear in their own forms of light.*

"A little distance from the prow
Those crimson shadows were;
I turned my eyes upon the deck—
O Christ! what saw I there!

"Each corse lay flat, lifeless and flat;
And, by the holy rood!
A man all light, a seraph-man,
On every corse there stood.

"This seraph-band, each waved his hand—
It was a heavenly sight!
They stood as signals to the land,
Each one a lovely light;

" This seraph-band, each waved his hand;
No voice did they impart—
No voice; but O! the silence sank
Like music on my heart.

" But soon I heard the dash of oars,
I heard the pilot's cheer;
My head was turned perforce away,
And I saw a boat appear.

" The pilot and the pilot's boy,
I heard them coming fast;
Dear Lord in Heaven! it was a joy
The dead men could not blast.

" I saw a third—I heard his voice;
It is the hermit good!
He singeth loud his godly hymns
That he makes in the wood;
He'll shrieve my soul—he'll wash away
The Albatross's blood.

### PART VII.

" This hermit good lives in that wood     The Hermit of
Which slopes down to the sea.     the wood
How loudly his sweet voice he rears!
He loves to talk with marineres
That come from a far countree.

He kneels at morn, and noon, and eve—
He hath a cushion plump;
It is the moss that wholly hides
The rotted old oak-stump.

"The skiff-boat neared—I heard them talk:
'Why, this is strange, I trow!
Where are those lights, so many and fair,
That signal made but now?

*Approacheth the ship with wonder.*

"'Strange, by my faith!' the hermit said—
'And they answered not our cheer!
The planks looked warped! and see those sails,
How thin they are and sere!
I never saw aught like to them,
Unless perchance it were

"'Brown skeletons of leaves that lag
My forest-brook along,
When the ivy-tod is heavy with snow,
And the owlet whoops to the wolf below,
That eats the she-wolf's young.'

"'Dear Lord! it hath a fiendish look,'
The pilot made reply—
'I am a-feared'—'Push on, push on!'
Said the hermit cheerily.

"The boat came closer to the ship,
But I nor spake nor stirred;
The boat came close beneath the ship,
And straight a sound was heard:

*The ship suddenly sinketh.*

"Under the water it rumbled on,
Still louder and more dread;
It reached the ship, it split the bay—
The ship went down like lead.

"Stunned by that loud and dreadful sound,　*The Ancient
Which sky and ocean smote,　　　　　　　Mariner is
Like one that hath been seven days drowned　saved in the
My body lay afloat;　　　　　　　　　　　pilot's boat.*
But, swift as dreams, myself I found
Within the pilot's boat.

"Upon the whirl where sank the ship
The boat span round and round;
And all was still, save that the hill
Was telling of the sound.

"I moved my lips—the pilot shrieked
And fell down in a fit;
The holy hermit raised his eyes,
And prayed where he did sit.

"I took the oars; the pilot's boy,
Who now doth crazy go,
Laughed loud and long; and all the while
His eyes went to and fro:
'Ha! ha!' quoth he, 'full plain I see,
The devil knows how to row.'

"And now, all in my own countree,
I stood on the firm land!
The hermit stepped forth from the boat,
And scarcely he could stand.

"'O shrieve me, shrieve me, holy man!'—　*The Ancient
The hermit crossed his brow:　　　　　　Mariner ear-
'Say quick,' quoth he, 'I bid thee say—　nestly entreat-
What manner of man art thou?'　　　　　eth the Hermit
　　　　　　　　　　　　　　　　　　　　to shrieve him;*

*and the penance of life falls on him.*

"Forthwith this frame of mine was wrenched
With a woful agony,
Which forced me to begin my tale—
And then it left me free.

*And ever and anon throughout his future life an agony constraineth him to travel from land to land.*

"Since then, at an uncertain hour,
That agony returns;
And till my ghastly tale is told
This heart within me burns.

"I pass, like night, from land to land;
I have strange power of speech;
That moment that his face I see
I know the man that must hear me—
To him my tale I teach.

"What loud uproar bursts from that door!
The wedding-guests are there;
But in the garden-bower the bride
And bride-maids singing are;
And hark the little vesper-bell,
Which biddeth me to prayer!

"O Wedding-Guest! this soul hath been
Alone on a wide, wide sea—
So lonely 'twas, that God himself
Scarce seemed there to be.

"O sweeter than the marriage-feast,
'Tis sweeter far to me,
To walk together to the kirk
With a goodly company!—

" To walk together to the kirk,
And all together pray,
While each to his great Father bends—
Old men, and babes, and loving friends,
And youths and maidens gay!

" Farewell! farewell! but this I tell    And to teach
To thee, thou Wedding-Guest!            by his own ex-
He prayeth well who loveth well         ample, love,
Both man and bird and beast.            and reverence
                                        to all things
                                        that God made
                                        and loveth.

" He prayeth best who loveth best
All things both great and small;
For the dear God who loveth us,
He made and loveth all."

The Mariner, whose eye is bright,
Whose beard with age is hoar,
Is gone. And now the Wedding-Guest
Turned from the bridegroom's door.

He went like one that hath been stunned,
And is of sense forlorn;
A sadder and a wiser man
He rose the morrow morn.

## GENEVIEVE.

ALL thoughts, all passions, all delights,
    Whatever stirs this mortal frame,
Are all but ministers of Love,
    And feed his sacred flame.

Oft in my waking dreams do I
    Live o'er again that happy hour,
When midway on the mount I lay,
    Beside the ruined tower.

The moonlight stealing o'er the scene,
    Had blended with the lights of eve;
And she was there, my hope, my joy,
    My own dear Genevieve!

She leant against the armèd man,
    The statue of the armèd knight;
She stood and listened to my lay,
    Amid the lingering light.

Few sorrows hath she of her own,
    My hope, my joy, my Genevieve!
She loves me best whene'er I sing
    The songs that make her grieve.

I played a soft and doleful air,
    I sang an old and moving story—
An old rude song, that suited well
    That ruin wild and hoary.

She listened with a flitting blush,
　With downcast eyes and modest grace,
For well she knew I could not choose
　But gaze upon her face.

I told her of the knight that wore
　Upon his shield a burning brand;
And that for ten long years he woo'd
　The lady of the land.

I told her how he pined, and—ah!
　The deep, the low, the pleading tone
With which I sang another's love,
　Interpreted my own.

She listened with a flitting blush,
　With downcast eyes and modest grace,
And she forgave me, that I gazed
　Too fondly on her face!

But when I told the cruel scorn
　That crazed that bold and lovely knight,
And that he crossed the mountain-woods,
　Nor rested day nor night:

That sometimes from the savage den,
　And sometimes from the darksome shade,
And sometimes starting up at once
　In green and sunny glade,

There came and looked him in the face
　An angel beautiful and bright;
And that he knew it was a fiend,
　This miserable knight!

And that, unknowing what he did,
   He leaped amid a murderous band,
And saved from outrage worse than death
   The lady of the land!

And how she wept and clasped his knees;
   And how she tended him in vain—
And ever strove to expiate
   The scorn that crazed his brain;

And that she nursed him in a cave;
   And how his madness went away,
When on the yellow forest leaves
   A dying man he lay.

His dying words—but when I reached
   That tenderest strain of all the ditty,
My faltering voice and pausing harp
   Disturbed her soul with pity.

All impulses of soul and sense
   Had thrilled my guileless Genevieve;
The music and the doleful tale,
   The rich and balmy eve;

And hopes, and fears that kindle hope,
   An undistinguishable throng,
And gentle wishes long subdued,
   Subdued and cherished long.

She wept with pity and delight,
   She blushed with love and virgin shame:
And like the murmur of a dream,
   I heard her breathe my name.

Her bosom heaved—she stept aside,
  As conscious of my look she stept—
Then suddenly, with timorous eye,
  She fled to me and wept.

She half enclosed me in her arms,
  She pressed me with a meek embrace:
And bending back her head, looked up.
  And gazed upon my face.

'Twas partly love and partly fear,
  And partly 'twas a bashful art
That I might rather feel than see,
  The swelling of her heart.

I calmed her fears, and she was calm,
  And told her love with virgin pride,
And so I won my Genevieve,
  My own, my beauteous bride.

---

## WORK WITHOUT HOPE.

ALL nature seems at work. Stags leave their lair—
  The bees are stirring—birds are on the wing—
And Winter, slumbering in the open air,
  Wears on his smiling face a dream of Spring!
And I, the while, the sole unbusy thing,
Nor honey make, nor pair, nor build, nor sing.
    \*    \*    \*    \*
Work without hope draws nectar in a sieve,
And hope without an object cannot live.

## Robert Southey.

### THE SCHOLAR.

MY days among the dead are passed;
   Around me I behold,
Where'er these casual eyes are cast,
   The mighty minds of old;
My never-failing friends are they,
With whom I converse day by day.

With them I take delight in weal,
   And seek relief in woe;
And while I understand and feel
   How much to them I owe,
My cheeks have often been bedewed
With tears of thoughtful gratitude.

My thoughts are with the dead; with them
   I live in long-past years;
Their virtues love, their faults condemn,
   Partake their hopes and fears,
And from their lessons seek and find
Instruction with an humble mind.

My hopes are with the dead; anon
   My place with them will be,
And I with them shall travel on
   Through all futurity:
Yet leaving here a name, I trust,
That will not perish in the dust.

## THE WELL OF ST. KEYNE.

A WELL there is in the west country,
   And a clearer one never was seen;
There is not a wife in the west country
   But has heard of the well of St. Keyne.

An oak and an elm-tree stand beside,
   And behind does an ash-tree grow;
And a willow from the bank above
   Droops to the water below.

A traveller came to the well of St. Keyne;
   Joyfully he drew nigh,
For from cock-crow he had been travelling,
   And there was not a cloud in the sky.

He drank of the water so cool and clear,
   For thirsty and hot was he;
And he sat down upon the bank
   Under the willow-tree.

There came a man from the neighbouring town,
   At the well to fill his pail;
On the well-side he rested it,
   And he bade the stranger hail.

"Now, art thou a bachelor, stranger?" quoth he;
   "For an if thou hast a wife,
The happiest draught thou hast drank this day
   That ever thou didst in thy life.

"Or has thy good woman, if one thou hast,
  Ever here in Cornwall been?
For an if she have, I'll venture my life
  She has drank of the well of St. Keyne."

"I have left a good woman who never was here,"
  The stranger he made reply;
"But that my draught should be the better for that,
  I pray you answer me why."

"St. Keyne," quoth the Cornish man, "many a time
  Drank of this crystal well;
And before the angel summoned her,
  She laid on the water a spell.

"If the husband of this gifted well
  Shall drink before his wife,
A happy man henceforth is he,
  For he shall be master for life.

"But if the wife should drink of it first,
  God help the husband then!"
The stranger stooped to the well of St. Keyne,
  And drank of the water again.

"You drank of the well I warrant betimes?"
  He to the Cornish man said;
But the Cornish man smiled as the stranger spoke,
  And sheepishly shook his head.

"I hastened as soon as the wedding was done,
  And left my wife in the porch;
But i' faith she had been wiser than I,
  For she took a bottle to church."

## JASPAR.

JASPAR was poor, and vice and want
    Had made his heart like stone:
And Jaspar looked with envious eyes
    On riches not his own.

On plunder bent, abroad he went
    Toward the close of day,
And loitered on the lonely road
    Impatient for his prey.

No traveller came, he loitered long,
    And often looked around,
And paused and listened eagerly
    To catch some coming sound.

He sate him down beside the stream
    That crossed the lonely way.
So fair a scene might well have charmed
    All evil thoughts away:

He sate beneath a willow-tree,
    Which cast a trembling shade;
The gentle river full in front
    A little island made—

Where pleasantly the moonbeam shone
    Upon the poplar-trees,
Whose shadow on the stream below
    Played slowly to the breeze.

He listened—and he heard the wind
　　That waved the willow-tree;
He heard the waters flow along,
　　And murmur quietly.

He listened for the traveller's tread,
　　The nightingale sang sweet;—
He started up, for now he heard
　　The sound of coming feet:

He started up, and grasped a stake,
　　And waited for his prey;
There came a lonely traveller,
　　And Jaspar crossed his way.

But Jaspar's threats and curses failed
　　The traveller to appal;
He would not lightly yield the purse
　　Which held his little all.

Awhile he struggled, but he strove
　　With Jaspar's strength in vain;
Beneath his blows he fell and groaned,
　　And never spake again.

Jaspar raised up the murdered man,
　　And plunged him in the flood,
And in the running water then
　　He cleansed his hands from blood.

The waters closed around the corpse,
　　And cleansed his hands from gore;
The willow waved, the stream flowed on,
　　And murmured as before.

There was no human eye had seen
  The blood the murderer spilt,
And Jaspar's conscience never felt
  The avenging goad of guilt.

And soon the ruffian had consumed
  The gold he gained so ill;
And years of secret guilt passed on,
  And he was needy still.

One eve beside the alehouse fire
  He sate as it befell,
When in there came a labouring man
  Whom Jaspar knew full well.

He sate him down by Jaspar's side,
  A melancholy man;
For, spite of honest toil, the world
  Went hard with Jonathan.

His toil a little earned, and he
  With little was content;
But sickness on his wife had fallen,
  And all was well-nigh spent.

Long, with his wife and little ones,
  He shared the scanty meal,
And saw their looks of wretchedness,
  And felt what wretches feel.

Their landlord, a hard man, that day
  Had seized the little left,
And now the sufferer found himself
  Of every thing bereft.

He leaned his head upon his hand,
 His elbow on his knee,
And so by Jaspar's side he sate,
 And not a word said he.

"Nay—why so downcast?" Jaspar cried,
 "Come—cheer up, Jonathan!
Drink, neighbour, drink! 'twill warm thy heart—
 Come! come! take courage, man!"

He took the cup that Jaspar gave,
 And down he drained it quick;
"I have a wife," said Jonathan,
 "And she is deadly sick.

"She has no bed to lie upon,
 I saw them take her bed—
And I have children—would to God
 That they and I were dead!

"Our landlord he goes home to-night,
 And he will sleep in peace—
I would that I were in my grave,
 For there all troubles cease.

"In vain I prayed him to forbear,
 Though wealth enough has he!
God be to him as merciless
 As he has been to me!"

When Jaspar saw the poor man's soul
 On all his ills intent,
He plied him with the heartening cup,
 And with him forth he went.

"This landlord on his homeward road
    'Twere easy now to meet:
The road is lonesome, Jonathan!
    And vengeance, man! is sweet."

He listened to the tempter's voice,
    The thought it made him start!—
His head was hot, and wretchedness
    Had hardened now his heart.

Along the lonely road they went,
    And waited for their prey;
They sate them down beside the stream
    That crossed the lonely way.

They sate them down beside the stream,
    And never a word they said:
They sate, and listened silently
    To hear the traveller's tread.

The night was calm, the night was dark,
    No star was in the sky;
The wind it waved the willow-boughs,
    The stream flowed quietly.

The night was calm, the air was still,
    Sweet sang the nightingale;
The soul of Jonathan was soothed,
    His heart began to fail.

"'Tis weary waiting here," he cried,
    "And now the hour is late;
Methinks he will not come to-night—
    No longer let us wait."

"Have patience, man!" the ruffian said,
  "A little we may wait;
But longer shall his wife expect
  Her husband at the gate."

Then Jonathan grew sick at heart:
  "My conscience yet is clear!
Jaspar—it is not yet too late—
  I will not linger here."

"How now!" cried Jaspar, "why, I thought
  Thy conscience was asleep;
No more such qualms!—the night is dark,
  The river here is deep."

"What matters that," said Jonathan,
  Whose blood began to freeze,
"When there is One above whose eye
  The deeds of darkness sees?"

"We are safe enough," said Jaspar then,
  "If that be all thy fear!
Nor eye above, nor eye below,
  Can pierce the darkness here."

That instant as the murderer spake,
  There came a sudden light;
Strong as the mid-day sun it shone,
  Though all around was night:

It hung upon the willow-tree,
  It hung upon the flood,
It gave to view the poplar-isle,
  And all the scene of blood.

The traveller who journeys there,
  He surely hath espied
A madman who has made his home
  Upon the river's side.

His cheek is pale, his eye is wild,
  His look bespeaks despair;
For Jaspar since that hour has made
  His home unsheltered there.

And fearful are his dreams at night,
  And dread to him the day;
He thinks upon his untold crime,
  And never dares to pray.

The summer suns, the winter storms,
  O'er him unheeded roll,
For heavy is the weight of blood
  Upon the maniac's soul.

---

## Thomas Campbell.

### HOHENLINDEN.

ON Linden, when the sun was low,
  All bloodless lay th' untrodden snow,
And dark as winter was the flow
  Of Iser, rolling rapidly.

But Linden saw another sight,
When the drum beat, at dead of night,
Commanding fires of death to light
    The darkness of her scenery.

By torch and trumpet fast arrayed,
Each horseman drew his battle-blade,
And furious every charger neighed,
    To join the dreadful revelry.

Then shook the hills with thunder riven,
Then rushed the steed to battle driven,
And louder than the bolts of heaven,
    Far flashed the red artillery.

But redder yet that light shall glow,
On Linden's hills of stainèd snow;
And bloodier yet the torrent flow
    Of Iser, rolling rapidly.

'Tis morn, but scarce yon level sun
Can pierce the war-clouds, rolling dun,
Where furious Frank and fiery Hun
    Shout in their sulph'rous canopy.

The combat deepens. On, ye brave,
Who rush to glory, or the grave!
Wave, Munich! all thy banners wave,
    And charge with all thy chivalry!

Few, few shall part where many meet!
The snow shall be their winding-sheet,
And every turf beneath their feet
    Shall be a soldier's sepulchre.

## THE SOLDIER'S DREAM.

OUR bugles sang truce—for the night-cloud had lowered,
    And the sentinel stars set their watch in the sky;
And thousands had sunk on the ground overpowered,
    The weary to sleep, and the wounded to die.

When reposing that night on my pallet of straw,
    By the wolf-scaring fagot that guarded the slain;
At the dead of the night a sweet vision I saw,
    And thrice ere the morning I dreamt it again.

Methought from the battle-field's dreadful array,
    Far, far I had roamed on a desolate track;
'Twas autumn—and sunshine arose on the way
    To the home of my fathers, that welcomed me back.

I flew to the pleasant fields traversed so oft
    In life's morning march, when my bosom was young;
I heard my own mountain-goats bleating aloft,
    And knew the sweet strain that the corn-reapers sung.

Then pledged we the wine-cup, and fondly I swore
    From my home and my weeping friends never to part;
My little ones kissed me a thousand times o'er,
    And my wife sobbed aloud in her fulness of heart.

"Stay, stay with us—rest, thou art weary and worn"—
    And fain was their war-broken soldier to stay;
But sorrow returned with the dawning of morn,
    And the voice in my dreaming ear melted away.

## LORD ULLIN'S DAUGHTER.

A CHIEFTAIN, to the Highlands bound,
    Cries, "Boatman, do not tarry!
And I'll give thee a silver pound
    To row us o'er the ferry."

"Now who be ye, would cross Lochgyle,
    This dark and stormy water?"
"Oh, I'm the chief of Ulva's isle,
    And this Lord Ullin's daughter.

"And fast before her father's men
    Three days we've fled together;
For should he find us in the glen,
    My blood would stain the heather.

"His horsemen hard behind us ride;
    Should they our steps discover,
Then who will cheer my bonny bride
    When they have slain her lover?"

Outspoke the hardy Highland wight:
    "I'll go, my chief—I'm ready.
It is not for your silver bright,
    But for your winsome lady.

"And by my word! the bonny bird
    In danger shall not tarry;
So, though the waves are raging white,
    I'll row you o'er the ferry."

By this the storm grew loud apace;
  The water-wraith was shrieking;
And in the scowl of heaven each face
  Grew dark as they were speaking.

But still as wilder blew the wind,
  And as the night grew drearer,
Adown the glen rode armèd men—
  Their trampling sounded nearer.

"O haste thee, haste!" the lady cries,
  "Though tempests round us gather;
I'll meet the raging of the skies,
  But not an angry father."

The boat has left a stormy land,
  A stormy sea before her—
When, oh! too strong for human hand,
  The tempest gathered o'er her.

And still they rowed amidst the roar
  Of waters fast prevailing—
Lord Ullin reached that fatal shore;
  His wrath was changed to wailing.

For sore dismayed, through storm and shade
  His child he did discover;
One lovely hand she stretched for aid,
  And one was round her lover.

"Come back! come back!" he cried in grief,
  "Across this stormy water;
And I'll forgive your Highland chief,
  My daughter!—O my daughter!"

Twas vain :—the loud waves lashed the shore,
  Return or aid preventing;
The waters wild went o'er his child,
  And he was left lamenting.

---

## BATTLE OF THE BALTIC.

### I.

OF Nelson and the North
  Sing the glorious day's renown,
When to battle fierce came forth
  All the might of Denmark's crown,
And her arms along the deep proudly shone;
  By each gun the lighted brand
  In a bold, determined hand,
  And the Prince of all the land
    Led them on.

### II.

Like leviathans afloat
  Lay their bulwarks on the brine;
While the sign of battle flew
  On the lofty British line—
It was ten of April morn by the chime.
  As they drifted on their path
  There was silence deep as death;
  And the boldest held his breath
    For a time.

### III.

But the might of England flushed
  To anticipate the scene;

And her van the fleeter rushed
   O'er the deadly space between.
"Hearts of oak!" our captain cried; when each gun
   From its adamantine lips
   Spread a death-shade round the ships,
   Like the hurricane eclipse
     Of the sun.

### IV.

Again! again! again!
   And the havoc did not slack,
Till a feeble cheer the Dane
   To our cheering sent us back;
Their shots along the deep slowly boom —
   Then ceased—and all is wail,
   As they strike the shattered sail,
   Or, in conflagration pale,
     Light the gloom.

### V.

Out spoke the victor then,
   As he hailed them o'er the wave:
"Ye are brothers! ye are men!
   And we conquer but to save;
So peace instead of death let us bring;
   But yield, proud foe, thy fleet,
   With the crews, at England's feet,
   And make submission meet
     To our king."

### VI.

Then Denmark blessed our chief,
   That he gave her wounds repose;

And the sounds of joy and grief
From her people wildly rose,
As Death withdrew his shades from the day--
While the sun looked smiling bright
O'er a wide and woeful sight,
Where the fires of funeral light
Died away.

### VII.

Now joy, Old England, raise!
For the tidings of thy might,
By the festal cities' blaze,
Whilst the wine-cup shines in light;
And yet, amidst that joy and uproar,
Let us think of them that sleep
Full many a fathom deep,
By thy wild and stormy steep,
Elsinore!

### VIII.

Brave hearts! to Britain's pride
Once so faithful and so true,
On the deck of fame that died,
With the gallant, good Riou—
Soft sigh the winds of heaven o'er their grave!
While the billow mournful rolls,
And the mermaid's song condoles,
Singing glory to the souls
Of the brave!

## VALEDICTORY STANZAS TO JOHN PHILIP KEMBLE.

PRIDE of the British stage,
   A long and last adieu !
Whose image brought the heroic age
   Revived to Fancy's view.
Like fields refreshed with dewy light
   When the sun smiles his last,
Thy parting presence makes more bright
   Our memory of the past;
And memory conjures feelings up
   That wine or music need not swell,
As high we lift the festal cup
   To Kemble! fare thee well!

His was the spell o'er hearts
   Which only acting lends,—
The youngest of the sister arts,
   Where all their beauty blends:
For ill can poetry express
   Full many a tone of thought sublime,
And painting, mute and motionless,
   Steals but a glance of time.
But by the mighty actor brought,
   Illusion's perfect triumphs come—
Verse ceases to be airy thought,
   And sculpture to be dumb.

Time may again revive,
   But ne'er eclipse the charm,
When Cato spoke in him alive,
   Or Hotspur kindled warm.

What soul was not resigned entire
   To the deep sorrows of the Moor,—
What English heart was not on fire
   With him at Agincourt?
And yet a majesty possessed
   His transport's most impetuous tone,
And to each passion of his breast
   The Graces gave their zone.

High were the task—too high,
   Ye conscious bosoms here!
In words to paint your memory
   Of Kemble and of Lear;
But who forgets that white, discrownèd head,
   Those bursts of reason's half-extinguished glare—
Those tears upon Cordelia's bosom shed,
   In doubt more touching than despair,
If 'twas reality he felt?
   Had Shakespeare's self amidst you been,
Friends, he had seen you melt,
   And triumphed to have seen!

And there was many an hour
   Of blended kindred fame,
When Siddons's auxiliar power
   And sister magic came.
Together at the Muse's side
   The tragic paragons had grown—
They were the children of her pride,
   The columns of her throne;
And undivided favour ran
   From heart to heart in their applause,

Save for the gallantry of man
   In lovelier woman's cause.


Fair as some classic dome,
   Robust and richly graced,
Your Kemble's spirit was the home
   Of genius and of taste :—
Taste like the silent dial's power,
   That, when supernal light is given,
Can measure inspiration's hour,
   And tell its height in heaven.
At once ennobled and correct,
   His mind surveyed the tragic page,
And what the actor could effect,
   The scholar could presage.

These were his traits of worth :—
   And must we lose them now!
And shall the scene no more show forth
   His sternly pleasing brow!
Alas, the moral brings a tear !—
   'Tis all a transient hour below;
And we that would detain thee here,
   Ourselves as fleetly go!
Yet shall our latest age
   This parting scene review :—
Pride of the British stage,
   A long and last adieu!

## Sir Walter Scott.

**THE LAY OF THE LAST MINSTREL.**

**THE MINSTREL.**

THE way was long, the wind was cold,
    The Minstrel was infirm and old;
His withered cheek, and tresses gray,
Seemed to have known a better day;
The harp, his sole remaining joy,
Was carried by an orphan boy.
The last of all the bards was he
Who sung of Border chivalry;
For, well-a-day! their date was fled,
His tuneful brethren all were dead;
And he, neglected and oppressed,
Wished to be with them, and at rest.
No more, on prancing palfrey borne,
He carolled, light as lark at morn;
No longer courted and caressed,
High placed in hall, a welcome guest,
He poured, to lord and lady gay,
The unpremeditated lay:
Old times were changed, old manners gone,
A stranger filled the Stuart's throne;
The bigots of the iron time
Had called his harmless art a crime.
A wandering harper, scorned and poor,
He begged his bread from door to door;

And tuned, to please a peasant's ear,
The harp, a king had loved to hear.

 He passed where Newark's stately tower
Looks out from Yarrow's birchen bower:
The Minstrel gazed with wishful eye—
No humbler resting-place was nigh;
With hesitating step, at last,
The embattled portal-arch he passed,
Whose ponderous grate, and massy bar,
Had oft rolled back the tide of war,
But never closed the iron door
Against the desolate and poor.
The Duchess[1] marked his weary pace,
His timid mien, and reverend face,
And bade her page the menials tell,
That they should tend the old man well:
For she had known adversity,
Though born in such a high degree;
In pride of power, in beauty's bloom,
Had wept o'er Monmouth's bloody tomb.

 When kindness had his wants supplied,
And the old man was gratified,
Began to rise his minstrel pride;
And he began to talk, anon,
Of good Earl Francis,[2] dead and gone,

---

[1] Anne, Duchess of Buccleuch and Monmouth, representative of the ancient lords of Buccleuch, and widow of the unfortunate James, Duke of Monmouth, who was beheaded in 1685.
[2] Francis Scott, Earl of Buccleuch, father to the Duchess.

And of Earl Walter,[1] rest him God!
A braver ne'er to battle rode;
And how full many a tale he knew,
Of the old warriors of Buccleuch:
And, would the noble Duchess deign
To listen to an old man's strain,
Though stiff his hand, his voice though weak,
He thought even yet, the sooth to speak,
That, if she loved the harp to hear,
He could make music to her ear.

The humble boon was soon obtained;
The Aged Minstrel audience gained.
But when he reached the room of state,
Where she, with all her ladies, sate,
Perchance he wished his boon denied;
For, when to tune his harp he tried,
His trembling hand had lost the ease
Which marks security to please;
And scenes, long past, of joy and pain,
Came wildering o'er his aged brain—
He tried to tune his harp in vain.
The pitying Duchess praised its chime,
And gave him heart and gave him time,
Till every string's according glee
Was blended into harmony.
And then, he said, he would full fain
He could recall an ancient strain
He never thought to sing again.

---

[1] Walter, Earl of Buccleuch, grandfather to the Duchess, and a celebrated warrior.

It was not framed for village churls,
But for high dames and mighty earls;
He had played it to King Charles the Good,
When he kept court at Holyrood;
And much he wished, yet feared, to try
The long-forgotten melody.

   Amid the strings his fingers strayed,
And an uncertain warbling made,
And oft he shook his hoary head.
But when he caught the measure wild,
The old man raised his face, and smiled,
And lightened up his faded eye
With all a poet's ecstasy!
In varying cadence, soft or strong,
He swept the sounding chords along:
The present scene, the future lot,
His toils, his wants, were all forgot:
Cold diffidence, and age's frost,
In the full tide of song were lost;
Each blank, in faithless memory void,
The poet's glowing thought supplied;
And, while his harp responsive rung,
'Twas thus the LATEST MINSTREL sung.

     \*     \*     \*     \*

HUSHED is the harp—the Minstrel gone.
And did he wander forth alone?
Alone, in indigence and age,
To linger out his pilgrimage?
No—close beneath proud Newark's tower
Arose the Minstrel's lowly bower;

A simple hut; but there was seen
The little garden hedged with green,
The cheerful hearth, and lattice clean.
There sheltered wanderers, by the blaze,
Oft heard the tale of other days;
For much he loved to ope his door,
And give the aid he begged before.
So passed the winter's day; but still,
When summer smiled on sweet Bowhill,
And July's eve, with balmy breath,
Waved the blue-bells on Newark-heath;
When throstles sung in Harehead-shaw,
And corn was green on Carterhaugh,
And flourished, broad, Blackandro's oak,
The aged Harper's soul awoke!
Then would he sing achievements high,
And circumstance of chivalry,
Till the rapt traveller would stay,
Forgetful of the closing day;
And noble youths, the strain to hear,
Forsook the hunting of the deer;
And Yarrow, as he rolled along,
Bore burden to the Minstrel's song.

---

## MARMION.

### THE TRIAL OF CONSTANCE.

WHILE round the fire such legends go,
    Far different was the scene of woe,
Where, in a secret aisle beneath,
Council was held of life and death.

It was more dark and lone, that vault,
    Than the worst dungeon-cell;
Old Colwulf built it,[1] for his fault,
    In penitence to dwell,
When he, for cowl and beads, laid down
The Saxon battle-axe and crown.
This den, which, chilling every sense
    Of feeling, hearing, sight,
Was called the Vault of Penitence,
    Excluding air and light,
Was, by the prelate Sexhelm, made
A place of burial, for such dead
As, having died in mortal sin,
Might not be laid the church within.
'Twas now a place of punishment;
Whence if so loud a shriek were sent,
    As reached the upper air,
The hearers blessed themselves, and said
The spirits of the sinful dead
    Bemoaned their torments there.

But though, in the monastic pile,
Did of this penitential aisle
    Some vague tradition go,
Few only, save the Abbot, knew

---

[1] Ceolwolf, or Colwulf, King of Northumberland, flourished in the eighth century. He abdicated the throne about 738, and retired to Holy Island, where he died in the odour of sanctity. These penitential vaults served as places of meeting for the chapter, when measures of uncommon severity were to be adopted. But their most frequent use, as implied by the name, was as places for performing penances, or undergoing punishment.

Where the place lay; and still more few
Were those, who had from him the clew
   To that dread vault to go.
Victim and executioner
Were blindfold when transported there.
In low, dark rounds the arches hung,
From the rude rock the side-walls sprung;
The grave-stones, rudely sculptured o'er,
Half sunk in earth, by time half wore,
Were all the pavement of the floor;
The mildew-drops fell one by one,
With tinkling plash, upon the stone.
A cresset,[1] in an iron chain,
Which served to light this drear domain,
With damp and darkness seemed to strive,
As if it scarce might keep alive;
And yet it dimly served to show
The awful conclave met below.

There, met to doom in secrecy,
Were placed the heads of convents three:
All servants of Saint Benedict,
The statutes of whose order strict
   On iron table lay;
In long black dress, on seats of stone,
Behind were these three judges shown,
   By the pale cresset's ray:
The Abbess of Saint Hilda's, there,
Sat for a space with visage bare,
Until, to hide her bosom's swell,
And tear-drops that for pity fell,

---

[1] Antique chandelier.

She closely drew her veil:
Yon shrouded figure, as I guess,
By her proud mien and flowing dress,
Is Tynemouth's haughty Prioress,[1]
    And she with awe looks pale:
And he, that Ancient Man, whose sight
Has long been quenched by age's night,
Upon whose wrinkled brow alone,
Nor ruth, nor mercy's trace, is shown,
    Whose look is hard and stern,—
Saint Cuthbert's Abbot is his style;
For sanctity called, through the isle,
    The Saint of Lindisfarne.

Before them stood a guilty pair;
But, though an equal fate they share,
Yet one alone deserves our care.
Her sex a page's dress belied;
The cloak and doublet, loosely tied,
Obscured her charms, but could not hide.
    Her cap down o'er her face she drew;
    And, on her doublet breast,
    She tried to hide the badge of blue,
        Lord Marmion's falcon crest.
But, at the Prioress' command,
A Monk undid the silken band
    That tied her tresses fair,
And raised the bonnet from her head,

---

[1] As in the case of Whitby and of Holy Island, the introduction of nuns at Tynemouth, in the reign of Henry VIII., is an anachronism.

And down her slender form they spread,
　　In ringlets rich and rare.
Constance de Beverley they know,
Sister professed of Fontevraud,
Whom the church numbered with the dead,
For broken vows and convent fled.

When thus her face was given to view
(Although so pallid was her hue,
It did a ghastly contrast bear
To those bright ringlets glistening fair),
Her look composed, and steady eye,
Bespoke a matchless constancy;
And there she stood so calm and pale,
That, but her breathing did not fail,
And motion slight of eye and head,
And of her bosom, warranted
That neither sense nor pulse she lacks,
You might have thought a form of wax,
Wrought to the life, was there;
So still she was, so pale, so fair.

Her comrade was a sordid soul,
　　Such as does murder for a meed;
Who, but of fear, knows no control,
Because his conscience, seared and foul,
　　Feels not the import of his deed;
One, whose brute-feeling ne'er aspires
Beyond his own more brute desires.
Such tools the tempter ever needs,
To do the savagest of deeds;
For them no visioned terrors daunt,
Their nights no fancied spectres haunt;

One fear with them, of all most base,
The fear of death,—alone finds place.
This wretch was clad in frock and cowl,
And shamed not loud to moan and howl,
His body on the floor to dash,
And crouch, like hound beneath the lash;
While his mute partner, standing near,
Waited her doom without a tear.

Yet well the luckless wretch might shriek,
Well might her paleness terror speak!
For there were seen, in that dark wall,
Two niches, narrow, deep, and tall.
Who enters at such grisly door,
Shall ne'er, I ween, find exit more.
In each a slender meal was laid,
Of roots, of water, and of bread:
By each, in Benedictine dress,
Two haggard monks stood motionless;
Who, holding high a blazing torch,
Showed the grim entrance of the porch:
Reflecting back the smoky beam,
The dark-red walls and arches gleam,
Hewn stones and cement were displayed,
And building tools in order laid.[1]

---

[1] It is well known, that the religious who broke their vows of chastity, were subjected to the same penalty as the Roman vestals in a similar case. A small niche, sufficient to inclose their bodies, was made in the massive wall of the convent; a slender pittance of food and water was deposited in it, and the awful words, VADE IN PACEM, were the signal for immuring the criminal.

These executioners were chose,
As men who were with mankind foes,
And, with despite and envy fired,
Into the cloister had retired;
  Or who, in desperate doubt of grace,
  Strove, by deep penance, to efface
    Of some foul crime the stain;
  For, as the vassals of her will,
  Such men the church selected still,
  As either joyed in doing ill,
    Or thought more grace to gain,
If, in her cause, they wrestled down
Feelings their nature strove to own.
By strange device were they brought there,
They knew not how, and knew not where.

And now that blind old Abbot rose,
  To speak the Chapter's doom
On those the wall was to inclose,
  Alive, within the tomb;
But stopped, because that woeful maid,
Gathering her powers, to speak essayed.
Twice she essayed, and twice in vain;
Her accents might no utterance gain;
Naught but imperfect murmurs slip
From her convulsed and quivering lip:
  'Twixt each attempt all was so still,
  You seemed to hear a distant rill—
    'Twas ocean's swells and falls;
  For though this vault of sin and fear
  Was to the sounding surge so near,
  A tempest there you scarce could hear,
    So massive were the walls.

At length, an effort sent apart
The blood that curdled to her heart,
   And light came to her eye,
And color dawned upon her cheek,
A hectic and a fluttered streak,
Like that left on the Cheviot peak
   By Autumn's stormy sky;
And when her silence broke at length,
Still as she spoke, she gathered strength,
   And armed herself to bear.
It was a fearful sight to see
Such high resolve and constancy,
   In form so soft and fair.

"I speak not to implore your grace;
Well know I, for one minute's space
   Successless might I sue:
Nor do I speak your prayers to gain;
For if a death of lingering pain,
To cleanse my sins, be penance vain,
   Vain are your masses too.—
I listened to a traitor's tale,
I left the convent and the veil;
For three long years I bowed my pride,
A horse-boy in his train to ride;
And well my folly's meed he gave,
Who forfeited, to be his slave,
All here, and all beyond the grave.—
He saw young Clara's face more fair,
He knew her of broad lands the heir,
Forgot his vows, his faith forswore,
And Constance was beloved no more.—

'Tis an old tale, and often told;
  But, did my fate and wish agree,
Ne'er had been read, in story old,
Of maiden true betrayed for gold,
    That loved, or was avenged, like me!

"The king approved his favorite's aim;
In vain a rival barred his claim,
  Whose faith with Clare's was plight,
For he attaints that rival's fame
With treason's charge—and on they came,
  In mortal lists to fight.
    Their oaths are said,
    Their prayers are prayed,
    Their lances in the rest are laid,
  They meet in mortal shock;
And hark! the throng, with thundering cry,
Shout, 'Marmion, Marmion, to the sky!
  De Wilton to the block!'
Say ye, who preach heaven shall decide,
When in the lists two champions ride,
  Say, was heaven's justice here?
When, loyal in his love and faith,
Wilton found overthrow or death,
  Beneath a traitor's spear.
How false the charge, how true he fell,
This guilty packet best can tell."—
Then drew a packet from her breast,
Paused, gathered voice, and spoke the rest.

"Still was false Marmion's bridal staid;
To Whitby's convent fled the maid,

The hated match to shun.
'Ho! shifts she thus?' King Henry cried,
'Sir Marmion, she shall be thy bride,
  If she were sworn a nun.'
One way remained—the king's command
Sent Marmion to the Scottish land:
I lingered here, and rescue planned
  For Clara and for me:
This caitiff Monk, for gold, did swear,
He would to Whitby's shrine repair,
And, by his drugs, my rival fair
  A saint in heaven should be.
But ill the dastard kept his oath,
Whose cowardice hath undone us both.

"And now my tongue the secret tells,
Not that remorse my bosom swells,
But to assure my soul, that none
Shall ever wed with Marmion.
Had fortune my last hope betrayed,
This packet, to the king conveyed,
Had given him to the headsman's stroke,
Although my heart that instant broke.—
Now, men of death, work forth your will,
For I can suffer, and be still;
And come he slow, or come he fast,
It is but death who comes at last.

"Yet dread me, from my living tomb,
Ye vassal slaves of bloody Rome!
If Marmion's late remorse should wake,
Full soon such vengeance will he take,

That you shall wish the fiery Dane
Had rather been your guest again.
Behind, a darker hour ascends!
The altars quake, the crosier bends,
The ire of a despotic king
Rides forth upon destruction's wing;
Then shall these vaults, so strong and deep,
Burst open to the sea-winds' sweep;
Some traveller then shall find my bones,
Whitening amid disjointed stones.
And, ignorant of priests' cruelty,
Marvel such relics here should be."—

Fixed was her look, and stern her air;
Back from her shoulders streamed her hair;
The locks, that wont her brow to shade,
Stared up erectly from her head;
Her figure seemed to rise more high;
Her voice, despair's wild energy
Had given a tone of prophecy.
Appalled the astonished conclave sate;
With stupid eyes, the men of fate
Gazed on the light inspired form,
And listened for the avenging storm;
The judges felt the victim's dread;
No hand was moved, no word was said,
Till thus the Abbot's doom was given,
Raising his sightless balls to heaven:—
"Sister, let thy sorrows cease;
Sinful brother, part in peace!"—
   From that dire dungeon, place of doom,
   Of execution too, and tomb,

  Paced forth the judges three;
Sorrow it were, and shame, to tell
The butcher-work that there befell,
When they had glided from the cell
  Of sin and misery.

An hundred winding steps convey
That conclave to the upper day;
But, ere they breathed the fresher air,
They heard the shriekings of despair,
  And many a stifled groan:
With speed their upward way they take
(Such speed as age and fear can make),
And crossed themselves for terror's sake,
  As hurrying, tottering on.
Even in the vesper's heavenly tone,
They seemed to hear a dying groan,
And bade the passing knell to toll
For welfare of a parting soul.
Slow o'er the midnight wave it swung,
Northumbrian rocks in answer rung;
To Warkworth cell the echoes rolled,
His beads the wakeful hermit told;
The Bamborough peasant raised his head,
But slept ere half a prayer he said:
So far was heard the mighty knell,
The stag sprung up on Cheviot Fell,
Spread his broad nostril to the wind,
Listed before, aside, behind;
Then couched him down beside the hind,
And quaked among the mountain fern,
To hear that sound so dull and stern.

## THE DEATH OF MARMION.

BLOUNT and Fitz-Eustace rested still
  With Lady Cláre upon the hill;
On which (for far the day was spent)
The western sunbeams now were bent.
The cry they heard, its meaning knew,
Could plain their distant comrades view.
Sadly to Blount did Eustace say,
" Unworthy office here to stay!
No hope of gilded spurs to-day.—
But, see! look up—on Flodden bent,
The Scottish foe has fired his tent."—
  And sudden, as he spoke,
From the sharp ridges of the hill,
All downward to the banks of Till,
  Was wreathed in sable smoke;
Volumed and vast, and rolling far,
The cloud enveloped Scotland's war,
  As down the hill they broke;
Nor martial shout, nor minstrel tone,
Announced their march; their tread alone,
At times one warning trumpet blown,
  At times a stifled hum,
Told England, from his mountain-throne,
  King James did rushing come.—
Scarce could they hear, or see their foes,
Until at weapon-point they close.—
They close, in clouds of smoke and dust,
With sword-sway, and with lance's thrust;
  And such a yell was there,

Of sudden and portentous birth,
As if men fought upon the earth,
   And fiends in upper air.
Long looked the anxious squires; their eye
Could in the darkness naught desery.

At length the freshening western blast
Aside the shroud of battle cast;
And, first, the ridge of mingled spears
Above the brightening cloud appears;
And in the smoke the pennons flew,
As in the storm the white sea-mew.
Then marked they, dashing broad and far,
The broken billows of the war,
And pluméd crests of chieftains brave,
Floating like foam upon the wave;
   But naught distinct they see:
Wide raged the battle on the plain;
Spears shook, and falchions flashed amain;
Fell England's arrow-flight like rain;
Crests rose, and stooped, and rose again,
   Wild and disorderly.
Amid the scene of tumult, high
They saw Lord Marmion's falcon fly:
And stainless Tunstall's banner white,
And Edmund Howard's lion bright,
Still bear them bravely in the fight;
   Although against them come,
Of gallant Gordons many a one,
And many a stubborn Highlandman,
And many a rugged Border clan,
   With Huntley, and with Home.

Far on the left, unseen the while,
Stanley broke Lennox and Argyle;
Though there the western mountaineer
Rushed with bare bosom on the spear,
And flung the feeble targe aside,
And with both hands the broadsword plied:
'Twas vain.—But Fortune, on the right,
With fickle smile, cheered Scotland's fight.
Then fell that spotless banner white,
    The Howard's lion fell;
Yet still Lord Marmion's falcon flew
With wavering flight, while fiercer grew
    Around the battle-yell.
The Border slogan rent the sky!
"A Home! a Gordon!" was the cry;
    Loud were the clanging blows;
Advanced,—forced back,—now low, now high
    The pennon sunk and rose;
As bends the bark's mast in the gale,
When rent are rigging, shrouds, and sail,
    It wavered 'mid the foes.
No longer Blount the view could bear:—
"By Heaven, and all its saints! I swear,
    I will not see it lost!
Fitz-Eustace, you with Lady Clare
May bid your beads, and patter prayer,—
    I gallop to the host."
And to the fray he rode amain,
Followed by all the archer train.
The fiery youth, with desperate charge,
Made, for a space, an opening large,—
    The rescued banner rose,—

But darkly closed the war around;
Like pine-tree, rooted from the ground,
　　It sunk among the foes.
Then Eustace mounted too;—yet staid,
As loth to leave the helpless maid,
　　When, fast as shaft can fly,
Bloodshot his eyes, his nostrils spread,
The loose rein dangling from his head,
Housing and saddle bloody red,
　　Lord Marmion's steed rushed by;
And Eustace, maddening at the sight,
　　A look and sign to Clara cast,
　　To mark he would return in haste,
Then plunged into the fight.

Ask me not what the maiden feels,
　　Left in that dreadful hour alone:
Perchance her reason stoops, or reels;
　　Perchance a courage, not her own,
　　Braces her mind to desperate tone.—
The scattered van of England wheels;
　　She only said, as loud in air
　　　The tumult roared, "Is Wilton there?"—
　　They fly, or, maddened by despair,
　　Fight but to die.—"Is Wilton there?"
With that, straight up the hill there rode
　　Two horsemen drenched with gore,
And in their arms, a helpless load,
　　A wounded knight they bore.
His hand still strained the broken brand;
His arms were smeared with blood and sand:
Dragged from among the horses' feet,

With dinted shield, and helmet beat,
The falcon-crest and plumage gone,
Can that be haughty Marmion!....
Young Blount his armour did unlace,
And, gazing on his ghastly face,
 Said—" By Saint George, he's gone!
That spear-wound has our master sped,
And see the deep cut on his head!
 Good-night to Marmion."—
" Unnurtured Blount!—thy brawling cease:
He opes his eyes," said Eustace; " peace!"—

When, doffed his casque, he felt free air,
Around 'gan Marmion wildly stare:—
" Where's Harry Blount? Fitz-Eustace where?
Linger ye here, ye hearts of hare!
Redeem my pennon,—charge again!
Cry—' Marmion to the rescue!'—Vain!
Last of my race, on battle-plain
That shout shall ne'er be heard again!—
Yet my last thought is England's:—fly,
 To Dacre bear my signet-ring;
 Tell him his squadrons up to bring.—
Fitz-Eustace, to Lord Surrey hie:
 Tunstall lies dead upon the field;
 His life-blood stains the spotless shield:
 Edmund is down;—my life is reft;—
 The Admiral alone is left.
Let Stanley charge with spur of fire,—
With Chester charge, and Lancashire,
Full upon Scotland's central host,
Or victory and England's lost.—

Must I bid twice ?—hence, varlets, fly !
Leave Marmion here alone—to die."
They parted, and alone he lay :
Clare drew her from the sight away,
Till pain wrung forth a lowly moan,
And half he murmured,—" Is there none,
 Of all my halls have nurst,
Page, squire, or groom, one cup to bring
Of blessed water from the spring,
 To slake my dying thirst ?"

O woman ! in our hours of ease,
Uncertain, coy, and hard to please,
And variable as the shade
By the light, quivering aspen made ;
When pain and anguish wring the brow,
A ministering angel thou !—
Scarce were the piteous accents said,
When, with the Baron's casque, the maid
 To the nigh streamlet ran :
Forgot were hatred, wrongs, and fears ;
The plaintive voice alone she hears,
 Sees but the dying man.
She stooped her by the runnel's side,
 But in abhorrence backward drew ;
For, oozing from the mountain wide,
Where raged the war, a dark-red tide
 Was curdling in the streamlet blue.
Where shall she turn !—behold her mark
 A little fountain-cell,
Where water, clear as diamond-spark,
 In a stone basin fell.

Above, some half-worn letters say—
"𝔇rink . 𝔴eary . 𝔭ilgrim . 𝔡rink . 𝔞nd . 𝔭ray.
𝔉or . 𝔱he . 𝔨ind . 𝔰oul . 𝔬f . 𝔖ybil . 𝔊rey.
    𝔚ho . 𝔟uilt . 𝔱his . 𝔠ross . 𝔞nd . 𝔴ell."
She filled the helm, and back she hied,
And with surprise and joy espied
    A Monk supporting Marmion's head:
A pious man, whom duty brought
To dubious verge of battle fought,
    To shrieve the dying, bless the dead.

Deep drank Lord Marmion of the wave,
And as she stooped his brow to lave—
"Is it the hand of Clare," he said,
"Or injured Constance, bathes my head?"
    Then, as remembrance rose,—
"Speak not to me of shrift or prayer!
    I must redress her woes.
Short space, few words, are mine to spare;
Forgive and listen, gentle Clare!"—
    "Alas!" she said, "the while,—
O think of your immortal weal!
In vain for Constance is your zeal;
    She——died at Holy Isle."—
Lord Marmion started from the ground,
As light as if he felt no wound;
Though in the action burst the tide,
In torrents, from his wounded side.
"Then it was truth," he said—"I knew
That the dark presage must be true.—
I would the Fiend, to whom belongs
The vengeance due to all her wrongs,
    Would spare me but a day!

For, wasting fire, and dying groan,
And priests slain on the altar-stone,
  Might bribe him for delay.
It may not be!—this dizzy trance—
Curse on yon base marauder's lance,
And doubly cursed my failing brand!
A sinful heart makes feeble hand."—
Then, fainting, down on earth he sunk,
Supported by the trembling Monk.

With fruitless labour, Clara bound
And strove to stanch the gushing wound:
The Monk, with unavailing cares,
Exhausted all the Church's prayers;
Ever, he said, that, close and near,
A lady's voice was in his ear,
And that the priest he could not hear,
  For that she ever sung,
"*In the lost battle, borne down by the flying,
Where mingles war's rattle with groans of the
    dying!*"
  So the notes rung;
"Avoid thee, Fiend!—with cruel hand,
Shake not the dying sinner's sand!—
O look, my son, upon yon sign
Of the Redeemer's grace divine;
  O, think on faith and bliss!—
By many a death-bed I have been,
And many a sinner's parting seen,
  But never aught like this."—
The war, that for a space did fail,
Now trebly thundering, swelled the gale,

And—"STANLEY!" was the cry;—
A light on Marmion's visage spread,
    And fired his glazing eye:
With dying hand, above his head
He shook the fragment of his blade,
    And shouted, "Victory!—
Charge, Chester, charge! on, Stanley, on!"
Were the last words of Marmion.

---

## THE LADY OF THE LAKE.

#### MEETING OF ELLEN AND FITZJAMES.

THE western waves of ebbing day
    Rolled o'er the glen their level way;
Each purple peak, each flinty spire,
Was bathed in floods of living fire.
But not a setting beam could glow
Within the dark ravines below,
Where twined the path in shadow hid,
Round many a rocky pyramid,
Shooting abruptly from the dell
Its thunder-splintered pinnacle;
Round many an insulated mass,
The native bulwarks of the pass,
Huge as the tower which builders vain
Presumptuous piled on Shinar's plain.
Their rocky summits, split and rent,
Formed turret, dome, or battlement,
Or seemed fantastically set
With cupola or minaret,

Wild crests as pagod ever decked,
Or mosque of Eastern architect.
Nor were these earth-born castles bare,
Nor lacked they many a banner fair;
For, from their shivered brows displayed,
Far o'er the unfathomable glade,
All twinkling with the dewdrops' sheen,
The brier-rose fell in streamers green;
And creeping shrubs, of thousand dyes,
Waved in the west-wind's summer sighs.

Boon Nature scattered, free and wild,
Each plant or flower, the mountain's child.
Here eglantine embalmed the air,
Hawthorn and hazel mingled there;
The primrose pale, and violet flower,
Found in each cliff a narrow bower;
Fox-glove and night-shade, side by side,
Emblems of punishment and pride,
Grouped their dark hues with every stain
The weather-beaten crags retain.
With boughs that quaked at every breath,
Gray birch and aspen wept beneath;
Aloft, the ash and warrior oak
Cast anchor in the rifted rock;
And, higher yet, the pine-tree hung
His shattered trunk, and frequent flung,
Where seemed the cliffs to meet on high,
His boughs athwart the narrowed sky.
Highest of all, where white peaks glanced,
Where glistening streamers waved and danced,
The wanderer's eye could barely view

The summer heaven's delicious blue;
So wondrous wild, the whole might seem
The scenery of a fairy dream.

Onward, amid the copse 'gan peep
A narrow inlet, still and deep,
Affording scarce such breadth of brim
As served the wild-duck's brood to swim.
Lost for a space, through thickets veering,
But broader when again appearing,
Tall rocks and tufted knolls their face
Could on the dark-blue mirror trace;
And farther as the hunter strayed,
Still broader sweep its channels made.
The shaggy mounds no longer stood,
Emerging from entangled wood,
But, wave-encircled, seemed to float,
Like castle girdled with its moat;
Yet broader floods extending still,
Divide them from their parent hill,
Till each, retiring, claims to be
An inslet in an inland sea.

And now, to issue from the glen,
No pathway meets the wanderer's ken,
Unless he climb, with footing nice,
A far-projecting precipice.[1]

---

[1] Until the present road was made through this romantic pass, there was no mode of issuing out of the defile called the Trosachs, except by a sort of ladder, composed of the branches and roots of the trees.

The broom's tough roots his ladder made,
The hazel saplings lent their aid;
And thus an airy point he won,
Where, gleaming with the setting sun,
One burnished sheet of living gold,
Loch Katrine lay beneath him rolled,
In all her length far winding lay,
With promontory, creek, and bay,
And islands that, empurpled bright,
Floated amid the livelier light;
And mountains, that like giants stand,
To sentinel enchanted land.
High on the south, huge Benvenue
Down on the lake in masses threw
Crags, knolls, and mounds, confusedly hurled,
The fragments of an earlier world;
A wildering forest feathered o'er
His ruined sides and summit hoar;
While on the north, through middle air,
Ben-an heaved high his forehead bare.

From the steep promontory gazed
The stranger, raptured and amazed;
And, "What a scene was here," he cried,
"For princely pomp, or churchman's pride!
On this bold brow, a lordly tower;
In that soft vale, a lady's bower;
On yonder meadow, far away,
The turrets of a cloister gray.
How blithely might the bugle-horn
Chide, on the lake, the lingering morn!
How sweet, at eve, the lover's lute

Chime, when the groves were still and mute!
And, when the midnight moon should lave
Her forehead in the silver wave,
How solemn on the ear would come
The holy matin's distant hum,
While the deep peal's commanding tone
Should wake, in yonder islet lone,
A sainted hermit from his cell,
To drop a bead with every knell!—
And bugle, lute, and bell, and all,
Should each bewildered stranger call
To friendly feast, and lighted hall.

" Blithe were it then to wander here!
But now—beshrew yon nimble deer,—
Like that same hermit's, thin and spare,
The copse must give my evening fare;
Some mossy bank my couch must be,
Some rustling oak my canopy.
Yet pass we that—the war and chase
Give little choice of resting-place;—
A summer night, in greenwood spent,
Were but to-morrow's merriment;
But hosts may in these wilds abound,
Such as are better missed than found;
To meet with Highland plunderers here
Were worse than loss of steed or deer.[1]
I am alone;—my bugle-strain
May call some straggler of the train;

---

[1] The clans in the neighbourhood of Loch Katrine, from their proximity to the Lowlands, were among the most warlike and predatory of the Highlanders.

Or, fall the worst that may betide,
Ere now this falchion has been tried."

But scarce again his horn he wound,
When lo! forth starting at the sound,
From underneath an aged oak,
That slanted from the islet rock,
A damsel, guider of its way,
A little skiff shot to the bay,
That round the promontory steep,
Led its deep line in graceful sweep,
Eddying, in almost viewless wave,
The weeping-willow twig to lave;
And kiss, with whispering sound and slow,
The beach of pebbles bright as snow.
The boat had touched this silver strand,
Just as the hunter left his stand,
And stood concealed amid the brake,
To view this Lady of the Lake.
The maiden paused, as if again
She thought to catch the distant strain,
With head up-raised, and look intent,
And eye and ear attentive bent,
And locks flung back, and lips apart,
Like monument of Grecian art.
In listening mood she seemed to stand,
The guardian Naiad of the strand.

And ne'er did Grecian chisel trace
A Nymph, a Naiad, or a Grace,
Of finer form, or lovelier face!
What though the sun, with ardent frown,

Had slightly tinged her cheek with brown,—
The sportive toil, which, short and light,
Had dyed her glowing hue so bright,
Served too in hastier swell to show
Short glimpses of a breast of snow;
What though no rule of courtly grace
To measured mood had trained her pace,—
A foot more light, a step more true,
Ne'er from the heath-flower dashed the dew;
E'en the slight hare-bell raised its head,
Elastic from her airy tread:
What though upon her speech there hung
The accents of the mountain tongue,—
Those silver sounds, so soft, so dear,
The listener held his breath to hear.

A chieftain's daughter seemed the maid;
Her satin snood, her silken plaid,
Her golden brooch, such birth betrayed.
And seldom was a snood amid
Such wild, luxuriant ringlets hid,
Whose glossy black to shame might bring
The plumage of the raven's wing;
And seldom o'er a breast so fair,
Mantled a plaid with modest care,
And never brooch the folds combined
Above a heart more good and kind.
Her kindness and her worth to spy,
You need but gaze on Ellen's eye;
Not Katrine, in her mirror blue,
Gives back the shaggy banks more true,
Than every free-born glance confessed

The guileless movements of her breast;
Whether joy danced in her dark eye,
Or woe or pity claimed a sigh,
Or filial love was glowing there,
Or meek devotion poured a prayer,
Or tale of injury called forth
The indignant spirit of the north.
One only passion, unrevealed,
With maiden pride the maid concealed,
Yet not less purely felt the flame;—
Oh, need I tell that passion's name!

Impatient of the silent horn,
Now on the gale her voice was borne:—
"Father!" she cried; the rocks around
Loved to prolong the gentle sound.
A while she paused, no answer came,—
"Malcolm, was thine the blast?" the name
Less resolutely uttered fell,
The echoes could not catch the swell.
"A stranger I," the Huntsman said,
Advancing from the hazel shade.
The maid, alarmed, with hasty oar
Pushed her light shallop from the shore,
And, when a space was gained between,
Closer she drew her bosom's screen
(So forth the startled swan would swing,
So turn to prune his ruffled wing).
Then safe, though fluttered and amazed,
She paused, and on the stranger gazed.
Not his the form, nor his the eye,
That youthful maidens wont to fly.

On his bold visage middle age
Had slightly pressed its signet sage,
Yet had not quenched the open truth
And fiery vehemence of youth;
Forward and frolic glee was there,
The will to do, the soul to dare,
The sparkling glance, soon blown to fire,
Of hasty love, or headlong ire.
His limbs were cast in manly mould,
For hardy sports, or contest bold;
And though in peaceful garb arrayed,
And weaponless, except his blade,
His stately mien as well implied
A high-born heart, a martial pride,
As if a Baron's crest he wore,
And sheathed in armour trod the shore.
Slighting the petty need he showed,
He told of his benighted road:
His ready speech flowed fair and free,
In phrase of gentlest courtesy;
Yet seemed that tone and gesture bland,
Less used to sue than to command.

A while the maid the stranger eyed,
And, reassured, at last replied,
That Highland halls were open still
To wildered wanderers of the hill.
"Nor think you unexpected come
To yon lone isle, our desert home:
Before the heath had lost the dew,
This morn a couch was pulled for you;
On yonder mountain's purple head

Have ptarmigan and heath-cock bled,
And our broad nets have swept the mere,
To furnish forth your evening cheer."
"Now, by the rood, my lovely maid,
Your courtesy has erred," he said;
"No right have I to claim, misplaced,
The welcome of expected guest.
A wanderer, here by fortune tossed,
My way, my friends, my courser lost,
I ne'er before, believe me, fair,
Have ever drawn your mountain air,
Till on this lake's romantic strand
I found a fay in fairy-land."

"I well believe," the maid replied,
As her light skiff approached the side—
"I well believe, that ne'er before
Your foot has trod Loch Katrine's shore;
But yet, as far as yesternight,
Old Allan-Bane foretold your plight—
A gray-haired sire, whose eye intent
Was on the visioned future bent.[1]
He saw your steed, a dappled gray,
Lie dead beneath the birchen way;
Painted exact your form and mien,
Your hunting-suit of Lincoln green,

---

[1] A superstitious belief in *second sight* prevailed in the Highlands: it was called in Gaelic *Taishitaraugh*, from *Taish*, an unreal or shadowy appearance; and those possessed of the faculty are called *Taishatrin*, which may be aptly translated *visionaries*. They pretended to see visions, and to be informed of future events, which obtained for them an extraordinary influence over their countrymen.

That tasselled horn so gayly gilt,
That falchion's crooked blade and hilt,
That cap with heron's plumage trim,
And yon two hounds so dark and grim.
He bade that all should ready be,
To grace a guest of fair degree;
But light I held his prophecy,
And deemed it was my father's horn,
Whose echoes o'er the lake were borne."

The stranger smiled:—"Since to your home
A destined errant-knight I come,
Announced by prophet sooth and old,
Doomed, doubtless, for achievement bold,
I'll lightly front each high emprize,
For one kind glance of those bright eyes:
Permit me, first, the task to guide
Your fairy frigate o'er the tide."
The maid, with smile suppressed and sly,
The toil unwonted saw him try;
For seldom, sure, if e'er before,
His noble hand had grasped an oar:
Yet with main strength his strokes he drew,
And o'er the lake the shallop flew;
With heads erect and whimpering cry,
The hounds behind their passage ply.
Nor frequent does the bright oar break
The darkening mirror of the lake,
Until the rocky isle they reach,
And moor their shallop on the beach.

## ROKEBY.

#### WILFRID, THE YOUTHFUL VISIONARY.

THE lovely heir of Rokeby's Knight
   Waits in his halls the event of fight;
For England's war revered the claim
Of every unprotected name,
And spared, amid its fiercest rage,
Childhood, and womanhood, and age.
But Wilfrid, son to Rokeby's foe,
Must the dear privilege forego,
By Greta's side, in evening gray,
To steal upon Matilda's way,
Striving, with fond hypocrisy,
For careless step and vacant eye;
Calming each anxious look and glance,
To give the meeting all to chance,
Or framing, as a fair excuse,
The book, the pencil, or the muse;
Something to give, to sing, to say,
Some modern tale, some ancient lay.
Then, while the longed-for minutes last,—
Ah! minutes quickly over-past!—
Recording each expression free,
Of kind or careless courtesy,
Each friendly look, each softer tone,
As food for fancy when alone.
All this is o'er—but still, unseen,
Wilfrid may lurk in Eastwood green,
To watch Matilda's wonted round,
While springs his heart at every sound.

She comes—'tis but a passing sight,
Yet serves to cheat his weary night;
She comes not—he will wait the hour,
When her lamp lightens in the tower;
'Tis something yet, if, as she passed,
Her shade is o'er the lattice cast.
" What is my life, my hope ?" he said;
" Alas! a transitory shade."

Thus wore his life, though reason strove
For mastery in vain with love,
Forcing upon his thoughts the sum
Of present woe and ills to come,
While still he turned impatient ear
From Truth's intrusive voice severe.
Gentle, indiff'rent, and subdued,
In all but this, unmoved he viewed
Each outward change of ill and good:
But Wilfrid, docile, soft, and mild,
Was Fancy's spoiled and wayward child;
In her bright car she bade him ride,
With one fair form to grace his side,
Or, in some wild and lone retreat,
Flung her high spells around his seat,
Bathed in her dews his languid head,
Her fairy mantle o'er him spread,
For him her opiates gave to flow,
Which he who tastes can ne'er forego,
And placed him in her circle, free
From every stern reality,
Till, to the Visionary, seem
Her day-dreams truth, and truth a dream.

Woe to the youth whom Fancy gains,
Winning from Reason's hand the reins,
Pity and woe! for such a mind
Is soft, contemplative, and kind;
And woe to those who train such youth,
And spare to press the rights of truth,
The mind to strengthen and anneal,
While on the stithy glows the steel!
O teach him, while your lessons last,
To judge the present by the past;
Remind him of each wish pursued,
How rich it glowed with promised good:
Remind him of each wish enjoyed,
How soon his hopes possession cloyed!
Tell him, we play unequal game,
Whene'er we shoot by Fancy's aim!
And, ere he strip him for her race,
Show the conditions of the chase.
Two sisters by the goal are set,
Cold Disappointment and Regret:
One disenchants the winner's eyes,
And strips of all its worth the prize;
While one augments its gaudy show
More to enhance the loser's woe.
The victor sees his fairy gold
Transformed, when won, to drossy mould,
But still the vanquished mourns his loss,
And rues, as gold, that glittering dross.

More wouldst thou know—yon tower survey,
Yon couch unpressed since parting day,
Yon untrimmed lamp, whose yellow gleam

Is mingling with the cold moonbeam,
And yon thin form!—the hectic red
On his pale cheek unequal spread;
The head reclined, the loosened hair,
The limbs relaxed, the mournful air.—
See, he looks up;—a woful smile
Lightens his woe-worn cheek a while,—
'Tis Fancy wakes some idle thought,
To gild the ruin she has wrought;
For, like the bat of Indian brakes,
Her pinions fan the wound she makes,
And soothing thus the dreamer's pain,
She drinks his life-blood from the vein.
Now to the lattice turn his eyes,
Vain hope! to see the sun arise.
The moon with clouds is still o'ercast;
Still howls by fits the stormy blast;
Another hour must wear away,
Ere the East kindle into day;
And hark! to waste that weary hour,
He tries the minstrel's magic power.

---

## James Hogg.

### TO THE SKYLARK.

BIRD of the wilderness,
    Blithesome and cumberless,
Sweet be thy matin o'er moorland and lea!
    Emblem of happiness,
    Blest is thy dwelling-place—

Oh to abide in the desert with thee!
  Wild is thy lay, and loud,
  Far in the downy cloud,
Love gives it energy, love gave it birth.
  Where, on thy dewy wing,
  Where art thou journeying?
Thy lay is in heaven, thy love is on earth.

  O'er fell and fountain sheen,
  O'er moor and mountain green,
O'er the red streamer that heralds the day,
  Over the cloudlet dim,
  Over the rainbow's rim,
Musical cherub, soar, singing away!
  Then, when the gloaming comes,
  Low in the heather blooms
Sweet will thy welcome and bed of love be!
  Emblem of happiness,
  Blest is thy dwelling-place—
Oh to abide in the desert with thee!

## Horace Smith.

### TO AN EGYPTIAN MUMMY.

AND thou hast walked about—how strange a story!—
 In Thebes's streets, three thousand years ago!
When the Memnonium was in all its glory,
 And time had not begun to overthrow
Those temples, palaces, and piles stupendous,
Of which the very ruins are tremendous!

Speak!—for thou long enough hast acted dummy,
    Thou hast a tongue, come—let us hear its tune!
Thou'rt standing on thy legs, above-ground, mummy!
    Revisiting the glimpses of the moon—
Not like thin, ghosts or disembodied creatures,
But with thy bones, and flesh, and limbs, and features!

Tell us—for doubtless thou canst recollect—
    To whom should we assign the Sphinx's fame?—
Was Cheops, or Cephrenes architect
    Of either pyramid that bears his name?—
Is Pompey's pillar really a misnomer?—
Had Thebes a hundred gates, as sung by Homer?

Perhaps thou wert a mason—and forbidden,
    By oath, to tell the mysteries of thy trade:
Then say, what secret melody was hidden
    In Memnon's statue, which at sunrise played?
Perhaps thou wert a priest;—if so, my struggles
Are vain—for priestcraft never owns its juggles!

Perchance that very hand, now pinioned flat,
    Hath hob-a-nobbed with Pharaoh, glass to glass—
Or dropped a halfpenny in Homer's hat—
    Or doffed thine own, to let Queen Dido pass—
Or held, by Solomon's own invitation,
A torch, at the great temple's dedication!

I need not ask thee if that hand, when armed,
    Has any Roman soldier mauled and knuckled?
For thou wert dead, and buried, and embalmed,
    Ere Romulus and Remus had been suckled:—
Antiquity appears to have begun
Long after thy primeval race was run.

Thou couldst develop, if that withered tongue
    Might tell us what those sightless orbs have seen,
How the world looked when it was fresh and young,
    And the great deluge still had left it green!—
Or was it then so old that history's pages
Contained no record of its early ages?

Still silent!—Incommunicative elf!
    Art sworn to secrecy? Then keep thy vows!
But, prithee, tell us something of thyself—
    Reveal the secrets of thy prison-house:—
Since in the world of spirits thou hast slumbered,
What hast thou seen—what strange adventures numbered?

Since first thy form was in this box extended,
    We have, above-ground, seen some strange mutations;
The Roman empire has begun and ended—
    New worlds have risen—we have lost old nations—
And countless kings have into dust been humbled,
While not a fragment of thy flesh has crumbled.

Didst thou not hear the pother o'er thy head,
    When the great Persian conqueror, Cambyses,
Marched armies o'er thy tomb, with thundering tread,
    O'erthrew Osiris, Orus, Apis, Isis—
And shook the pyramids with fear and wonder,
When the gigantic Memnon fell asunder?

If the tomb's secrets may not be confessed,
    The nature of thy private life unfold!
A heart hath throbbed beneath that leathern breast,
    And tears adown that dusky cheek have rolled:—
Have children climbed those knees, and kissed that face?
What was thy name and station, age and race?

Statue of flesh!—Immortal of the dead!
    Imperishable type of evanescence!
Posthumous man—who quitt'st thy narrow bed,
    And standest undecayed within our presence!
Thou wilt hear nothing till the judgment morning,
When the great trump shall thrill thee with its warning!

Why should this worthless tegument endure,
    If its undying guest be lost for ever?
Oh! let us keep the soul embalmed and pure
    In living virtue—that when both must sever,
Although corruption may our fame consume,
The immortal spirit in the skies may bloom!

---

## Thomas Moore.

### PARADISE AND THE PERI.

(From "LALLA ROOKH.")

ONE morn a Peri at the gate
    Of Eden stood disconsolate;
And as she listened to the Springs
    Of Life within, like music flowing,
And caught the light upon her wings
    Through the half-open portal glowing,
She wept to think her recreant race
Should e'er have lost that glorious place!

"How happy," exclaimed this child of air,
"Are the holy Spirits who wander there,
    Mid flowers that never shall fade or fall;

Though mine are the gardens of earth and sea,
And the stars themselves have flowers for me,
  One blossom of Heaven outblooms them all!

" Though sunny the Lake of cool Cashmere,
With its plane-tree isle reflected clear,
  And sweetly the founts of that Valley fall;
Though bright are the waters of Sing-su-hay,
And the golden floods that thitherward stray,
Yet—oh! 'tis only the Blest can say
  How the waters of Heaven outshine them all!

" Go, wing thy flight from star to star,
From world to luminous world, as far
  As the universe spreads its flaming wall;
Take all the pleasures of all the spheres,
And multiply each through endless years,
  One minute of Heaven is worth them all!"

The glorious Angel, who was keeping
The gates of Light, beheld her weeping;
And, as he nearer drew and listened
To her sad song, a tear-drop glistened
Within his eyelids, like the spray
  From Eden's fountain, when it lies
On the blue flower, which—Brahmins say—
  Blooms nowhere but in Paradise.

" Nymph of a fair but erring line!"
Gently he said—" One hope is thine.
'Tis written in the Book of Fate,
  *The Peri yet may be forgiven*
*Who brings to this Eternal gate*
  *The Gift that is most dear to Heaven!*

Go, seek it, and redeem thy sin—
'Tis sweet to let the pardoned in!"

Rapidly as comets run
To th' embraces of the sun;—
Fleeter than the starry brands
Flung at night from angel hands
At those dark and daring sprites
Who would climb th' empyreal heights,
Down the blue vault the Peri flies,
   And, lighted earthward by a glance
That just then broke from morning's eyes,
   Hung hov'ring o'er our world's expanse.

But whither shall the Spirit go
To find this gift for Heaven?—"I know
The wealth," she cries, "of every urn
In which unnumbered rubies burn,
Beneath the pillars of Chilminar;
I know where the Isles of Perfume are,
Many a fathom down in the sea,
To the south of sun-bright Araby;
I know, too, where the Genii hid
The jewelled cup of their King Jamshid,
With Life's elixir sparkling high—
But gifts like these are not for the sky.
Where was there ever a gem that shone
Like the steps of Allah's wonderful Throne?
And the Drops of Life—oh! what would they be
In the boundless Deep of Eternity?"

While thus she mused, her pinions fann'd
The air of that sweet Indian land,

Whose air is balm; whose ocean spreads
O'er coral rocks, and amber beds;
Whose mountains, pregnant by the beam
Of the warm sun, with diamonds teem;
Whose rivulets are like rich brides,
Lovely, with gold beneath their tides;
Whose sandal groves and bowers of spice
Might be a Peri's Paradise!
But crimson now her rivers ran
   With human blood—the smell of death
Came reeking from those spicy bowers,
And man, the sacrifice of man,
   Mingled his taint with every breath
Upwafted from the innocent flowers.

Land of the Sun! what foot invades
Thy Pagods and thy pillared shades—
Thy cavern shrines, and Idol stones,
Thy Monarchs and their thousand Thrones?
'Tis He of Gazna—fierce in wrath
   He comes, and India's diadems
Lie scattered in his ruinous path.—
   His bloodhounds he adorns with gems
Torn from the violated necks
   Of many a young and loved Sultana;
   Maidens, within their pure Zenana,
   Priests in the very fane he slaughters,
And chokes up with the glittering wrecks
   Of golden shrines the sacred waters!

Downward the Peri turns her gaze,
And, through the war-field's bloody haze

Beholds a youthful warrior stand,
    Alone beside his native river,—
The red blade broken in his hand,
    And the last arrow in his quiver.
"Live," said the Conq'ror, "live to share
The trophies and the crowns I bear!"
Silent that youthful warrior stood—
Silent he pointed to the flood
All crimson with his country's blood,
Then sent his last remaining dart,
For answer, to th' Invader's heart.

False flew the shaft, though pointed well;
The Tyrant lived, the Hero fell!—
Yet marked the Peri where he lay,
    And, when the rush of war was past,
Swiftly descending on a ray
    Of morning light, she caught the last—
Last glorious drop his heart had shed,
Before its free-born spirit fled!

"Be this," she cried, as she winged her flight,
"My welcome gift at the Gates of Light.
Though foul are the drops that oft distil
    On the field of warfare, blood like this,
    For Liberty shed, so holy is,
It would not stain the purest rill
    That sparkles among the Bowers of Bliss!
Oh, if there be, on this earthly sphere,
A boon, an offering Heaven holds dear,
'Tis the last libation Liberty draws
From the heart that bleeds and breaks in her cause."

"Sweet," said the Angel, as she gave
   The gift into his radiant hand,
"Sweet is our welcome of the Brave
   Who die thus for their native land.—
But see—alas!—the crystal bar
Of Eden moves not—holier far
Than ev'n this drop the boon must be
That opes the Gates of Heaven for thee!"

Her first fond hope of Eden blighted,
   Now among Afric's lunar Mountains,
Far to the South, the Peri lighted;
   And sleeked her plumage at the fountains
Of that Egyptian tide—whose birth
Is hidden from the sons of earth
Deep in those solitary woods
Where oft the Genii of the Floods
Dance round the cradle of their Nile,
And hail the new-born Giant's smile.
Thence over Egypt's palmy groves,
   Her grots, and sepulchres of Kings,
The exiled Spirit sighing roves;
And now hangs list'ning to the doves
In warm Rosetta's vale—now loves
   To watch the moonlight on the wings
Of the white pelicans that break
The azure calm of Mœris' Lake.
'Twas a fair scene—a Land more bright
   Never did mortal eye behold!
Who could have thought, that saw this night
   Those valleys and their fruits of gold
Basking in Heaven's serenest light;—

Those groups of lovely date-trees bending
　　Languidly their leaf-crowned heads,
Like youthful maids, when sleep descending
　　Warns them to their silken beds;—
Those virgin lilies, all the night
　　Bathing their beauties in the lake,
That they may rise more fresh and bright,
　　When their belovèd Sun's awake;—
Those ruined shrines and towers that seem
The relics of a splendid dream;
　　Amid whose fairy loneliness
Naught but the lapwing's cry is heard,
Naught seen but (when the shadows, flitting
Fast from the moon, unsheath its gleam)
Some purple-winged Sultana sitting
　　Upon a column, motionless -
And glitt'ring like an Idol bird:—
Who could have thought, that there, ev'n there,
Amid those scenes so still and fair,
　　The Demon of the Plague hath cast
　　From his hot wing a deadlier blast,
More mortal far than ever came
From the red Desert's sands of flame!
So quick, that ev'ry living thing
Of human shape, touched by his wing,
　　Like plants, where the Simoon hath passed,
At once falls black and withering!
The sun went down on many a brow
　　Which, full of bloom and freshness then,
Is rankling in the pest-house now,
　　And ne'er will feel that sun again.
And, oh! to see th' unburied heaps

On which the lonely moonlight sleeps—
The very vultures turn away,
And sicken at so foul a prey!
Only the fierce hyena stalks
Throughout the city's desolate walks
At midnight, and his carnage plies:—
   Woe to the half-dead wretch, who meets
The glaring of those large blue eyes
   Amid the darkness of the streets!

" Poor race of men!" said the pitying Spirit,
   " Dearly ye pay for your primal Fall—
Some flow'rets of Eden ye still inherit,
   But the trail of the Serpent is over them all!

She wept—the air grew pure and clear
   Around her, as the bright drops ran;
For there's a magic in each tear
   Such kindly Spirits weep for man!

Just then, beneath some orange-trees,
Whose fruit and blossoms in the breeze
Were wantoning together, free,
Like age at play with infancy—
Beneath that fresh and springing bower,
   Close by the Lake, she heard the moan
Of one who, at this silent hour,
   Had thither stol'n to die alone.
One who in life, where'er he moved,
   Drew after him the hearts of many;
Yet now, as though he ne'er were loved,
   Dies here unseen, unwept by any!

None to watch near him—none to slake
   The fire that in his bosom lies,
With ev'n a sprinkle from that lake,
   Which shines so cool before his eyes.
No voice, well known through many a day,
   To speak the last, the parting word,
Which, when all other sounds decay,
   Is still like distant music heard;—
That tender farewell on the shore
Of this rude world, when all is o'er,
Which cheers the spirit, ere its bark
Puts off into the unknown Dark.

Deserted youth! one thought alone
   Shed joy around his soul in death,—
That she, whom he for years had known,
And loved, and might have called his own,
   Was safe from this foul midnight's breath,—
Safe in her father's princely halls,
Where the cool airs from fountain falls,
Freshly perfumed by many a brand
Of the sweet wood from India's land,
Were pure as she whose brow they fann'd.

But see—who yonder comes by stealth,
   This melancholy bower to seek,
Like a young envoy, sent by Health,
   With rosy gifts upon her cheek?
'Tis she—far off, through moonlight dim,
   He knew his own betrothed bride,
She, who would rather die with him,
   Than live to gain the world beside!—

Her arms are round her lover now,
  His livid cheek to hers she presses,
And dips, to bind his burning brow,
  In the cool lake her loosened tresses.
Ah! once, how little did he think
An hour would come, when he should shrink
With horror from that dear embrace,
  Those gentle arms, that were to him
Holy as is the cradling place
  Of Eden's infant cherubim!
And now he yields—now turns away
Shudd'ring as if the venom lay
All in those proffered lips alone—
Those lips that, then so fearless grown,
Never until that instant came
Near his unmasked or without shame.
"Oh! let me only breathe the air,
  The blessèd air, that's breathed by thee,
And, whether on its wings it bear
  Healing or death, 'tis sweet to me!
There—drink my tears, while yet they fall—
  Would that my bosom's blood were balm,
And, well thou know'st, I'd shed it all,
  To give thy brow one minute's calm.
Nay, turn not from me that dear face—
  Am I not thine—thy own loved bride—
The one, the chosen one, whose place
  In life or death is by thy side?
Think'st thou that she, whose only light,
  In this dim world, from thee hath shone,
Could bear the long, the cheerless night,
  That must be hers when thou art gone?

That I can live, and let thee go,
Who art my life itself?—No, no—
When the stem dies, the leaf that grew
Out of its heart must perish too!
Then turn to me, my own love, turn,
Before, like thee, I fade and burn;
Cling to these yet cool lips, and share
The last pure life that lingers there!"
She fails—she sinks—as dies the lamp
In charnel airs, or cavern-damp,
So quickly do his baleful sighs
Quench all the sweet light of her eyes.
One struggle—and his pain is past—
  Her lover is no longer living!
One kiss the maiden gives, one last,
  Long kiss, which she expires in giving!

"Sleep," said the Peri, as softly she stole
The farewell sigh of that vanishing soul,
As true as e'er warmed a woman's breast—
"Sleep on, in visions of odour rest,
In balmier airs than ever yet stirred
Th' enchanted pile of that lonely bird,
Who sings at the last his own death-lay,
And in music and perfume dies away."

Thus saying, from her lips she spread
  Unearthly breathings through the place,
And shook her sparkling wreath, and shed
  Such lustre o'er each paly face,
That like two lovely saints they seemed,
  Upon the eve of doomsday taken

From their dim graves, in odour sleeping;
    While that benevolent Peri beamed
Like their good angel, calmly keeping
    Watch o'er them till their souls should waken.

But morn is blushing in the sky;
    Again the Peri soars above,
Bearing to Heaven that precious sigh
    Of pure, self-sacrificing love.
High throbb'd her heart, with hope elate,
    Th' Elysian palm she soon shall win,
For the bright Spirit at the gate
    Smiled as she gave that off'ring in;
And she already hears the trees
    Of Eden, with their crystal bells
Ringing in that ambrosial breeze
    That from the throne of Allah swells;
And she can see the starry bowls
    That lie around that lucid lake,
Upon whose banks admitted Souls
    Their first sweet draught of glory take!

But, ah! ev'n Peri's hopes are vain—
Again the Fates forbade, again
Th' immortal barrier closed—" Not yet,"
The Angel said, as, with regret,
He shut from her that glimpse of glory.
" True was the maiden, and her story,
Written in light o'er Allah's head,
By seraph eyes shall long be read.
But Peri, see—the crystal bar
Of Eden moves not—holier far

Than ev'n this sigh the boon must be
That opes the Gates of Heaven for thee."

Now, upon Syria's land of roses
Softly the light of Eve reposes,
And, like a glory, the broad sun
Hangs over sainted Lebanon;
Whose head in wintry grandeur towers,
   And whitens with eternal sleet,
While summer, in a vale of flowers,
   Is sleeping rosy at his feet.

To one, who looked from upper air
O'er all th' enchanted regions there,
How beauteous must have been the glow,
The light, the sparkling from below!
Fair gardens, shining streams, with ranks
Of golden melons on their banks,
More golden where the sun-light falls;—
Gay lizards, glitt'ring on the walls
Of ruined shrines, busy and bright
As they were all alive with light;
And yet, more splendid, numerous flocks
Of pigeons, settling on the rocks,
With their rich restless wings, that gleam
Variously in the crimson beam
Of the warm West,—as if inlaid
With brilliants from the mine, or made
Of tearless rainbows, such as span
Th' unclouded skies of Peristan.
And then the mingling sounds that come
Of shepherd's ancient reed, with hum

Of the wild bees of Palestine,
  Banqueting through the flowery vales;
And, Jordan, those sweet banks of thine,
  And woods, so full of nightingales.

But naught can charm the luckless Peri;
Her soul is sad—her wings are weary—
Joyless she sees the Sun look down
On that great Temple, once his own,
Whose lonely columns stand sublime,
  Flinging their shadows from on high,
Like dials, which the wizard, Time,
  Had raised to count his ages by!

Yet haply there may lie concealed
  Beneath those Chambers of the Sun,
Some amulet of gems, annealed
In upper fires, some tablet sealed
  With the great name of Solomon,
  Which, spelled by her illumined eyes,
May teach her where, beneath the moon,
In earth or ocean, lies the boon,
The charm, that can restore so soon
  An erring Spirit to the skies.

Cheered by this hope, she bends her thither;
  Still laughs the radiant eye of Heaven,
  Nor have the golden bowers of Even
In the rich West begun to wither;
When, o'er the vale of Balbec winging
  Slowly, she sees a child at play
Among the rosy wild-flowers singing,
  As rosy and as wild as they;

Chasing, with eager hands and eyes,
The beautiful blue damsel-flies,
That fluttered round the jasmine stems,
Like wingèd flowers or flying gems:—
And near the boy, who, tired with play,
Now nestling 'mid the roses lay,
She saw a wearied man dismount
   From his hot steed, and on the brink
Of a small imaret's rustic fount
   Impatient fling him down to drink.
Then swift his haggard brow he turned
   To the fair child, who fearless sat,
Though never yet hath day-beam burned
   Upon a brow more fierce than that,—
Sullenly fierce—a mixture dire,
Like thunder-clouds of gloom and fire;
In which the Peri's eye could read
Dark tales of many a ruthless deed;
The ruined maid—the shrine profaned—
Oaths broken—and the threshold stained
With blood of guests!—*there* written, all
Black as the damning drops that fall
From the denouncing Angel's pen,
Ere Mercy weeps them out again.

Yet tranquil now that man of crime
(As if the balmy evening time
Softened his spirit) looked and lay,
Watching the rosy infant's play;—
Though still, whene'er his eye by chance
Fell on the boy's, its lurid glance
   Met that unclouded, joyous gaze,

As torches, that have burned all night
Through some impure and godless rite,
   Encounter morning's glorious rays.

But, hark! the vesper call to prayer,
   As slow the orb of daylight sets,
Is rising sweetly on the air,
   From Syria's thousand minarets.
The boy has started from the bed
Of flowers, where he had laid his head,
And down upon the fragrant sod
   Kneels with his forehead to the south,
Lisping th' eternal name of God
   From Purity's own cherub mouth,
And looking, while his hands and eyes
Are lifted to the glowing skies,
Like a stray babe of Paradise,
Just lighted on that flowery plain,
And seeking for its home again.
Oh! 'twas a sight—that Heaven—that child—
A scene, which might have well beguiled
Ev'n haughty Eblis of a sigh,
For glories lost and peace gone by!

And how felt *he*, the wretched Man
Reclining there—while memory ran
O'er many a year of guilt and strife,
Flew o'er the dark flood of his life,
Nor found one sunny resting-place,
Nor brought him back one branch of grace,
"There *was* a time," he said, in mild,
Heart-humbled tones—"thou blessèd child!

When, young, and haply pure as thou,
I looked and prayed like thee—but now—"
He hung his head—each nobler aim,
    And hope, and feeling, which had slept
From boyhood's hour, that instant came
    Fresh o'er him, and he wept—he wept

Blest tears of soul-felt penitence!
    In whose benign, redeeming flow
Is felt the first, the only sense
    Of guiltless joy that guilt can know.
"There's a drop," said the Peri, "that down from
        the moon
Falls through the withering airs of June
Upon Egypt's land, of so healing a power,
So balmy a virtue, that ev'n in the hour
That drop descends, contagion dies,
And health reanimates earth and skies!
Oh, is it not thus, thou man of sin,
    The precious tears of repentance fall?
Though foul thy fiery plagues within,
    One heavenly drop hath dispelled them all!"

And now—behold him kneeling there
By the child's side, in humble prayer,
While the same sunbeam shines upon
The guilty and the guiltless one,
And hymns of joy proclaim through Heaven
The triumph of a Soul Forgiven!

'Twas when the golden orb had set,
While on their knees they lingered yet,

There fell a light more lovely far
Than ever came from sun or star,
Upon the tear that, warm and meek,
Dewed that repentant sinner's cheek.
To mortal eye this light might seem
A northern flash or meteor beam—
But well th' enraptured Peri knew
'Twas a bright smile the Angel threw
From Heaven's gate, to hail that tear,
The harbinger of glory near!

"Joy, joy forever! my task is done—
The gates are passed, and Heaven is won!
Oh! am I not happy? I am, I am—
   To thee, sweet Eden! how dark and sad
Are the diamond turrets of Shadukiam,
   And the fragrant bowers of Amberabad!

"Farewell, ye odours of Earth, that die
Passing away like a lover's sigh;—
My feast is now of the Tooba Tree,
Whose scent is the breath of Eternity!

"Farewell, ye vanishing Flowers, that shone
   In my fairy wreath, so bright and brief;—
Oh! what are the brightest that e'er have blown
To the lote-tree, springing by Allah's throne,
   Whose flowers have a soul in every leaf!
Joy, joy forever!—my task is done—
The Gates are passed, and Heaven is won!"

## THE DEATH OF HAFED AND HINDA.

### (From "The Fire-Worshippers.")

THERE was a deep ravine, that lay
   Yet darkling in the Moslem's way;
Fit spot to make invaders rue
The many fallen before the few.
The torrents from that morning's sky
Had filled the narrow chasm breast-high,
And on each side, aloft and wild,
Huge cliffs and toppling crags were piled,—
The guards with which young Freedom lines
The pathways to her mountain-shrines.
Here, at this pass, the scanty band
Of Iran's last avengers stand;
Here wait, in silence like the dead,
And listen for the Moslem's tread
So anxiously, the carrion-bird
Above them flaps his wing unheard!

They come—that plunge into the water
Gives signal for the work of slaughter.
Now, Ghebers, now—if e'er your blades
   Had point or prowess, prove them now,—
Woe to the file that foremost wades!
   They come—a falchion greets each brow,
And, as they tumble, trunk on trunk,
Beneath the gory waters sunk,
Still o'er their drowning bodies press
New victims quick and numberless;

Till scarce an arm in Hafed's band,
  So fierce their toil, hath power to stir,
But listless from each crimson hand
  The sword hangs, clogged with massacre.
Never was horde of tyrants met
With bloodier welcome—never yet
To patriot vengeance hath the sword
More terrible libations poured!

All up the dreary, long ravine,
By the red, murky glimmer seen
Of half-quenched brands, that o'er the flood
Lie scattered round and burn in blood,
What ruin glares! what carnage swims!
Heads, blazing turbans, quiv'ring limbs,
Lost swords that, dropped from many a hand,
In that thick pool of slaughter stand;—
Wretches who, wading, half on fire
  From the tossed brands that round them fly,
'Twixt flood and flame in shrieks expire;—
  And some who, grasped by those that die,
Sink woundless with them, smothered o'er
In their dead brethren's gushing gore!

But vainly hundreds, thousands bleed,
Still hundreds, thousands more succeed;
Countless as tow'rds some flame at night
The North's dark insects wing their flight,
And quench or perish in its light,
To this terrific spot they pour—
Till, bridged with Moslem bodies o'er,
It bears aloft their slippery tread,

And o'er the dying and the dead,
Tremendous causeway! on they pass.—
Then, hapless Ghebers, then, alas,
What hope was left for you? for you,
Whose yet warm pile of sacrifice
Is smoking in their vengeful eyes;—
Whose swords how keen, how fierce they knew,
And burn with shame to find how few?

Crushed down by that vast multitude,
Some found their graves where first they stood:
While some with hardier struggle died,
And still fought on by Hafed's side,
Who, fronting to the foe, trod back
Tow'rds the high towers his gory track;
And, as a lion swept away
   By sudden swell of Jordan's pride
From the wild covert where he lay,
   Long battles with th' o'erwhelming tide,
So fought he back with fierce delay,
And kept both foes and fate at bay.

But whither now? their track is lost,
   Their prey escaped—guide, torches gone
By torrent beds and labyrinths crossed,
   The scattered crowd rush blindly on—
"Curse on those tardy lights that wind,"
They panting cry, "so far behind;
Oh for a bloodhound's precious scent,
To track the way the Gheber went!"
Vain wish—confusedly along
They rush, more desp'rate as more wrong

Till, wildered by the far-off lights,
Yet glitt'ring up those gloomy heights,
Their footing, mazed and lost, they miss,
And down the darkling precipice
Are dashed into the deep abyss;
Or midway hang, impaled on rocks,
A banquet, yet alive, for flocks
Of rav'ning vultures,—while the dell
Re-echoes with each horrid yell.

Those sounds—the last, to vengeance dear,
That e'er shall ring in Hafed's ear,—
Now reached him, as aloft, alone,
Upon the steep way breathless thrown,
He lay beside his reeking blade,
   Resigned, as if life's task were o'er,
Its last blood-offering amply paid,
   And Iran's self could claim no more.
One only thought, one ling'ring beam
Now broke across his dizzy dream
Of pain and weariness—'twas she,
   His heart's pure planet, shining yet
Above the waste of memory,
   When all life's other lights were set.
And never to his mind before
Her image such enchantment wore.
It seemed as if each thought that stained,
   Each fear that chill'd their loves was past,
And not one cloud of earth remained
   Between him and her radiance cast;—
As if to charms, before so bright,
   New grace from other worlds was given,

And his soul saw her by the light
  Now breaking o'er itself from heaven.
A voice spoke near him—'twas the tone
Of a loved friend, the only one
Of all his warriors left with life
From that short night's tremendous strife.—
"And must we then, my Chief, die here?
Foes round us, and the Shrine so near!"
These words have roused the last remains
  Of life within him—"What! not yet
Beyond the reach of Moslem chains!"
  The thought could make ev'n Death forget
His icy bondage—with a bound
He springs, all bleeding, from the ground,
And grasps his comrade's arm, now grown
Ev'n feebler, heavier than his own,
And up the painful pathway leads,
Death gaining on each step he treads.
Speed them, thou God, who heardst their vow!
They mount—they bleed—oh save them now!
The crags are red they've clambered o'er,
The rock-weed's dripping with their gore;—
Thy blade too, Hafed, false at length,
Now breaks beneath thy tott'ring strength:
Haste, haste—the voices of the Foe
Come near and nearer from below—
One effort more—thank Heaven! 'tis past,
They've gained the topmost steep at last.
And now they touch the temple's walls,
  Now Hafed sees the Fire divine—
When, lo! his weak, worn comrade falls
  Dead on the threshold of the Shrine.

"Alas, brave soul, too quickly fled!
　And must I leave thee with'ring here,
The sport of every ruffian's tread,
　The mark for every coward's spear?
No, by yon altar's sacred beams!"
He cries, and, with a strength that seems
Not of this world, uplifts the frame
Of the fallen Chief, and tow'rds the flame
Bears him along;—with death-damp hand
　The corpse upon the pyre he lays,
Then lights the consecrated brand,
　And fires the pile, whose sudden blaze
Like lightning bursts o'er Oman's Sea.—
"Now, Freedom's God! I come to Thee,"
The youth exclaims, and with a smile
Of triumph vaulting on the pile,
In that last effort, ere the fires
Have harmed one glorious limb, expires!

What shriek was that on Oman's tide?
　It came from yonder drifting bark,
That just hath caught upon her side
　The death-light—and again is dark.
It is the boat—ah! why delay'd?—
That bears the wretched Moslem maid
Confided to the watchful care
　Of a small veteran band, with whom
Their gen'rous Chieftain would not share
　The secret of his final doom,
But hoped when Hinda, safe and free,
　Was rendered to her father's eyes,
Their pardon, full and prompt, would be

The ransom of so dear a prize.—
Unconscious, thus, of Hafed's fate,
And proud to guard their beauteous freight,
Scarce had they cleared the surfy waves
That foam around those frightful caves,
When the cursed war-whoops, known so well,
Came echoing from the distant dell—
Sudden each oar, upheld and still,
   Hung dripping o'er the vessel's side,
And, driving at the current's will,
   They rocked along the whisp'ring tide;
While every eye, in mute dismay,
   Was tow'rd that fatal mountain turned
Where the dim altar's quiv'ring ray
   As yet all lone and tranquil burned.

Oh! 'tis not, Hinda, in the power
   Of Fancy's most terrific touch
To paint thy pangs in that dread hour—
   Thy silent agony—'twas such
As those who feel could paint too well,
But none e'er felt and lived to tell!
'Twas not alone the dreary state
Of a lorn spirit, crushed by fate,
When, though no more remains to dread,
   The panic chill will not depart;—
When, though the inmate Hope be dead,
   Her ghost still haunts the mould'ring heart.
No—pleasures, hopes, affections gone,
The wretch may bear, and yet live on,
Like things, within the cold rock found
Alive, when all's congealed around.

But there's a blank repose in this,
A calm stagnation, that were bliss
To the keen, burning, harrowing pain
Now felt through all thy breast and brain;—
That spasm of terror, mute, intense,
That breathless, agonized suspense,
From whose hot throb, whose deadly aching,
The heart hath no relief but breaking!

Calm is the wave—heaven's brilliant lights
   Reflected dance beneath the prow;
Time was when, on such lovely nights,
   She who is there, so desolate now,
Could sit all cheerful, though alone,
   And ask no happier joy than seeing
That starlight o'er the waters thrown—
No joy but that, to make her blest,
   And the fresh, buoyant, sense of Being,
Which bounds in youth's yet careless breast,
Itself a star, not borrowing light,
But in its own glad essence bright.
How different now!—but, hark! again
The yell of havoc rings—brave men!
In vain, with beating hearts, ye stand
On the bark's edge—in vain each hand
Half draws the falchion from its sheath;
   All's o'er—in rust your blades may lie:—
He, at whose word they've scattered death,
   Ev'n now, this night, himself must die!
Well may ye look to yon dim tower,
   And ask, and wondering guess what means
The battle-cry at this dead hour—

Ah! she could tell you—she, who leans
Unheeded there, pale, sunk, aghast,
With brow against the dew-cold mast;
   Too well she knows—her more than life,
Her soul's first idol and its last,
   Lies bleeding in that murd'rous strife.

But see—what moves upon the height?
Some signal!—'tis a torch's light.
   What bodes its solitary glare?
In gasping silence tow'rd the Shrine
All eyes are turned—thine, Hinda, thine
   Fix their last fading life-beams there.
'Twas but a moment—fierce and high
The death-pile blazed into the sky,
And far away, o'er rock and flood
   Its melancholy radiance sent;
While Hafed, like a vision, stood
Revealed before the burning pyre,
Till, shadowy, like a Spirit of Fire
   Shrined in its own grand element!
" 'Tis he!"—the shudd'ring maid exclaims.
   But, while she speaks, he's seen no more;
High burst in air the funeral flames,
   And Iran's hopes and hers are o'er!

One wild, heart-broken shriek she gave;
   Then sprung, as if to reach that blaze,
   Where still she fixed her dying gaze,
And, gazing, sunk into the wave,—
   Deep, deep,—where never care or pain
   Shall reach her innocent heart again!

Farewell—farewell to thee, Araby's daughter!
  (Thus warbled a Peri beneath the dark sea),
No pearl ever lay, under Oman's green water,
  More pure in its shell than thy Spirit in thee.

Oh! fair as the sea-flower close to thee growing,
  How light was thy heart till Love's witchery came,
Like the wind of the south o'er a summer lute blowing,
  And hushed all its music, and withered its frame!

But long, upon Araby's green sunny highlands,
  Shall maids and their lovers remember the doom
Of her who lies sleeping among the Pearl Islands,
  With naught but the sea-star to light up her tomb!

And still, when the merry date-season is burning,
  And calls to the palm-groves the young and the old,
The happiest there, from their pastime returning
  At sunset, will weep when thy story is told.

The young village-maid, when with flowers she dresses
  Her dark flowing hair for some festival-day,
Will think of thy fate till, neglecting her tresses,
  She mournfully turns from the mirror away.

Nor shall Iran, beloved of her Hero! forget thee—
  Though tyrants watch over her tears as they start,
Close, close by the side of that Hero she'll set thee,
  Embalmed in the innermost shrine of her heart.

Farewell—be it ours to embellish thy pillow
  With every thing beauteous that grows in the deep;
Each flower of the rock and each gem of the billow
  Shall sweeten thy bed and illumine thy sleep.

Around thee shall glisten the loveliest amber
  That ever the sorrowing sea-bird has wept;
With many a shell, in whose hollow-wreathed chamber
  We, Peris of Ocean, by moonlight have slept.

We'll dive where the gardens of coral lie darkling,
  And plant all the rosiest stems at thy head;
We'll seek where the sands of the Caspian are sparkling,
  And gather their gold to strew over thy bed.

Farewell—farewell—until Pity's sweet fountain
  Is lost in the hearts of the fair and the brave;
They'll weep for the Chieftain who died on that mountain,
  They'll weep for the Maiden who sleeps in this wave.

---

### BEAUTY, WIT, AND GOLD.

IN her bower a widow dwelt,
  At her feet three suitors knelt;
Each adored the widow much,
Each essayed her heart to touch.
One had wit, and one had gold,
And one was cast in beauty's mould.
Guess which was it won the prize—
Purse, or tongue, or handsome eyes?

First appeared the handsome man,
Proudly peeping o'er her fan;
Red his lips and white his skin—
Could such beauty fail to win?
Then stepped forth the man of gold,
Cash he counted, coin he told;

Wealth the burden of his tale,
Could such golden projects fail?

Then the man of wit and sense
Wooed her with his eloquence;
Now, she heard him with a sigh!
Now, she blushed, she knew not why;
Then she smiled to hear him speak—
Then a tear was on her cheek!
Beauty, vanish! gold, depart!
Wit has won the widow's heart!

---

REASON, FOLLY, AND BEAUTY.

REASON, and Folly, and Beauty, they say,
   Went on a party of pleasure one day.
      Folly played
      Around the maid,
The bells of his cap rung merrily out;
      While Reason took
      To his sermon-book—
Oh! which was the pleasanter no one need doubt,
Which was the pleasanter no one need doubt.

Beauty, who likes to be thought very sage,
Turned for a moment to Reason's dull page,
      Till Folly said,
      "Look here, sweet maid!"—
The sight of his cap brought her back to herself,
      While Reason read
      His leaves of lead,
With no one to mind him, poor sensible elf!
No —no one to mind him, poor sensible elf!

Then Reason grew jealous of Folly's gay cap;
Had he that on, he her heart might entrap—
    "There it is,"
    Quoth Folly, "old quiz!"
(Folly was always good-natured, 'tis said,)
    "Under the sun
    There's no such fun,
As Reason with my cap and bells on his head,
Reason with my cap and bells on his head!"

But Reason the head-dress so awkwardly wore,
That Beauty now liked him still less than before;
    While Folly took
    Old Reason's book,
And twisted the leaves in a cap of such *ton*,
    That Beauty vowed
    (Though not aloud)
She liked him still better in that than his own,
Yes,—liked him still better in that than his own.

---

### THOSE EVENING BELLS.

THOSE evening bells! those evening bells!
    How many a tale their music tells,
Of youth, and home, and that sweet time
When last I heard their soothing chime.

Those joyous hours are passed away;
And many a heart that then was gay,
Within the tomb now darkly dwells,
And hears no more those evening bells.

And so 'twill be when I am gone—
That tuneful peal will still ring on;
While other bards shall walk these dells,
And sing your praise, sweet evening bells.

---

## A CANADIAN BOAT-SONG.

Faintly as tolls the evening chime,
  Our voices keep tune, and our oars keep time.
Soon as the woods on shore look dim,
We'll sing at St. Ann's our parting hymn.
Row, brothers, row! the stream runs fast,
The rapids are near, and the daylight's past!

Why should we yet our sail unfurl?—
There is not a breath the blue wave to curl!
But when the wind blows off the shore,
O! sweetly we'll rest our weary oar.
Blow, breezes, blow! the stream runs fast,
The rapids are near, and the daylight's past!

Utawa's tide! this trembling moon
Shall see us float over thy surges soon.
Saint of this green isle, hear our prayers—
O! grant us cool heavens and favouring airs!
Blow, breezes, blow! the stream runs fast,
The rapids are near, and the daylight's past!

## Lord Byron.

### EXTRACTS FROM "CHILDE HAROLD."

#### ANCIENT GREECE.

Ancient of days! august Athena! where,
  Where are thy men of might? thy grand in soul?
Gone—glimmering thro' the dream of things that were:
First in the race that led to Glory's goal,
They won, and passed away—is this the whole?
A schoolboy's tale, the wonder of an hour!
The warrior's weapon, and the sophist's stole,
Are sought in vain, and o'er each mouldering tower,
Dim with the mist of years, gray flits the shade of power.

Son of the morning, rise! approach you here!
Come, but molest not yon defenceless urn:
Look on this spot—a nation's sepulchre!
Abode of gods, whose shrines no longer burn.
Even gods must yield—religions take their turn:
'Twas Jove's—'tis Mahomet's—and other creeds
Will rise with other years, till man shall learn
Vainly his incense soars, his victim bleeds;
Poor child of Doubt and Death, whose hope is built on
    reeds.

Bound to the earth, he lifts his eye to heaven—
Is't not enough, unhappy thing! to know
Thou art? Is this a boon so kindly given,
That being, thou wouldst be again, and go,
Thou know'st not, reck'st not, to what region, so
On earth no more, but mingled with the skies?

Still wilt thou dream on future joy and woe?
Regard and weigh yon dust before it flies:
That little urn saith more than thousand homilies.

Or burst the vanished hero's lofty mound:
Far on the solitary shore he sleeps:
He fell, and falling, nations mourned around;
But now not one of saddening thousands weeps,
Nor warlike worshipper his vigil keeps
Where demi-gods appeared, as records tell.
Remove yon skull from out the scattered heaps:
Is that a temple where a god may dwell?
Why, even the worm at last disdains her shattered cell.

Look on its broken arch, its ruined wall,
Its chambers desolate, and portals foul:
Yes, this was once ambition's airy hall,
The dome of thought, the palace of the soul:
Behold through each lack-lustre eyeless hole,
The gay recess of wisdom and of wit,
And passion's host, that never brooked control:
Can all saint, sage, or sophist ever writ,
People this lonely tower, this tenement refit?

Well didst thou speak, Athena's wisest son!
"All that we know is, nothing can be known."
Why should we shrink from what we cannot shun!
Each hath his pang, but feeble sufferers groan
With brain-born dreams of evil all their own.
Pursue what chance or fate proclaimeth best;
Peace waits us on the shores of Acheron:
There no forced banquet claims the sated guest,
But silence spreads the couch of ever-welcome rest.

Yet if, as holiest men have deemed, there be
A land of souls beyond that sable shore,
To shame the doctrine of the Sadducee
And sophists, madly vain of dubious lore,
How sweet it were in concert to adore
With those who made our mortal labours light!
To hear each voice we feared to hear no more!
Behold each mighty shade revealed to sight,
The Bactrian, Samian sage, and all who taught the right!

---

### EVENING ON LAKE LEMAN.

IT is the hush of night; and all between
  Thy margin and the mountains, dusk, yet clear,
Mellowed and mingling, yet distinctly seen—
Save darkened Jura, whose capped heights appear
Precipitously steep; and drawing near,
There breathes a living fragrance from the shore,
Of flowers yet fresh with childhood: on the ear
Drops the light drip of the suspended oar,
Or chirps the grasshopper one good-night carol more;

He is an evening reveller, who makes
His life an infancy, and sings his fill!
At intervals, some bird from out the brakes
Starts into voice a moment—then is still.
There seems a floating whisper on the hill—
But that is fancy, for the star-light dews
All silently their tears of love instil,
Weeping themselves away, till they infuse
Deep into Nature's breast the spirit of her hues.

## STORM ON LAKE LEMAN.

THE sky is changed!—and such a change! O night,
And storm, and darkness, ye are wondrous strong,
Yet lovely in your strength, as is the light
Of a dark eye in woman! Far along
From peak to peak, the rattling crags among,
Leaps the live thunder! not from one lone cloud,
But every mountain now hath found a tongue,
And Jura answers, through her misty shroud,
Back to the joyous Alps, who call to her aloud.

And this is in the night: most glorious night!
Thou wert not sent for slumber! let me be
A sharer in thy fierce and far delight—
A portion of the tempest and of thee!
How the lit lake shines, a phosphoric sea,
And the big rain comes dancing to the earth!
And now again 'tis black—and now the glee
Of the loud hill shakes with its mountain-mirth,
As if they did rejoice o'er a young earthquake's birth.

---

## THE COLISEUM.

### THE DYING GLADIATOR.

THE seal is set.—Now welcome, thou dread power!
Nameless, yet thus omnipotent, which here
Walk'st in the shadow of the midnight hour
With a deep awe, yet all distinct from fear;
Thy haunts are ever where the dead walls rear
Their ivy mantles, and the solemn scene

Derives from thee a sense so deep and clear,
That we become a part of what has been,
And grow unto the spot, all-seeing, but unseen.

And here the buzz of eager nations ran,
In murmured pity, or loud-roared applause,
As man was slaughtered by his fellow-man.
And wherefore slaughtered? wherefore, but because
Such were the bloody circus' genial laws,
And the imperial pleasure.  Wherefore not?
What matters where we fall to fill the maws
Of worms—on battle-plains or listed spot?
Both are but theatres where the chief actors rot.

I see before me the Gladiator lie:
He leans upon his hand; his manly brow
Consents to death, but conquers agony,
And his drooped head sinks gradually low:
And through his side the last drops, ebbing slow
From the red gash, fall heavy, one by one,
Like the first of a thunder-shower; and now
The arena swims around him; he is gone,
Ere ceased the inhuman shout which hailed the wretch who won.

He heard it, but he heeded not; his eyes
Were with his heart, and that was far away:
He recked not of the life he lost nor prize,
But where his rude hut by the Danube lay;
*There* were his young barbarians all at play,
*There* was their Dacian mother—he, their sire,
Butchered to make a Roman holiday.
All this rushed with his blood.  Shall he expire,
And unavenged?  Arise, ye Goths, and glut your ire!

## THE DREAM.

OUR life is twofold: sleep hath its own world,
　　A boundary between the things misnamed
Death and existence; sleep hath its own world,
And a wide realm of wild reality,
And dreams in their development have breath,
And tears, and tortures, and the touch of joy:
They leave a weight upon our waking thoughts,
They take a weight from off our waking toils,
They do divide our being; they become
A portion of ourselves as of our time,
And look like heralds of eternity;
They pass like spirits of the past,—they speak
Like sibyls of the future; they have power—
The tyranny of pleasure and of pain;
They make us what we were not—what they will,
And shake us with the vision that's gone by,—
The dread of vanished shadows. Are they so?
Is not the past all shadow? What are they?
Creations of the mind? The mind can make
Substance, and people planets of its own
With beings brighter than have been,—and give
A breath to forms which can outlive all flesh.
I would recall a vision which I dreamed
Perchance in sleep,—for in itself a thought,
A slumbering thought, is capable of years,
And curdles a long life into one hour.

　I saw two beings in the hues of youth
Standing upon a hill, a gentle hill,
Green and of mild declivity,—the last

As 'twere the cape of a long ridge of such,
Save that there was no sea to lave its base,
But a most living landscape, and the wave
Of woods and corn-fields, and the abodes of men
Scattered at intervals, and wreathing smoke
Arising from such rustic roofs; the hill
Was crowned with a peculiar diadem
Of trees, in circular array, so fixed,—
Not by the sport of nature, but of man:
These two, a maiden and a youth, were there
Gazing; the one, on all that was beneath—
Fair as herself—but the boy gazed on her;
And both were young, and one was beautiful;
And both were young, yet not alike in youth.
As the sweet moon on the horizon's verge,
The maid was on the eve of womanhood;—
The boy had fewer summers, but his heart
Had far outgrown his years; and, to his eye,
There was but one beloved face on earth—
And that was shining on him: he had looked
Upon it till it could not pass away;
He had no breath, no being, but in hers:
She was his voice;—he did not speak to her,
But trembled on her words: she was his sight,
For his eye followed hers, and saw with hers,
Which coloured all his objects;—he had ceased
To live within himself; she was his life,—
The ocean to the river of his thoughts,
Which terminated all! upon a tone,
A touch of hers, his blood would ebb and flow,
And his cheek change tempestuously;—his heart
Unknowing of its cause of agony.

But she in these fond feelings had no share:
Her sighs were not for him! to her he was
Even as a brother,—but no more: 'twas much,
For brotherless she was, save in the name
Her infant friendship had bestowed on him;
Herself the solitary scion left
Of a time-honoured race.   It was a name
Which pleased him, and yet pleased him not—and why?
Time taught him a deep answer—when she loved
Another! even *now* she loved another;
And on the summit of that hill she stood
Looking afar, if yet her lover's steed
Kept pace with her expectancy, and flew.

   A change came o'er the spirit of my dream.
There was an ancient mansion, and before
Its walls there was a steed caparisoned:
Within an antique oratory stood
The boy of whom I spake;—he was alone,
And pale, and pacing to and fro: anon
He sate him down, and seized a pen, and traced
Words which I could not guess of; then he leaned
His bowed head on his hands, and shook as 'twere
With a convulsion,—then arose again,
And, with his teeth and quivering hands, did tear
What he had written; but he shed no tears.
And he did calm himself, and fix his brow
Into a kind of quiet: as he paused,
The lady of his love re-entered there;
She was serene and smiling then,—and yet
She knew she was by him beloved! she knew,
For quickly comes such knowledge, that his heart

Was darkened with her shadow; and she saw
That he was wretched,—but she saw not all.
He rose, and, with a cold and gentle grasp,
He took her hand; a moment o'er his face
A tablet of unutterable thoughts
Was traced,—and then it faded as it came:
He dropped the hand he held, and with slow steps
Retired,—but not as bidding her adieu;
For they did part with mutual smiles: he passed
From out the massy gate of that old hall,
And mounting on his steed he went his way,
And ne'er repassed that hoary threshold more.

A change came o'er the spirit of my dream.
The boy was sprung to manhood: in the wilds
Of fiery climes he made himself a home,
And his soul drank their sunbeams; he was girt
With strange and dusky aspects; he was not
Himself like what he had been: on the sea
And on the shore he was a wanderer!
There was a mass of many images
Crowded like waves upon me; but he was
A part of all,—and in the last he lay
Reposing from the noontide sultriness,
Couched among fallen columns, in the shade
Of ruined walls, that had survived the names
Of those who reared them: by his sleeping side
Stood camels grazing, and some goodly steeds
Were fastened near a fountain; and a man,
Clad in a flowing garb, did watch the while,
While many of his tribe slumbered around;
And they were canopied by the blue sky—

So cloudless, clear, and purely beautiful,
That God alone was to be seen in heaven.

   A change came o'er the spirit of my dream.
The lady of his love was wed with one
Who did not love her better: in her home,
A thousand leagues from his,—her native home,
She dwelt begirt with growing infancy,
Daughters and sons of beauty,—but behold!
Upon her face there was the tint of grief,
The settled shadow of an inward strife,
And an unquiet drooping of the eye,
As if its lid were charged with unshed tears.
What could her grief be?—she had all she loved;
And he who had so loved her was not there
To trouble with bad hopes, or evil wish,
Or ill-repressed affliction, her pure thoughts.
What could her grief be?—she had loved him not,
Nor given him cause to deem himself beloved;
Nor could he be a part of that which preyed
Upon her mind,—a spectre of the past.
   A change came o'er the spirit of my dream.
The wanderer was returned.  I saw him stand
Before an altar, with a gentle bride:
Her face was fair,—but was not that which made
The starlight of his boyhood! as he stood
Even at the altar, o'er his brow there came
The selfsame aspect and the quivering shock
That in the antique oratory shook
His bosom in its solitude; and then,
As in that hour, a moment o'er his face
The tablet of unutterable thoughts

Was traced,—and then it faded as it came;
And he stood calm and quiet, and he spoke
The fitting vows,—but heard not his own words;
And all things reeled around him! he could see
Not that which was, nor that which should have been;
But the old mansion, and the accustomed hall,
And the remembered chambers, and the place,
The day, the hour, the sunshine, and the shade,—
All things pertaining to that place and hour,
And her who was his destiny, came back,
And thrust themselves between him and the light:
What business had they there at such a time?

A change came o'er the spirit of my dream.
The lady of his love,—oh! she was changed
As by the sickness of the soul: her mind
Had wandered from its dwelling, and her eyes,—
They had not their own lustre, but the look
Which is not of the earth: she was become
The queen of a fantastic realm; her thoughts
Were combinations of disjointed things;
And forms—impalpable and unperceived
Of others' sight—familiar were to hers,
And this the world calls frenzy! but the wise
Have a far deeper madness; and the glance
Of melancholy is a fearful gift:
What is it but the telescope of truth!
Which strips the distance of its fantasies,
And brings life near in utter nakedness,
Making the cold reality too real!

A change came o'er the spirit of my dream.
The wanderer was alone as heretofore;

The beings that surrounded him were gone,
Or were at war with him! he was a mark
For blight and desolation,—compassed round
With hatred and contention: pain was mixed
In all which was served up to him, until,
Like to the Pontic monarch of old days,
He fed on poisons, and they had no power,—
But were a kind of nutriment: he lived
Through that which had been death to many men,
And made him friends of mountains: with the stars
And the quick spirit of the universe
He held his dialogues; and they did teach
To him the magic of their mysteries;
To him the book of night was opened wide,
And voices from the deep abyss revealed
A marvel and a secret—be it so.

   My dream was past; it had no further change.
It was of a strange order, that the doom
Of these two creatures should be thus traced out
Almost like a reality—the one
To end in madness—both in misery.

---

### THE SHIPWRECK.

#### (From "Don Juan.")

'TWAS twilight, and the sunless day went down
   Over the waste of waters; like a veil
Which, if withdrawn, would but disclose the frown
   Of one whose hate is masked but to assail.

Thus to their hopeless eyes the night was shown,
  And grimly darkled o'er the faces pale,
And the dim desolate deep: twelve days had Fear
Been their familiar, and now Death was here.

\*   \*   \*   \*

Then rose from sea to sky the wild farewell—
  Then shrieked the timid, and stood still the brave—
Then some leaped overboard with dreadful yell,
  As eager to anticipate their grave;
And the sea yawned around her like a hell,
  And down she sucked with her the whirling wave,
Like one who grapples with his enemy,
And strives to strangle him before he die.

And first one universal shriek there rushed,
  Louder than the loud ocean, like a crash
Of echoing thunder; and then all was hushed,
  Save the wild wind and the remorseless dash
Of billows; but at intervals there gushed,
  Accompanied with a convulsive splash,
A solitary shriek, the bubbling cry
Of some strong swimmer in his agony.

\*   \*   \*   \*

There were two fathers in this ghastly crew,
  And with them their two sons, of whom the one
Was more robust and hardy to the view;
  But he died early; and when he was gone,
His nearest messmate told his sire, who threw
  One glance on him, and said, "Heaven's will be done!
I can do nothing;" and he saw him thrown
Into the deep without a tear or groan.

The other father had a weaklier child,
   Of a soft cheek, and aspect delicate;
But the boy bore up long, and with a mild
   And patient spirit held aloof his fate;
Little he said, and now and then he smiled,
   As if to win a part from off the weight
He saw increasing on his father's heart,
With the deep deadly thought that they must part.

And o'er him bent his sire, and never raised
   His eyes from off his face, but wiped the foam
From his pale lips, and ever on him gazed:
   And when the wished-for shower at length was come,
And the boy's eyes, which the dull film half glazed,
   Brightened, and for a moment seemed to roam,
He squeezed from out a rag some drops of rain
Into his dying child's mouth; but in vain!

The boy expired—the father held the clay,
   And looked upon it long; and when at last
Death left no doubt, and the dead burthen lay
   Stiff on his heart, and pulse and hope were past,
He watched it wistfully, until away
   'Twas borne by the rude wave wherein 'twas cast;
Then he himself sunk down all dumb and shivering,
And gave no sign of life, save his limbs quivering.

---

### "THERE'S NOT A JOY," ETC.

THERE'S not a joy the world can give like that it takes away
When the glow of early thought declines in feeling's dull decay;

'Tis not on youth's smooth cheek the blush alone which fades so fast,
But the tender bloom of heart is gone, ere youth itself be past.

Then the few whose spirits float above the wreck of happiness
Are driven o'er the shoals of guilt or ocean of excess:
The magnet of their course is gone, or only points in vain
The shore to which their shivered sail shall never stretch again.

Then the mortal coldness of the soul like death itself comes down;
It cannot feel for others' woes, it dare not dream its own;
That heavy chill has frozen o'er the fountain of our tears,
And though the eye may sparkle still, 'tis where the ice appears.

Though wit may flash from fluent lips, and mirth attract the breast,
Through midnight hours that yield no more their former hope of rest;
'Tis but as ivy-leaves around the ruined turret wreath,
All green and wildly fresh without, but worn and gray beneath.

O could I feel as I have felt, or be what I have been,
Or weep as I could once have wept o'er many a vanished scene,—
As springs in deserts found seem sweet, all brackish though they be,
So midst the withered waste of life, those tears would flow to me!

# Leigh Hunt.

### SPRING IN RAVENNA.

#### (From "Rimini.")

THE sun is up, and 'tis a morn of May
    Round old Ravenna's clear-shown towers and bay,
A morn, the loveliest which the year has seen,
Last of the Spring, yet fresh with all its green;
For a warm eve, and gentle rains at night,
Have left a sparkling welcome for the light,
And there's a crystal clearness all about;
The leaves are sharp, the distant hills look out;
A balmy briskness comes upon the breeze;
The smoke goes dancing from the cottage trees;
And when you listen, you may hear a coil,
Of bubbling springs about the grassy soil:
And all the scene, in short—sky, earth, and sea—
Breathes like a bright-eyed face, that laughs out openly.

'Tis Nature, full of spirits, waked and springing:—
The birds to the delicious time are singing,
Darting with freaks and snatches up and down,
Where the light woods go seaward from the town;
While happy faces, striking through the green
Of leafy roads, at every turn are seen;
And the far ships, lifting their sails of white
Like joyful hands, come up with scattery light,
Come gleaming up, true to the wished-for day,
And chase the whistling brine, and swirl into the bay.

## ABOU BEN ADHEM.

ABOU Ben Adhem (may his tribe increase!)
  Awoke one night from a deep dream of peace,
And saw, within the moonlight in his room,
Making it rich, and like a lily in bloom,
An angel, writing in a book of gold;
Exceeding peace had made Ben Adhem bold:
And to the presence in the room he said,
"What writest thou?" The vision raised its head,
And with a look made of all sweet accord,
Answered, "The names of those who love the Lord."
"And is mine one?" said Abou. "Nay, not so,"
Replied the angel. Abou spoke more low,
But cheerily still; and said, "I pray thee, then,
Write me as one that loves his fellow-men."

The angel wrote and vanished. The next night
It came again, with a great wakening light,
And showed the names whom love of God had blessed,
And, lo! Ben Adhem's name led all the rest.

---

## Percy Bysshe Shelley.

### TO THE SKYLARK.

HAIL to thee, blithe spirit!
  Bird thou never wert,
That from heaven, or near it,
  Pourest thy full heart
In profuse strains of unpremeditated art.

Higher still and higher,
    From the earth thou springest,
Like a cloud of fire;
    The blue deep thou wingest,
And singing still dost soar, and soaring ever singest.

    In the golden lightning
        Of the setting sun,
    O'er which clouds are brightening,
        Thou dost float and run;
Like an embodied joy whose race is just begun.

    The pale, purple even
        Melts around thy flight;
    Like a star of heaven,
        In the broad daylight,
Thou art unseen, but yet I hear thy shrill delight.

    Keen as are the arrows
        Of that silver sphere,
    Whose intense lamp narrows
        In the white dawn clear,
Until we hardly see, we feel that it is there.

    All the earth and air
        With thy voice is loud,
    As, when night is bare,
        From one lonely cloud
The moon rains out her beams, and heaven is overflowed.

    What thou art we know not;
        What is most like thee?
    From rainbow-clouds there flow not
        Drops so bright to see,
As from thy presence showers a rain of melody.

Like a poet hidden
   In the light of thought,
Singing hymns unbidden,
   Till the world is wrought
To sympathy with hopes and fears it heeded not:

Like a high-born maiden,
   In a palace tower,
Soothing her love-laden
   Soul in secret hour
With music sweet as love, which overflows her bower:

Like a glow-worm golden,
   In a dell of dew,
Scattering unbeholden
   Its aërial hue
Among the flowers and grass which screen it from the view:

Like a rose embowered
   In its own green leaves,
By warm winds deflowered,
   Till the scent it gives
Makes faint with too much sweet these heavy-wingèd thieves.

Sound of vernal showers
   On the twinkling grass,
Rain-awakened flowers,
   All that ever was
Joyous, and clear, and fresh, thy music doth surpass.

Teach no sprite or bird
   What sweet thoughts are thine:
I have never heard
   Praise of love or wine
That panted forth a flood of rapture so divine.

Chorus hymeneal,
    Or triumphant chant,
Matched with thine would be all
    But an empty vaunt—
A thing wherein we feel there is some hidden want.

What objects are the fountains
    Of thy happy strain?
What fields, or waves, or mountains?
    What shapes of sky or plain?
What love of thine own kind? what ignorance of pain?

With thy clear, keen joyance
    Languor cannot be;
Shades of annoyance
    Never come near thee:
Thou lovest, but ne'er knew love's sad satiety.

Waking, or asleep,
    Thou of death must deem
Things more true and deep
    Than we mortals dream;
Or how could thy notes flow in such a crystal stream?

We look before and after,
    And pine for what is not:
Our sincerest laughter
    With some pain is fraught;
Our sweetest songs are those that tell of saddest thought.

Yet if we could scorn
    Hate, and pride, and fear;
If we were things born
    Not to shed a tear,
I know not how thy joy we ever should come near.

> Better than all measures
> Of delightful sound;
> Better than all treasures
> That in books are found,
> Thy skill to poet were, thou scorner of the ground!
>
> Teach me half the gladness
> That thy brain must know,
> Such harmonious madness
> From my lips would flow,
> The world should listen then, as I am listening now.

---

### THE SENSITIVE PLANT.

A SENSITIVE Plant in a garden grew,
And the young winds fed it with silver dew,
And it opened its fan-like leaves to the light,
And closed them beneath the kisses of night.

And the spring arose on the garden fair,
Like the Spirit of Love felt everywhere;
And each flower and herb on earth's dark breast
Rose from the dreams of its wintry rest.

But none ever trembled and panted with bliss
In the garden, the field, or the wilderness,
Like a doe in the noontide with love's sweet want,
As the companionless Sensitive Plant.

The snow-drop, and then the violet,
Arose from the ground with warm rain wet,
And their breath was mixed with fresh odour, sent
From the turf, like the voice and the instrument.

Then the pied wind-flowers and the tulip tall,
And narcissi, the fairest among them all,
Who gaze on their eyes in the stream's recess,
Till they die of their own dear loveliness;

And the Naiad-like lily of the vale,
Whom youth makes so fair, and passion so pale,
That the light of its tremulous bells is seen
Through their pavilions of tender green;

And the hyacinth purple, and white, and blue,
Which flung from its bells a sweet peal anew
Of music so delicate, soft, and intense,
It was felt like an odour within the sense;

And the rose like a nymph to the bath addressed,
Which unveiled the depth of her glowing breast,
Till, fold after fold, to the fainting air
The soul of her beauty and love lay bare;

And the wand-like lily, which lifted up,
As a Mænad, its moonlight-coloured cup,
Till the fiery star, which is its eye,
Gazed through clear dew on the tender sky;

And the jessamine faint, and the sweet tuberose,
The sweetest flower for scent that blows;
And all rare blossoms from every clime,
Grew in that garden in perfect prime.

And on the stream whose inconstant bosom
Was prankt under boughs of embowering blossom,
With golden and green light slanting through
Their heaven of many a tangled hue.

Broad water-lilies lay tremulously,
And starry river-buds glimmered by,
And around them the soft stream did glide and dance
With a motion of sweet sound and radiance.

And the sinuous path of lawn and of moss,
Which led through the garden along and across,
Some open at once to the sun and the breeze,
Some lost among bowers of blossoming trees—

Were all paved with daisies and delicate bells
As fair as the fabulous asphodels;
And flow'rets which, drooping as day drooped too,
Fell into pavilions, white, purple, and blue,
To roof the glow-worm from the evening dew.

And from this undefilèd Paradise
The flowers (as an infant's awakening eyes
Smile on its mother, whose singing sweet
Can first lull, and at last must awaken it)—

When heaven's blithe winds had unfolded them,
As mine-lamps enkindle a hidden gem,
Shone smiling to heaven, and every one
Shared joy in the light of the gentle sun;

For each one was interpenetrated
With the light and the odour its neighbour shed,
Like young lovers whom youth and love make dear,
Wrapt and filled by their mutual atmosphere.

But the Sensitive Plant, which could give small fruit
Of the love which it felt from the leaf to the root,
Received more than all, it loved more than ever,
Where none wanted but it, could belong to the giver;

For the Sensitive Plant has no bright flower;
Radiance and odour are not its dower:
It loves, even like Love, its deep heart is full,
It desires what it has not—the beautiful!

The light winds which, from unsustaining wings,
Shed the music of many murmurings;
The beams which dart from many a star
Of the flowers whose hues they bear afar;

The plumèd insects swift and free,
Like golden boats on a sunny sea,
Laden with light and odour, which pass
Over the gleam of the living grass;

The unseen clouds of the dew, which lie
Like fire in the flowers till the sun rides high,
Then wander like spirits among the spheres,
Each cloud faint with the fragrance it bears;

The quivering vapours of dim noontide,
Which like a sea o'er the warm earth glide,
In which every sound, and odour, and beam,
Move as reeds in a single stream;

Each and all like ministering angels were
For the Sensitive Plant sweet joy to bear,
Whilst the lagging hours of the day went by,
Like windless clouds o'er a tender sky.

And when evening descended from heaven above,
And the earth was all rest, and the air was all love,
And delight, though less bright, was far more deep,
And the day's veil fell from the world of sleep—

And the beasts, and the birds, and the insects were drowned
In an ocean of dreams without a sound;
Whose waves never mark, though they ever impress
The light sand which paves it—consciousness;

(Only overhead the sweet nightingale
Ever sang more sweet as the day might fail,
And snatches of its Elysian chant
Were mixed with the dreams of the Sensitive Plant).

The Sensitive Plant was the earliest
Up-gathered into the bosom of rest;
A sweet child weary of its delight,
The feeblest and yet the favourite,
Cradled within the embrace of Night.

---

### THE POET'S DREAM.

ON a Poet's lips I slept,
    Dreaming like a love-adept
In the sound his breathing kept;
Nor seeks nor finds he mortal blisses,
But feeds on the aërial kisses
Of shapes that haunt Thought's wildernesses.
He will watch from dawn to gloom
The lake-reflected sun illume
The yellow bees in the ivy-bloom,
    Nor heed nor see what things they be—
But from these create he can
Forms more real than living Man,
    Nurslings of Immortality!

# John Keats.

## THE EVE OF ST. AGNES.[1]

### I.

ST. AGNES' Eve—Ah! bitter chill it was:
*The owl, for all his feathers, was a-cold;*
The hare limped trembling through the frozen grass,
And silent was the flock in woolly fold;
Numb were the beadsman's fingers while he told
His rosary, and while his frosted breath,
*Like pious incense from a censer old,*
Seemed taking flight for heaven without a death
Past the sweet Virgin's picture, while his prayer he saith.

### II.

His prayer he saith, this patient, holy man,
Then takes his lamp, and riseth from his knees,
And back returneth, meagre, barefoot, wan,
Along the chapel-aisle by slow degrees:

---

[1] St. Agnes was a Roman virgin, who suffered martyrdom in the reign of Dioclesian. Her parents, a few days after her decease, are said to have had a vision of her, surrounded by angels and attended by a white lamb, which afterwards became sacred to her. In the Catholic Church, formerly, the nuns used to bring a couple of lambs to her altar during mass. The superstition is, that, by taking certain measures of divination, damsels may get a sight of their future husbands in a dream. The ordinary process seems to have been by fasting. Aubrey (as quoted in "Brand's Popular Antiquities") mentions another, which is, to take a row of pins, and pull them out one by one, saying a Paternoster; after which, upon going to bed, the dream is sure to ensue.

The sculptured dead on each side seemed to freeze,
  *Imprisoned in black, purgatorial rails:*
Knights, ladies, praying in dumb orat'ries,
  He passeth by; and his weak spirit fails
*To think how they may ache in icy hoods and mails.*

### III.

Northward he turneth through a little door,
  And scarce three steps, ere music's golden tongue
*Flattered* to tears this aged man and poor:
  But no; already had his death-bell rung:
  The joys of all his life were said and sung:
His was harsh penance on St. Agnes' Eve.
  Another way he went, and soon among
Rough ashes sat he, for his soul's reprieve;
And all night kept awake, for sinners' sake to grieve.

### IV.

That ancient beadsman heard the prelude soft;
  And so it chanced (for many a door was wide,
From hurry to and fro) soon up aloft
  *The silver-snarling trumpets* 'gan to chide;
  The level chambers ready with their pride,
Were glowing to receive a thousand guests:
  *And carvèd angels, ever eager-eyed,*
Stared, where upon their heads the cornice rests,
*With hair blown back, and wings put crosswise on their breasts.*

### V.

At length burst in the argent revelry
  With plume, tiara, and all rich array,
Numerous as shadows haunting fairily
  The brain, new stuffed, in youth, with triumphs gay

Of old romance. These let us wish away,
  And turn, sole-thoughted, to one lady there,
  Whose heart had brooded all that wintry day
  On love, and winged St. Agnes' saintly care,
As she had heard old dames full many times declare.

### VI.

They told her how, upon St. Agnes' Eve,
  Young virgins might have visions of delight;
  And soft adorings from their loves receive
  *Upon the honeyed middle of the night,*
  If ceremonies due they did aright;
  As, supperless to bed they must retire,
  And couch supine their beauties, lily white:
  Nor look behind or sideways, but require
Of Heaven with upward eyes for all that they desire.

### VII.

Full of this whim was youthful Madeline:
  *The music, yearning, like a god in pain,*
  She scarcely heard; her maiden eyes divine,
  Fixed on the floor, saw many a sweeping train
  Pass by, she heeded not at all; in vain
  Came many a tip-toe amorous cavalier,
  And back retired, not cooled by high disdain,
  But she saw not; her heart was otherwhere;
She sighed for Agnes' dreams, the sweetest of the year.

### VIII.

She danced along with vague, regardless eyes,
  Anxious her lips, her breathing quick and short;
  The hallowed hour was near at hand: she sighs
  Amid the timbrels and the thronged resort

Of whisperers in anger or in sport;
　'Mid looks of love, defiance, hate, and scorn;
　*Hoodwinked with faery fancy;* all amort,
　Save to St. Agnes' and her lambs unshorn,
And all the bliss to be before to-morrow morn.

### IX.

So, purposing each moment to retire,
　She lingered still.　Meantime, across the moors,
　Had come young Porphyro, with heart on fire
　For Madeline.　Beside the portal doors
　Buttressed from moonlight, stands he, and implores
All saints to give him sight of Madeline,
　But for one moment in the tedious hours,
　That he might gaze and worship all unseen,
Perchance speak, kneel, touch, kiss;—in sooth such things have been.

### X.

He ventures in—let no buzzed whisper tell;
　All eyes be muffled, or a hundred swords
　Will storm his heart, Love's feverous citadel.
　For him those chambers had barbarian hordes,
　Hyæna foemen, and hot-blooded lords,
Whose very dogs would execrations howl
　Against his lineage.　Not one breast affords
　Him any mercy, in that mansion foul,
*Save one old beldame, weak in body and in soul.*

### XI.

Ah! happy chance! the aged creature came
　Shuffling along with ivory-headed wand,
　To where he stood, hid from the torches' light,
　Behind a broad hall pillar, far beyond

The sound of merriment and chorus bland.
He startled her; but soon she knew his face,
And grasped his fingers in her palsied hand:
Saying, "Mercy, Porphyro! hie thee from this place.
They are all here to-night, the whole blood-thirsty race.

### XII.

"Get hence! get hence! there's dwarfish Hildebrand,
He had a fever late, and in the fit
He cursèd thee and thine, both house and land:
Then there's that old Lord Maurice, *not a whit
More tame for his gray hairs*—Alas, me! flit;
Flit like a ghost away!"—"Ah, gossip dear,
We're safe enough; here in this arm-chair sit,
And tell me how—"—"Good Saints! not here, not here!
Follow me, child, or else these stones will be thy bier!"

### XIII.

He followed through a lowly, archèd way,
Brushing the cobwebs with his lofty plume;
And as she muttered, "Well-a-well-a-day!"
He found him *in a little moonlight room,
Pale, latticed, chill,* and silent as a tomb.
"Now tell me where is Madeline," said he;
"Oh, tell me, Angela, by the holy loom
Which none but secret sisterhood may see,
When they St. Agnes' wool are weaving piously."

### XIV.

"St. Agnes! Ah! it is St. Agnes' Eve—
Yet men will murder upon holidays;
Thou must hold water in a witch's sieve,
And be the liege lord of all elves and fays,

To venture so: it fills me with amaze
To see thee, Porphyro!—St. Agnes' Eve!
God's help! my lady fair the conjurer plays
This very night: good angels her deceive!
But let me laugh awhile; I've mickle time to grieve."

### XV.

*Feebly she laugheth in the languid moon,*
While Porphyro upon her face doth look,
Like puzzled urchin on an aged crone,
Who keepeth closed a wondrous riddle-book,
As spectacled she sits in chimney nook;
But soon his eyes grow brilliant, when she told
His lady's purpose; and he scarce could brook
Tears, at the thought of those enchantments cold,
*And Madeline asleep in lap of legends old.*

### XVI.

Sudden a thought came, *like a full-blown rose*,
Flushing his brow, and in his painèd heart
Made purple riot; then doth he propose
A stratagem, that makes the beldame start.
"A cruel man and impious thou art;
Sweet lady! let her pray, and sleep and dream,
Alone with her good angels far apart
From wicked men like thee.—Go! go! I deem
Thou canst not, surely, be the same that thou dost seem."

### XVII.

"I will not harm her, by all saints, I swear!"
Quoth Porphyro. "Oh, may I ne'er find grace,
When my weak voice shall whisper its last prayer,
If one of her soft ringlets I displace,

Or look with *ruffian passion* in her face!
Good Angela, believe me, by these tears,
Or I will, even in a moment's space,
Awake with horrid shout my foemen's ears,
And beard them, though they be more fanged than wolves and bears!"

#### XVIII.

"Ah! why wilt thou affright a feeble soul?—
A poor, weak, palsy-stricken, *churchyard* thing,
Whose passing bell may ere the midnight toll;
Whose prayers for thee, each morn and evening,
Were never missed?" Thus plaining, doth she bring
A gentler speech from burning Porphyro,
So woful and of such deep sorrowing,
That Angela gives promise she will do
Whatever he shall wish, betide or weal or woe:

#### XIX.

Which was, to lead him in close secrecy
Even to Madeline's chamber, and there hide
Him in a closet, of such privacy
That he might see her beauty unespied,
And win perhaps that night a peerless bride,
*While legioned fairies paced the coverlet,*
*And pale Enchantment held her sleepy-eyed.*
Never on such a night have lovers met,
Since Merlin paid his demon all the monstrous debt.

#### XX.

"It shall be as thou wishest," said the dame;
"All cates and dainties shall be storèd there,
Quickly on this feast-night; by the tambour-frame
Her own lute thou wilt see: no time to spare,

For I am slow and feeble, and scarce dare,
On such a catering, trust my dizzy head.
Wait here, my child, with patience; kneel in prayer
The while; ah! thou must needs the lady wed;
Or may I never leave my grave among the dead!"

### XXI.

So saying, she hobbled off with busy fear;
The lover's endlesss minute slowly passed,
The dame returned, and whispered in his ear
To follow her, with aged eyes aghast
From fright of dim espial. Safe at last
Through many a dusky gallery, they gain
The maiden's chamber, *silken, hushed, and chaste,*
Where Porphyro took covert, pleased amain:
His poor guide hurried back with agues in her brain.

### XXII.

Her faltering hand upon the balustrade,
Old Angela was feeling for the stair,
When Madeline, St. Agnes' charmèd maid,
Rose, like a missioned spirit, unaware;
With silver taper-light, and pious care
She turned, and down the aged gossip led
To a safe, level matting. Now prepare,
Young Porphyro, for gazing on that bed;
She comes, she comes again, like ring-dove frayed and fled.

### XXIII.

Out went the taper as she hurried in;
*Its little smoke in pallid moonshine died:*
She closed the door, she panteth all akin
To spirits of the air, and visions wide;

Nor uttered syllable, or "Woe betide!"
*But to her heart her heart was voluble,
Paining with eloquence her balmy side:*
As though a tongueless nightingale should swell
Her throat in vain, and die heart-stifled in her dell.

### XXIV.

*A casement high and triple-arched there was,
All garlanded with carven images
Of fruits, and flowers, and bunches of knot-grass,
And diamonded with panes of quaint device,
Innumerable of stains and splendid dyes,
As are the tiger-moth's deep damasked wings;*
And in the midst, 'mong thousand heraldries,
And twilight saints, and dim emblazonings,
A shielded scutcheon blushed with blood of queens and
    kings.

### XXV.

Full on this casement shone the wintry moon,
And threw warm *gales* on Madeline's fair breast,
As down she knelt for Heaven's grace and boon:
*Rose-bloom fell on her hands together pressed,
And on her silver cross soft amethyst,
And on her hair a glory like a saint;*
She seemed a *splendid angel, newly dressed,
Save wings for heaven:*—Porphyro grew faint—
She knelt so pure a thing, so free from mortal taint.

### XXVI.

Anon his heart revives: her vespers done,
Of all its wreathèd pearls her hair she frees;
Unclasps her *warmèd* jewels one by one;
Loosens her fragrant bodice; *by degrees*

*Her rich attire creeps rustling to her knees:*
Half hidden, *like a mermaid in sea-weed,*
Pensive awhile she dreams awake, and sees
  In fancy fair St. Agnes in her bed,
But dares not look behind, or all the charm is fled.

### XXVII.

Soon, trembling in her soft and chilly nest,
In sort of wakeful swoon, perplexed she lay,
Until the poppied warmth of sleep oppressed
Her smoothèd limbs, and soul, fatigued away,
*Flown, like a thought, until the morrow day;*
*Blissfully havened both from joy and pain;*
*Clasped like a missal, where swart Paynims pray;*
*Blinded alike from sunshine and from rain,*
As though a rose should shut, and be a bud again.

### XXVIII.

Stol'n to this paradise, and so entranced,
Porphyro gazed upon her empty dress,
And listened to her breathing if it chanced
To wake unto a slumb'rous tenderness:
Which when he heard, that minute did he bless,
And breathed himself; then from the closet crept,
*Noiseless as fear in a wild wilderness,*
And over the hushed carpet silent stepped,
And 'tween the curtains peeped, where lo! how fast she
  slept.

### XXIX.

Then by the bedside, *where the faded moon*
*Made a dim, silver twilight,*—soft he set
A table, and, half-anguished, threw thereon
A cloth of *woven crimson, gold, and jet:*—

O, for some drowsy Morphean amulet!
The boist'rous, midnight, festive clarion,
The kettle-drum, and far-heard clarionet,
Affray his ears, though but in dying tone:—
The hall-door shuts again, and all the noise is gone.

### XXX.

And still she slept *an azure-lidded sleep*
In blanchèd linen, smooth and lavendered,
While he from forth the closet brought a heap
Of candied apple, quince, and plum, and gourd,
With jellies soother than the creamy curd,
*And lucent sirups tinct with cinnamon:*
Manna and dates, in argosy transferred
From Fez; and spicèd dainties every one,
*From silken Samarcand to cedared Lebanon.*

### XXXI.

These delicates he heaped with glowing hand
On golden dishes and in baskets bright
Of wreathèd silver; sumptuously they stand
In the retirèd quiet of the night,
*Filling the chilly room with perfume light.*
"And now, my love, my seraph fair, awake!
Thou art my heaven, and I thine eremite.
Open thine eyes for meek St. Agnes' sake,
Or I shall drowse beside thee, so my soul doth ache."

### XXXII.

Thus whispering, his warm, unnervèd arm
Sank in her pillow. Shaded was her dream
By the dusk curtains;—'twas a midnight charm
Impossible to melt as icèd stream:

The lustrous salvers in the moonlight gleam;
Broad golden fringe upon the carpet lies;
It seemed he never, never could redeem
From such a steadfast spell his lady's eyes;
So mused awhile, entoiled in woofèd fantasies.

### XXXIII.

Awakening up, he took her hollow lute,—
Tumultuous,—and, in chords that tenderest be,
He played an ancient ditty, long since mute,
In Provence called "*La Belle Dame sans Merci:*"
Close to her ear touching the melody;—
Wherewith disturbed, she uttered a soft moan:
He ceased—she panted quick—and suddenly
Her blue affrayèd eyes wide open shone:
Upon his knees he sank, pale as smooth sculptured stone.

### XXXIV.

Her eyes were open, but she still beheld,
Now wide awake, the vision of her sleep;
There was a painful change that nigh expelled
The blisses of her dream, so pure and deep,
At which fair Madeline began to weep,
And moan forth witless words with many a sigh;
While still her gaze on Porphyro would keep;
Who knelt, with joinèd hands and piteous eye,
Fearing to move or speak, she looked so dreamingly.

### XXXV.

"Ah, Porphyro!" said she, "but even now
Thy voice was a sweet tremble in mine ear,
Made tunable with every sweetest vow;
And those sad eyes were spiritual and clear;

How changed thou art! how pallid, chill, and drear!—
Give me that voice again, my Porphyro,
Those looks immortal, those complainings dear;
Oh! leave me not in this eternal woe,—
For if thou diest, my love, I know not where to go."

### XXXVI.

*Beyond a mortal man impassioned far*
*At these voluptuous accents he arose,*
*Ethereal, flushed, and like a throbbing star*
*Seen 'mid the sapphire heaven's deep repose;*
*Into her dream he melted, as the rose*
*Blendeth its odours with the violet,—*
*Solution sweet.* Meantime the frost wind blows
Like love's alarum, pattering the sharp sleet
Against the window-panes: St. Agnes' moon hath set.

### XXXVII.

'Tis dark; quick pattereth the flaw-blown sleet:
"This is no dream; my bride, my Madeline!"
'Tis dark: the icèd gusts still rave and beat.
"No dream, alas! alas! and woe is mine;
Porphyro will leave me here to rave and pine;
Cruel! what traitor could thee hither bring?
I curse not, for my heart is lost in thine,
Though thou forsakest a deceivèd thing;—
A dove, forlorn and lost, with sick, unprunèd wing!"

### XXXVIII.

"My Madeline, sweet dreamer! lovely bride!
Say, may I be for aye thy vassal blest?
*Thy beauty's shield, heart-shaped, and vermeil-dyed?*
Ah! silver shrine, here will I take my rest,

After so many hours of toil and quest—
A famished pilgrim, saved by miracle:
Though I have found, I will not rob thy nest,
Saving of thy sweet self; if thou think'st well
To trust, fair Madeline, to no rude infidel.

### XXXIX.

"Hark! 'tis an elfin storm from faery-land,
Of haggard seeming, but a boon indeed.
Arise,—arise!—the morning is at hand;
The bloated wassailers will never heed;
Let us away, my love, with happy speed;
There are no ears to hear, nor eyes to see,—
Drowned all in Rhenish and the sleepy mead:
Awake! arise! my love, and fearless be;
For o'er the southern moors I have a home for thee."

### XL.

She hurried at his words, beset with fears,
For there were sleeping dragons all around
At glaring watch, perhaps with ready spears.
Down the wide stairs a darkling way they found.—
In all the house was heard no human sound.
A chain-drooped lamp was flickering by each door;
The arras, rife with horseman, hawk, and hound,
Fluttered in the besieging winds' uproar;
*And the long carpets rose along the gusty floor.*

### XLI.

They glide like phantoms into the wide hall;
Like phantoms to the inner porch they glide,
Where lay the porter, in uneasy sprawl,
With a huge empty flagon by his side;

The watchful blood-hound rose, and shook his hide,
But his sagacious eye an inmate owns:
By one, and one, the bolts full easy slide:
The chains lie silent on the foot-worn stones:
The key turns, and the door upon its hinges groans.

### XLII.

And they are gone; ay, ages long ago,
These lovers fled away *into the storm.*
That night the Baron dreamt of many a woe,
And all his warrior guests, with shade and form
Of witch, and demon, and large coffin-worm,
Were long benightmared. Angela the old
Died palsy-twitched, with meagre face deform:
The beadsman, after thousand aves told,
For aye unsought-for slept among his ashes cold.

---

## BARDS OF PASSION.

BARDS of Passion and of Mirth,
  Ye have left your souls on earth!
Have ye souls in heaven too,
Double-lived in regions new?
Yes, and those of heaven commune
With the spheres of sun and moon;
With the noise of fountains wondrous,
And the parle of voices thund'rous;
With the whisper of heaven's trees
And one another, in soft ease
Seated on Elysian lawns
Browsed by none but Dian's fawns;

Underneath large blue-bells tented,
Where the daisies are rose-scented,
And the rose herself has got
Perfume which on earth is not;
Where the nightingale doth sing
Not a senseless, trancèd thing,
But divine, melódious truth—
Philosophic numbers smooth—
Tales and golden histories
Of heaven and its mysteries.

Thus ye live on high, and then
On the earth ye live again;
And the souls ye left behind you
Teach us, here, the way to find you,
Where your other souls are joying,
Never slumbered, never cloying.
Here your earth-born souls still speak
To mortals, of their little week;
Of their sorrows and delights;
Of their passions and their spites;
Of their glory and their shame;
What doth strengthen and what maim.
Thus ye teach us, every day,
Wisdom, though fled far away.

Bards of Passion and of Mirth,
Ye have left your souls on earth!
Ye have souls in heaven too,
Double-lived in regions new!

## LINES ON THE MERMAID TAVERN.

Souls of Poets dead and gone,
  What Elysium have ye known,
Happy field or mossy cavern,
Choicer than the Mermaid Tavern?

Have ye tippled drink more fine
Than mine host's Canary wine?
Or are fruits of Paradise
Sweeter than those dainty pies
Of Venison? O generous food!
Drest as though bold Robin Hood
Would, with his Maid Marian,
Sup and bouse from horn and can.

I have heard that on a day
Mine host's signboard flew away
Nobody knew whither, till
An astrologer's old quill
To a sheepskin gave the story—
Said he saw you in your glory
Underneath a new-old Sign
Sipping beverage divine,
And pledging with contented smack
The Mermaid in the Zodiac!

Souls of Poets dead and gone,
What Elysium have ye known,
Happy field or mossy cavern,
Choicer than the Mermaid Tavern?

## John Wilson (Christopher North).

### EXTRACTS FROM "CITY OF THE PLAGUE."

WHY does the finger,
    Yellow mid the sunshine, on the minster clock,
Point at that hour? It is most horrible,
Speaking of midnight in the face of day.
During the very dead of night it stopped,
Even at the moment when a hundred hearts
Paused with it suddenly, to beat no more.
Yet, wherefore should it run its idle round?
There is no need that men should count the hours
Of time, thus standing on eternity.
It is a death-like image. How can I,
When round me silent nature speaks of death,
Withstand such monitory impulses?
When yet far off I thought upon the plague,
Sometimes my mother's image struck my soul,
In unchanged meekness and serenity,
And all my fears were gone. But these green banks,
With an unwonted flush of flowers o'ergrown,
Brown, when I left them last, with frequent feet
From morn till evening hurrying to and fro,
In mournful beauty seem encompassing
A still forsaken city of the dead.

O unrejoicing Sabbath! not of yore
Did thy sweet evenings die along the Thames
Thus silently! Now every sail is furled,
The oar hath dropped from out the rower's hand,

And on thou flowest in lifeless majesty,
River of a desert lately filled with joy!
O'er all that mighty wilderness of stone
The air is clear and cloudless, as at sea
Above the gliding ship.   All fires are dead,
And not one single wreath of smoke ascends
Above the stillness of the towers and spires.
How idly hangs that arch magnificent
Across the idle river!   Not a speck
Is seen to move along it.   There it hangs,
Still as a rainbow in the pathless sky.

\*       \*       \*       \*       \*

Know ye what ye will meet with in the city?
Together will ye walk through long, long streets,
All standing silent as a midnight church.
You will hear nothing but the brown red grass
Rustling beneath your feet; the very beating
Of your own hearts will awe you; the small voice
Of that vain bauble, idly counting time,
Will speak a solemn language in the desert.
Look up to heaven, and there the sultry clouds,
Still threatening thunder, lower with grim delight,
As if the spirit of the plague dwelt there,
Darkening the city with the shades of death.
Know ye that hideous hubbub?   Hark, far off
A tumult like an echo! on it comes,
Weeping and wailing, shrieks and groaning prayer,
And, louder than all, outrageous blasphemy.
The passing storm hath left the silent streets,
But are these houses near you tenantless?
Over your heads from a window, suddenly

A ghastly face is thrust, and yells of death
With voice not human. Who is he that flies,
As if a demon dogged him on his path?
With ragged hair, white face, and bloodshot eyes,
Raving, he rushes past you; till he falls,
As if struck by lightning, down upon the stones,
Or, in blind madness, dashed against the wall,
Sinks backward into stillness. Stand aloof,
And let the pest's triumphal chariot
Have open way advancing to the tomb;
See how he mocks the pomp and pageantry
Of earthly kings! a miserable cart,
Heaped up with human bodies; dragged along
By pale steeds, skeleton anatomies!
And onwards urged by a wan, meagre wretch,
Doomed never to return from the foul pit,
Whither, with oaths, he drives his load of horror.
Would you look in? Gray hairs and golden tresses,
Wan shrivelled cheeks, that have not smiled for years,
And many a rosy visage smiling still;
Bodies in the noisome weeds of beggary wrapt,
With age decrepit, and wasted to the bone;
And youthful frames, august and beautiful,
In spite of mortal pangs—there lie they all,
Embraced in ghastliness! But look not long,
For haply mid the faces glimmering there,
The well-known cheek of some belovèd friend
Will meet thy gaze, or some small snow-white hand,
Bright with the ring that holds her lover's hair.

## "Barry Cornwall" (Bryan W. Proctor).

### THE SEA.

THE sea! the sea! the open sea!
  The blue, the fresh, the ever free!
Without a mark, without a bound,
It runneth the earth's wide regions round;
It plays with the clouds; it mocks the skies;
Or like a cradled creature lies.

I'm on the sea!  I'm on the sea!
I am where I would ever be,
With the blue above, and the blue below,
And silence wheresoe'er I go:
If a storm should come, and awake the deep,
What matter? I shall ride and sleep.

I love, oh! how I love to ride
On the fierce, foaming, bursting tide,
When every mad wave drowns the moon,
Or whistles aloft his tempest tune,
And tells how goeth the world below,
And why the sou'west blasts do blow

I never was on the dull tame shore,
But I loved the great sea more and more,
And backward flew to her billowy breast,
Like a bird that seeketh its mother's nest;
And a mother she was and is to me,
For I was born on the open sea!

The waves were white, and red the morn,
In the noisy hour when I was born;
And the whale it whistled, the porpoise rolled,
And the dolphins bared their backs of gold;
And never was heard such an outcry wild
As welcomed to life the ocean child!

I've lived since then, in calm and strife,
Full fifty summers a sailor's life,
With wealth to spend and a power to range,
But never have sought, nor sighed for change;
And death, whenever he comes to me,
Shall come on the wild unbounded sea!

---

## Rev. George Croly.

### THE SEVENTH PLAGUE OF EGYPT.

'TWAS morn—the rising splendour rolled
On marble towers and roofs of gold;
Hall, court, and gallery below,
Were crowded with a living flow;
Egyptian, Arab, Nubian there,
The bearers of the bow and spear;
The hoary priest, the Chaldee sage,
The slave, the gemmed and glittering page—
Helm, turban, and tiara, shone
A dazzling ring round Pharaoh's throne.

There came a man—the human tide
Shrank backward from his stately stride:
His cheek with storm and time was tanned;
A shepherd's staff was in his hand;
A shudder of instinctive fear
Told the dark king what step was near;
On through the host the stranger came,
It parted round his form like flame.

He stooped not at the footstool stone,
He clasped not sandal, kissed not throne;
Erect he stood amid the ring,
His only words—" Be just, O king!"
On Pharaoh's cheek the blood flushed high,
A fire was in his sullen eye;
Yet on the chief of Israel
No arrow of his thousands fell:
All mute and moveless as the grave
Stood chilled the satrap and the slave.

"Thou'rt come," at length the monarch spoke;
Haughty and high the words outbroke:
" Is Israel weary of its lair,
The forehead peeled, the shoulder bare?
Take back the answer to your band;
Go, reap the wind; go, plough the sand;
Go, vilest of the living vile,
To build the never-ending pile,
Till, darkest of the nameless dead,
The vulture on their flesh is fed.
What better asks the howling slave
Than the base life our bounty gave?"

Shouted in pride the turbaned peers,
Upclashed to heaven the golden spears.
"King! thou and thine are doomed!—Behold!"
The prophet spoke—the thunder rolled!
Along the pathway of the sun
Sailed vapory mountains, wild and dun.
"Yet there is time," the prophet said:
He raised his staff—the storm was stayed:
"King! be the word of freedom given:
What art thou, man, to war with Heaven?"

There came no word—the thunder broke!
Like a huge city's final smoke,
Thick, lurid, stifling, mixed with flame,
Through court and hall the vapours came.
Loose as the stubble in the field,
Wide flew the men of spear and shield;
Scattered like foam along the wave,
Flew the proud pageant, prince and slave:
Or, in the chains of terror bound,
Lay, corpse-like, on the smouldering ground.
"Speak, king!—the wrath is but begun—
Still dumb?—then, Heaven, thy will be done!"

Echoed from earth a hollow roar
Like ocean on the midnight shore,
A sheet of lightning o'er them wheeled,
The solid ground beneath them reeled;
In dust sank roof and battlement;
Like webs the giant walls were rent;
Red, broad, before his startled gaze,
The monarch saw his Egypt blaze.

Still swelled the plague—the flame grew pale;
Burst from the clouds the charge of hail;
With arrowy keenness, iron weight,
Down poured the ministers of fate;
Till man and cattle, crushed, congealed,
Covered with death the boundless field.

Still swelled the plague—uprose the blast,
The avenger, fit to be the last;
On ocean, river, forest, vale,
Thundered at once the mighty gale.
Before the whirlwind flew the tree,
Beneath the whirlwind roared the sea;
A thousand ships were on the wave—
Where are they?—ask that foaming grave!
Down go the hope, the pride of years,
Down go the myriad mariners;
The riches of Earth's richest zone,
Gone, like a flash of lightning, gone!

And, lo! that first fierce triumph o'er,
Swells Ocean on the shrinking shore;
Still onward, onward, dark and wide,
Ingulfs the land the furiest tide.
Then bowed thy spirit, stubborn king,
Thou serpent, reft of fang and sting;
Humbled before the prophet's knee,
He groaned, "Be injured Israel free!"

To heaven the sage upraised his wand;
Back rolled the deluge from the land;

Back to its caverns sank the gale;
Fled from the noon the vapours pale;
Broad burned again the joyous sun:
The hour of wrath and death was done.

---

## Bishop Heber.

**PASSAGE OF THE RED SEA.**

(From "Palestine.")

For many a coal-black tribe and cany spear,
    The hireling guards of Misraim's throne, were there.
From distant Cush they trooped, a warrior train,
Siwah's green isle and Senaar's marly plain;
On either wing their fiery coursers check
The parched and sinewy sons of Amalek;
While close behind, inured to feast on blood,
Decked in Behemoth's spoils, the tall Shangalla strode.
'Mid blazing helms, and bucklers rough with gold,
Saw ye how swift the scythèd chariots rolled?
Lo, these are they whom, lords of Afric's fates,
Old Thebes hath poured through all her hundred gates,
Mother of armies! How the emeralds glowed,
Where, flushed with power and vengeance, Pharaoh rode!
And stoled in white, those brazen wheels before,
Osiris' ark his swarthy wizards bore;
And still responsive to the trumpet's cry,
The priestly sistrum murmured—Victory!
Why swell these shouts that rend the desert's gloom?
Whom come ye forth to combat?—warriors, whom?

These flocks and herds—this faint and weary train—
Red from the scourge, and recent from the chain?
God of the poor, the poor and friendless save!
Giver and Lord of freedom, help the slave!
North, south, and west, the sandy whirlwinds fly,
The circling horns of Egypt's chivalry.
On earth's last margin throng the weeping train;
Their cloudy guide moves on:—" And must we swim the main?"
'Mid the light spray their snorting camels stood,
Nor bathed a fetlock in the nauseous flood;
He comes—their leader comes!—the man of God
O'er the wide waters lifts his mighty rod,
And onward treads. The circling waves retreat,
In hoarse, deep murmurs, from his holy feet;
And the chased surges, inly roaring, show
The hard wet sand and coral hills below.

With limbs that falter, and with hearts that swell,
Down, down they pass—a steep and slippery dell;
Around them rise, in pristine chaos hurled,
The ancient rocks, the secrets of the world;
And flowers that blush beneath the ocean green,
And caves, the sea-calves' low-roofed haunt, are seen.
Down, safely down the narrow pass they tread;
The beetling waters storm above their head;
While far behind retires the sinking day,
And fades on Edom's hills its latest ray.

Yet not from Israel fled the friendly light,
Or dark to them or cheerless came the night.
Still in their van, along that dreadful road,
Blazed broad and fierce the brandished torch of God.

Its meteor glare a tenfold lustre gave
On the long mirror of the rosy wave;
While its blest beams a sunlike heat supply,
Warm every cheek, and dance in every eye—
To them alone—for Misraim's wizard train
Invoke for light their monster-gods in vain;
Clouds heaped on clouds their struggling sight confine,
And tenfold darkness broods above their line.
Yet on they fare, by reckless vengeance led,
And range unconscious through the ocean's bed;
Till midway now—that strange and fiery form
Showed his dread visage lightening through the storm;
With withering splendour blasted all their might,
And brake their chariot wheels, and marred their coursers'
    flight.
" Fly, Misraim, fly!" The ravenous floods they see,
And, fiercer than the floods, the Deity.
" Fly, Misraim, fly!" From Edom's coral strand
Again the prophet stretched his dreadful wand.
With one wild crash the thundering waters sweep,
And all is waves—a dark and lonely deep;
Yet o'er those lonely waves such murmurs passed,
As mortal wailing swelled the nightly blast.
And strange and sad the whispering breezes bore
The groans of Egypt to Arabia's shore.

  Oh! welcome came the morn, where Israel stood
In trustless wonder by the avenging flood!
Oh! welcome came the cheerful morn, to show
The drifted wreck of Zoan's pride below!
The mangled limbs of men—the broken car—
A few sad relics of a nation's war;

Alas, how few! Then, soft as Elim's well,
The precious tears of new-born freedom fell.
And he, whose hardened heart alike had borne
The house of bondage and the oppressor's scorn,
The stubborn slave, by hope's new beams subdued,
In faltering accents sobbed his gratitude,
Till, kindling into warmer zeal, around
The virgin timbrel waked its silver sound;
And in fierce joy, no more by doubt suppressed,
The struggling spirit throbbed in Miriam's breast.
She, with bare arms, and fixing on the sky
The dark transparence of her lucid eye,
Poured on the winds of heaven her wild sweet harmony.
"Where now," she sang, "the tall Egyptian spear?
On's sunlike shield, and Zoan's chariot, where?
Above their ranks the whelming waters spread.
Shout, Israel, for the Lord hath triumphèd!"
And every pause between, as Miriam sang,
From tribe to tribe the martial thunder rang,
And loud and far their stormy chorus spread—
"Shout, Israel, for the Lord hath triumphèd!"

## MISSIONARY HYMN.

FROM Greenland's icy mountains,
   From India's coral strand,
Where Afric's sunny fountains
   Roll down their golden sand—
From many an ancient river,
   From many a palmy plain,

They call us to deliver
    Their land from error's chain.

What though the spicy breezes
    Blow soft o'er Ceylon's isle,
Though every prospect pleases,
    And only man is vile:
In vain, with lavish kindness,
    The gifts of God are strown—
The heathen, in his blindness,
    Bows down to wood and stone.

Shall we, whose souls are lighted
    With wisdom from on high—
Shall we to man benighted
    The lamp of life deny?
Salvation! O, Salvation!
    The joyful sound proclaim,
Till earth's remotest nation
    Has learned Messiah's name.

Waft, waft, ye winds, the story,
    And you, ye waters, roll,
Till, like a sea of glory,
    It spreads from pole to pole—
Till o'er our ransomed nature
    The Lamb for sinners slain—
Redeemer, King, Creator—
    In bliss returns to reign.

## Mrs. Hemans.

### THE LANDING OF THE PILGRIM FATHERS IN NEW ENGLAND.

" Look now abroad—another race has filled
   Those populous borders—wide the wood recedes,
And towns shoot up, and fertile realms are tilled ;
   The land is full of harvests and green meads."
BRYANT.

THE breaking waves dashed high
   On a stern and rock-bound coast,
And the woods against a stormy sky
   Their giant branches tossed;

And the heavy night hung dark
   The hills and waters o'er,
When a band of exiles moored their bark
   On the wild New England shore.

Not as the conqueror comes,
   They, the true-hearted, came;
Not with the roll of the stirring drums,
   And the trumpet that sings of fame;

Not as the flying come,
   In silence and in fear;—
They shook the depths of the desert gloom
   With their hymns of lofty cheer.

Amidst the storm they sang,
   And the stars heard, and the sea;
And the sounding aisles of the dim woods rang
   To the anthem of the free!

The ocean eagle soared
  From his nest by the white wave's foam;
And the rocking pines of the forest roared—
  This was their welcome home!

There were men with hoary hair
  Amidst that pilgrim band:
Why had they come to wither there,
  Away from their childhood's land?

There was woman's fearless eye,
  Lit by her deep love's truth;
There was manhood's brow serenely high,
  And the fiery heart of youth.

What sought they thus afar?
  Bright jewels of the mine?
The wealth of seas, the spoils of war?—
  They sought a faith's pure shrine!

Ay, call it holy ground,
  The soil where first they trod.
They have left unstained what there they found—
  Freedom to worship God.

## THE HOMES OF ENGLAND.

THE stately homes of England,
  How beautiful they stand!
Amidst their tall ancestral trees,
  O'er all the pleasant land.
The deer across their greensward bound
  Through shade and sunny gleam,

And the swan glides past them with the sound
  Of some rejoicing stream.

The merry homes of England!
  Around their hearths by night,
What gladsome looks of household love
  Meet in the ruddy light!
There woman's voice flows forth in song,
  Or childhood's tale is told;
Or lips move tunefully along
  Some glorious page of old.

The blessed homes of England!
  How softly on their bowers
Is laid the holy quietness
  That breathes from Sabbath hours!
Solemn, yet sweet, the church-bell's chime
  Floats through their woods at morn;
All other sounds, in that still time,
  Of breeze and leaf are born.

The cottage homes of England!
  By thousands on her plains,
They are smiling o'er the silvery brooks
  And round the hamlet-fanes.
Through glowing orchards forth they peep,
  Each from its nook of leaves,
And fearless there the lowly sleep,
  As the bird beneath their eaves.

The free, fair homes of England!
  Long, long, in hut and hall,
May hearts of native proof be reared
  To guard each hallowed wall!

And green forever be the groves,
    And bright the flowery sod,
Where first the child's glad spirit loves
    Its country and its God!

---

### WASHINGTON'S STATUE.

YES! rear thy guardian hero's form
    On thy proud soil, thou Western World!
A watcher through each sign of storm,
    O'er freedom's flag unfurl'd.

There, as before a shrine to bow,
Bid thy true sons their children lead:
The language of that noble brow
    For all things good shall plead.

The spirit reared in patriot fight,
The virtue born of home and hearth,
There calmly throned, a holy light
    Shall pour o'er chainless earth.

And let that work of England's hand,
Sent through the blast and surge's roar,
So girt with tranquil glory, stand
    For ages on thy shore!

Such through all time the greetings be,
That with the Atlantic billows sweep!
Telling the mighty and the free
    Of brothers o'er the deep!

## Thomas Davis.

### THE WELCOME.

COME in the evening, or come in the morning—
   Come when you're looked for, or come without warning;
Kisses and welcome you'll find here before you,
And the oftener you come here the more I'll adore you!
   Light is my heart since the day we were plighted;
   Red is my cheek that they told me was blighted;
   The green of the trees looks far greener than ever,
   And the linnets are singing, "True lovers, don't sever!"

I'll pull you sweet flowers, to wear if you choose them!
Or, after you've kissed them, they'll lie on my bosom;
I'll fetch from the mountain its breeze to inspire you;
I'll fetch from my fancy a tale that won't tire you.
   O! your step's like the rain to the summer-vexed farmer,
   Or sabre and shield to a knight without armour;
   I'll sing you sweet songs till the stars rise above me,
   Then, wandering, I'll wish you, in silence, to love me.

We'll look through the trees at the cliff and the eyry;
We'll tread round the rath on the track of the fairy;
We'll look on the stars, and we'll list to the river,
Till you ask of your darling what gift you can give her—
   O! she'll whisper you—"Love, as unchangeably beaming,
   And trust, when in secret, most tunefully streaming;
   Till the starlight of heaven above us shall quiver,
   As our souls flow in one down Eternity's river."

So come in the evening, or come in the morning—
Come when you're looked for, or come without warning;
Kisses and welcome you'll find here before you,
And the oftener you come here the more I'll adore you!
 Light is my heart since the day we were plighted;
 Red is my cheek that they told me was blighted;
 The green of the trees looks far greener than ever,
 And the linnets are singing, " True lovers, don't sever!"

---

## John Sterling.

### SHAKESPEARE.

HOW little fades from earth when sink to rest
 The hours and cares that move a great man's breast
Though naught of all we saw the grave may spare,
His life pervades the world's impregnate air;
Though Shakespeare's dust beneath our footsteps lies,
His spirit breathes amid his native skies;
With meaning won from him forever glows
Each air that England feels, and star it knows;
His whispered words from many a mother's voice
Can make her sleeping child in dreams rejoice;
And gleams from spheres he first conjoined to earth
Are blent with rays of each new morning's birth.
Amid the sights and tales of common things,
Leaf, flower, and bird, and wars, and deaths of kings,—
Of shore, and sea, and nature's daily round,
Of life that tills, and tombs that load, the ground,
His visions mingle, swell, command, pace by,
And haunt with living presence heart and eye;

And tones from him, by other bosoms caught,
Awaken flush and stir of mounting thought;
And the long sigh, and deep impassioned thrill,
Rouse custom's trance and spur the faltering will.
Above the goodly land, more his than ours,
He sits supreme, enthroned in skyey towers;
And sees the heroic brood of his creation
Teach larger life to his ennobled nation.
O shaping brain! O flashing fancy's hues!
O boundless heart, kept fresh by pity's dews!
O wit humane and blithe! O sense sublime!
For each dim oracle of mantled Time!
Transcendent Form of Man! in whom we read
Mankind's whole tale of Impulse, Thought, and Deed!
Amid the expanse of years, beholding thee,
We know how vast our world of life may be;
Wherein, perchance, with aims as pure as thine,
Small tasks and strengths may be no less divine.

---

## Walter Savage Landor.

### THE MAID'S LAMENT.

I LOVED him not; and yet, now he is gone,
    I feel I am alone.
I checked him while he spoke; yet, could he speak
    Alas! I would not check.

For reasons not to love him once I sought,
    And wearied all my thought

To vex myself and him: I now would give
    My love could he but live
Who lately lived for me, and, when he found
    'Twas vain, in holy ground
He hid his face amid the shades of death!

    I waste for him my breath
Who wasted his for me! but mine returns,
    And this lorn bosom burns
With stifling heat, heaving it up in sleep,
    And waking me to weep
Tears that had melted his soft heart: for years
    Wept he as bitter tears!

"Merciful God!" such was his latest prayer,
    "These may she never share!"
Quieter is his breath, his breast more cold
    Than daisies in the mould,
Where children spell, athwart the churchyard gate,
    His name and life's brief date.
Pray for him, gentle souls, whoe'er you be,
    And, oh! pray, too, for me!

---

### THE BRIER.

MY brier that smelledst sweet,
    When gentle Spring's first heat
  Ran through thy quiet veins;
Thou that couldst injure none,
But wouldst be left alone,
Alone thou leavest me, and naught of thine remains.

  What! hath no poet's lyre
  O'er thee, sweet breathing brier,
   Hung fondly, ill or well?
  And yet, methinks, with thee
  A poet's sympathy,
Whether in weal or woe, in life or death, might dwell.

  Hard usage both must bear,
  Few hands your youth will rear,
   Few bosoms cherish you;
  Your tender prime must bleed
  Ere you are sweet, but freed
From life, you then are prized; thus prized are poets too.

---

## Allan Cunningham.

### "AWAKE, MY LOVE!"

AWAKE, my love! ere morning's ray
 Throws off night's weed of pilgrim gray;
Ere yet the hare, cowered close from view,
Licks from her fleece the clover dew:
Or wild swan shakes her snowy wings,
By hunters roused from secret springs:
Or birds upon the boughs awake,
Till green Arbigland's woodlands shake.

She combed her curling ringlets down,
Laced her green jupes, and clasped her shoon;
And from her home, by Preston-burn,
Came forth the rival light of morn.

The lark's song dropped,—now loud, now hush,
The goldspink answered from the bush;
The plover, fed on heather crop,
Called from the misty mountain top.

'Tis sweet, she said, while thus the day
Grows into gold from silvery gray,
To hearken heaven, and bush, and brake,
Instinct with soul of song awake;—
To see the smoke, in many a wreath,
Stream blue from hall and bower beneath,
Where yon blithe mower hastes along
With glittering scythe and rustic song.

Yes, lovely one! and dost thou mark
The moral of yon carolling lark?
Takest thou from Nature's counsellor tongue
The warning precept of her song?
Each bird that shakes the dewy grove
Warms its wild note with nuptial love;
The bird, the bee, with various sound,
Proclaim the sweets of wedlock round.

---

## "A WET SHEET AND A FLOWING SEA."

A WET sheet and a flowing sea—
    A wind that follows fast,
And fills the white and rustling sail,
    And bends the gallant mast—
And bends the gallant mast, my boys,
    While, like the eagle free,
Away the good ship flies, and leaves
    Old England on the lee.

O for a soft and gentle wind!
   I heard a fair one cry;
But give to me the snoring breeze,
   And white waves heaving high—
And white waves heaving high, my boys—
   The good ship tight and free;
The world of waters is our home,
   And merry men are we.

There's tempest in yon hornèd moon,
   And lightning in yon cloud;
And hark the music, mariners!
   The wind is piping loud—
The wind is piping loud, my boys,
   The lightning flashing free;
While the hollow oak our palace is,
   Our heritage the sea.

---

## Thomas Haynes Bailey.

### THE SOLDIER'S TEAR.

UPON the hill he turned,
   To take a last fond look
Of the valley and the village church,
   And the cottage by the brook;
He listened to the sounds,
   So familiar to his ear,
And the soldier leant upon his sword,
   And wiped away a tear.

Beside that cottage porch
    A girl was on her knees,
She held aloft a snowy scarf,
    Which fluttered in the breeze;
She breathed a prayer for him,
    A prayer he could not hear,
But he paused to bless her as she knelt,
    And wiped away a tear.

He turned and left the spot—
    Oh, do not deem him weak;
For dauntless was the soldier's heart,
    Though tears were on his cheek:
Go watch the foremost rank
    In danger's dark career,
Be sure the hand most daring there
    Has wiped away a tear.

---

## "OH, NO! WE NEVER MENTION HER."

OH, no! we never mention her;
    Her name is never heard;
My lips are now forbid to speak
    That once familiar word.
From sport to sport they hurry me,
    To banish my regret;
And when they win a smile from me,
    They think that I forget.

They bid me seek in change of scene
    The charms that others see;

But were I in a foreign land,
   They'd find no change in me.
'Tis true that I behold no more
   The valley where we met;
I do not see the hawthorn tree—
   But how can I forget!

They tell me she is happy now—
   The gayest of the gay;
They hint that she forgets me now,
   But heed not what they say;
Like me, perhaps she struggles with
   Each feeling of regret;
But if she loves as I have loved,
   She never can forget.

---

## "I'D BE A BUTTERFLY."

I'D be a butterfly born in a bower,
   Where roses and lilies and violets meet;
Roving for ever from flower to flower,
   Kissing all buds that are pretty and sweet.
I'd never languish for wealth or for power,
   I'd never sigh to see slaves at my feet;
I'd be a butterfly born in a bower,
   Kissing all buds that are pretty and sweet.

Oh! could I pilfer the wand of a fairy,
   I'd have a pair of those beautiful wings;
Their summer day's ramble is sportive and airy,
   They sleep in a rose when the nightingale sings.

Those who have wealth must be watchful and wary,
  Power, alas! naught but misery brings;
I'd be a butterfly, sportive and airy,
  Rocked in a rose when the nightingale sings.

What though you tell me each gay little rover
  Shrinks from the breath of the first autumn day;
Surely 'tis better, when summer is over,
  To die, when all fair things are fading away.
Some in life's winter may toil to discover
  Means of procuring a weary delay:
I'd be a butterfly, living a rover,
  Dying when fair things are fading away.

---

## "SHE WORE A WREATH OF ROSES."

She wore a wreath of roses
  The night that first we met,
Her lovely face was smiling
  Beneath her curls of jet;
Her footstep had the lightness,
  Her voice the joyous tone,
The tokens of a youthful heart,
  Where sorrow is unknown;
I saw her but a moment—
  Yet, methinks, I see her now,
With the wreath of summer flowers
  Upon her snowy brow.

A wreath of orange blossoms,
  When next we met, she wore;
The expression of her features
  Was more thoughtful than before;

And standing by her side was one
    Who strove, and not in vain,
To soothe her, leaving that dear home
    She ne'er might view again.
I saw her but a moment—
    Yet, methinks, I see her now,
With the wreath of orange blossoms
    Upon her snowy brow.

And once again I see that brow,
    No bridal wreath is there,
The widow's sombre cap conceals
    Her once luxuriant hair;
She weeps in silent solitude,
    And there is no one near
To press her hand within his own,
    And wipe away the tear.
I see her broken-hearted!
    Yet, methinks, I see her now
In the pride of youth and beauty,
    With a garland on her brow.

## Rev. Charles Wolfe.

### THE BURIAL OF SIR JOHN MOORE AT CORUNNA.

Not a drum was heard, not a funeral note,
    As his corse to the rampart we hurried;
Not a soldier discharged his farewell shot
    O'er the grave where our hero we buried.

We buried him darkly at dead of night,
    The sods with our bayonets turning;
By the struggling moonbeam's misty light
    And the lantern dimly burning.

No useless coffin enclosed his breast,
    Not in sheet or in shroud we wound him;
But he lay like a warrior taking his rest
    With his martial cloak around him.

Few and short were the prayers we said,
    And we spoke not a word of sorrow;
But we steadfastly gazed on the face that was dead,
    And we bitterly thought of the morrow.

We thought, as we hollowed his narrow bed,
    And smoothed down his lonely pillow,
That the foe and the stranger would tread o'er his head,
    And we far away on the billow!

Lightly they'll talk of the spirit that's gone,
    And o'er his cold ashes upbraid him,—
But little he'll reck, if they let him sleep on
    In the grave where a Briton has laid him.

But half of our heavy task was done
    When the clock struck the hour for retiring;
And we heard the distant and random gun
    That the foe was sullenly firing.

Slowly and sadly we laid him down,
    From the field of his fame fresh and gory;
We carved not a line, and we raised not a stone—
    But we left him alone with his glory.

## John Keble.

### ADVENT SUNDAY.

AWAKE!—again the Gospel-trump is blown—
   From year to year it swells with louder tone;
     From year to year the signs of wrath
     Are gathering round the Judge's path:
Strange words fulfilled, and mighty works achieved,
And truth in all the world both hated and believed.

Awake! why linger in the gorgeous town,
   Sworn liegemen of the Cross and thorny crown?
     Up from your beds of sloth, for shame!
     Speed to the eastern mount like flame,
Nor wonder, should ye find your King in tears,
E'en with the loud Hosanna ringing in his ears.

Alas! no need to rouse them: long ago
   They are gone forth to swell Messiah's show;
     With glittering robes and garlands sweet
     They strew the ground beneath his feet:
All but your hearts are there—O doomed to prove
The arrows winged in heaven for faith that will not love!

Meanwhile He paces through the adoring crowd,
   Calm as the march of some majestic cloud,
     That o'er wild scenes of ocean-war
     Holds its course in heaven afar:
Even so, heart-searching Lord, as years roll on,
Thou keepest silent watch from thy triumphal throne;

Even so, the world is thronging round to gaze
On the dread vision of the latter days,
   Constrained to own Thee, but in heart
   Prepared to take Barabbas' part:
"Hosanna" now, to-morrow "Crucify,"
The changeful burden still of their rude lawless cry.

Yet, in that throng of selfish hearts untrue,
Thy sad eye rests upon thy faithful few;
   Children and childlike souls are there,
   Blind Bartimeus' humble prayer,
And Lazarus wakened from his four days' sleep,
Enduring life again, that Passover to keep.

And fast beside the olive-bordered way
Stands the blest home where Jesus deigned to stay,
   And peaceful home, to Zeal sincere
   The heavenly Contemplation dear,
Where Martha loved to wait with reverence meet,
And wiser Mary lingered at thy sacred feet.

Still, through decaying ages as they glide,
Thou lovest thy chosen remnant to divide;
   Sprinkled along the waste of years,
   Full many a soft green isle appears:
Pause where we may upon the desert road,
Some shelter is in sight, some sacred, safe abode.

When withering blasts of error swept the sky,
And Love's last flower seemed fain to droop and die,
   How sweet, how lone, the ray benign,
   On sheltered nooks of Palestine!
Then to his early home did Love repair,
And cheered his sickening heart with his own native air.

Years roll away: again the tide of crime
Has swept thy footsteps from the favoured clime.
   Where shall the holy Cross find rest?
   On a crowned monarch's[1] mailèd breast:
Like some bright angel o'er the darkling scene,
Through court and camp he holds his heavenward course
     serene.

A fouler vision yet; an age of light,
Light without love, glares on the aching sight:
   Oh, who can tell how calm and sweet,
   Meek Walton! shows thy green retreat,
When, wearied with the tale thy times disclose,
The eye first finds thee out in thy secure repose?

## THE FLOWERS OF THE FIELD.

SWEET nurslings of the vernal skies,
   Bathed in soft airs, and fed with dew,
What more than magic in you lies,
   To fill the heart's fond view!
In childhood's sports, companions gay;
In sorrow, on life's downward way,
How soothing! in our last decay
   Memorials prompt and true.

Relics ye are of Eden's bowers,
   As pure, as fragrant, and as fair,
As when ye crowned the sunshine hours
   Of happy wanderers there.

---

[1] St. Louis, in the thirteenth century.

Fall'n all beside—the world of life,
How is it stained with fear and strife!
In Reason's world what storms are rife,
    What passions range and glare!

But cheerful and unchanged the while
    Your first and perfect form ye show,
The first that won Eve's matron smile
    In the world's opening glow.
The same of heaven a course are taught
Too high above our human thought;—
Ye may be found if ye are sought,
    And as we gaze, we know.

Ye dwell beside our paths and homes—
    Our paths of sin, our homes of sorrow;
And guilty man, where'er he roams,
    Your innocent mirth may borrow.
The birds of air before us fleet,
They cannot brook our shame to meet—
But we may taste your solace sweet,
    And come again to-morrow.

Ye fearless in your nests abide—
    Nor may we scorn, too proudly wise,
Your silent lessons, undescried
    By all but lowly eyes:
For ye could draw the admiring gaze
Of Him who worlds and hearts surveys;
Your order wild, your fragrant maze,
    He taught us how to prize.

Ye felt your Maker's smile that hour,
    As when He paused and owned you good;

His blessing on earth's primal bower,
  Ye felt it all renewed.
What care ye now, if winter's storm
Sweep ruthless o'er each silken form?
Christ's blessing at your heart is warm—
  Ye fear no vexing mood.

Alas! of thousand bosoms kind,
  That daily court you and caress,
How few the happy secret find
  Of your calm loveliness!
"Live for to-day! to-morrow's light
To-morrow's cares shall bring to sight;
Go sleep like closing flowers at night,
  And Heaven thy morn will bless."

---

## Richard Monckton Milnes.

### THE VOICE OF THE PEOPLE.

WHO is this man whose words have might
  To lead you from your rest or care,
Who speaks as if the earth were right
  To stop its course and listen there?
Where is the symbol of command
  By which he claims this lofty tone?
His hand is as another's hand—
  His speech no stronger than your own.

He bids you wonder, weep, rejoice,
  Saying,—"It is yourselves, not I;

I speak but with the people's voice,
   I see but with the people's eye."—
Words of imposing pride and strength;
   Words that contain, in little span,
The secret of the height and length
   Of all the intelligence of man.

Yet, brothers! God has given to few,
   Through the long progress of our kind,
To read with eyes undimmed and true
   The blotted book of public mind;
To separate from the moment's will
   The heart's enduring, real desires;
To tell the steps of coming ill,
   And seek the good the time requires.

These are the prophets, these the kings
   And lawgivers of human thought,
Who in our being's deepest springs
   The engines of their might have sought;
Whose utterance comes, we know not whence,
   Being no more their own than ours,
With instantaneous evidence
   Of titles just and sacred powers.

But bold usurpers may arise
   Of this as of another's throne;
Persuasion waits upon the wise,
   But waits not on the wise alone:
An echo of your evil self
   No better than the voice can be,
And appetites of fame or pelf
   Grow not in good as in degree.

Then try the speaker, try the cause,
   With prudent care, as men who know
The subtle nature of the laws
   By which our feelings ebb and flow:
Lest virtue's void and reason's lack
   Be hid beneath a specious name,
And on the people's helpless back
   Rest all the punishment and shame.

## Thomas Hood.

### THE DREAM OF EUGENE ARAM.[1]

'TWAS in the prime of summer time,
   An evening calm and cool,
And four-and-twenty happy boys
   Came bounding out of school:
There were some that ran and some that leaped,
   Like troutlets in a pool.

Away they sped with gamesome minds,
   And souls untouched by sin;
To a level mead they came, and there
   They drave the wickets in:
Pleasantly shone the setting sun
   Over the town of Lynn.

---

[1] The late Admiral Burney went to school at an establishment where the unhappy Eugene Aram was usher, subsequent to his crime. The admiral stated, that Aram was generally liked by the boys; and that he used to discourse to them about *murder*, in somewhat of the spirit which is attributed to him in this poem.

Like sportive deer they coursed about,
    And shouted as they ran,
Turning to mirth all things of earth,
    As only boyhood can;
But the usher sat remote from all,
    A melancholy man!

His hat was off, his vest apart,
    To catch heaven's blessed breeze;
For a burning thought was in his brow,
    And his bosom ill at ease;
So he leaned his head on his hands, and read
    The book between his knees!

Leaf after leaf he turned it o'er,
    Nor ever glanced aside;
For the peace of his soul he read that book
    In the golden eventide:
Much study had made him very lean,
    And pale, and leaden-eyed.

At last he shut the ponderous tome;
    With a fast and fervent grasp
He strained the dusky covers close,
    And fixed the brazen hasp:
"O God, could I so close my mind,
    And clasp it with a clasp!"

Then leaping on his feet upright,
    Some moody turns he took—
Now up the mead, then down the mead,
    And past a shady nook—
And, lo! he saw a little boy
    That pored upon a book!

" My gentle lad, what is't you read—
   Romance or fairy tale ?
Or is it some historic page,
   Of kings and crowns unstable ?"
The young boy gave an upward glance—
   " It is ' The Death of Abel.' "

The usher took six hasty strides,
   As smit with sudden pain—
Six hasty strides beyond the place,
   Then slowly back again;
And down he sat beside the lad,
   And talked with him of Cain.

He told how murderers walked the earth,
   Beneath the curse of Cain—
With crimson clouds before their eyes,
   And flames about their brain:
For blood has left upon their souls
   Its everlasting stain !

"And well," quoth he, " I know, for truth,
   Their pangs must be extreme—
Woe, woe, unutterable woe—
   Who spill life's sacred stream !
For why ?   Methought, last night, I wrought
   A murder in a dream !

" One that had never done me wrong—
   A feeble man, and old ;
I led him to a lonely field,
   The moon shone clear and cold :
' Now here,' said I, ' this man shall die,
   And I will have his gold !'

"Two sudden blows with a ragged stick,
　And one with a heavy stone,
One hurried gash with a hasty knife—
　And then the deed was done:
There was nothing lying at my foot
　But lifeless flesh and bone.

"Nothing but lifeless flesh and bone,
　That could not do me ill;
And yet I feared him all the more,
　For lying there so still:
There was a manhood in his look,
　That murder could not kill!

"And, lo! the universal air
　Seemed lit with ghastly flame—
Ten thousand thousand dreadful eyes
　Were looking down in blame:
I took the dead man by the hand,
　And called upon his name!

"O God, it made me quake to see
　Such sense within the slain!
But when I touched the lifeless clay,
　The blood gushed out amain!
For every clot, a burning spot
　Was scorching in my brain!

"And now from forth the frowning sky,
　From the heaven's topmost height,
I heard a voice—the awful voice
　Of the blood-avenging sprite:—
'Thou guilty man! take up thy dead
　And hide it from my sight!'

"I took the dreary body up,
  And cast it in a stream—
A sluggish water, black as ink,
  The depth was so extreme.
My gentle boy, remember this
  Is nothing but a dream!

"Down went the corse with a hollow plunge,
  And vanished in the pool;
Anon I cleansed my bloody hands
  And washed my forehead cool,
And sat among the urchins young,
  That evening in the school!

"O Heaven, to think of their white souls,
  And mine so black and grim!
I could not share in childish prayer,
  Nor join in evening hymn:
Like a devil of the pit I seemed,
  'Mid holy cherubim!

"And Peace went with them one and all,
  And each calm pillow spread:
But Guilt was my grim chamberlain
  That lighted me to bed,
And drew my midnight curtains round,
  With fingers bloody red!

"All night I lay in agony,
  From weary chime to chime,
With one besetting, horrid hint,
  That racked me all the time—
A mighty yearning, like the first
  Fierce impulse unto crime!

"One stern, tyrannic thought, that made
    All other thoughts its slave;
Stronger and stronger every pulse
    Did that temptation crave—
Still urging me to go and see
    The dead man in his grave!

"Heavily I rose up—as soon
    As light was in the sky—
And sought the black, accursèd pool
    With a wild, misgiving eye;
And I saw the dead in the river-bed,
    For the faithless stream was dry.

"Merrily rose the lark, and shook
    The dew-drop from its wing:
But I never marked its morning flight,
    I never heard it sing:
For I was stooping once again
    Under the horrid thing.

"With breathless speed, like a soul in chase,
    I took him up and ran—
There was no time to dig a grave
    Before the day began:
In a lonesome wood, with heaps of leaves,
    I hid the murdered man!

"And all that day I read in school,
    But my thought was otherwhere:
As soon as the mid-day task was done,
    In secret I was there:
And a mighty wind had swept the leaves,
    And still the corse was bare!

"Then down I cast me on my face,
　And first began to weep,
For I knew my secret then was one
　That earth refused to keep;
Or land or sea, though he should be
　Ten thousand fathoms deep!

"O God, that horrid, horrid dream
　Besets me now awake!
Again—again, with a dizzy brain,
　The human life I take;
And my red right hand grows raging hot,
　Like Cranmer's at the stake.

"And still no peace for the restless clay
　Will wave or mould allow;
The horrid thing pursues my soul—
　It stands before me now!"—
The fearful boy looked up, and saw
　Huge drops upon his brow!

That very night, while gentle Sleep
　The urchin eyelids kissed,
Two stern-faced men set out from Lynn,
　Through the cold and heavy mist;
And Eugene Aram walked between,
　With gyves upon his wrist.

## THE SONG OF THE SHIRT.

WITH fingers weary and worn,
    With eyelids heavy and red,
A woman sat, in unwomanly rags,
    Plying her needle and thread—
       Stitch! stitch! stitch!
In poverty, hunger, and dirt;
    And still, with a voice of dolorous pitch,
She sang the "Song of the Shirt:"

"Work! work! work!
    While the cock is crowing aloof!
And work—work—work,
    Till the stars shine through the roof!
It's oh! to be a slave
    Along with the barbarous Turk,
Where woman has never a soul to save,
    If this is Christian work!

"Work—work—work,
    Till the brain begins to swim!
Work—work—work,
    Till the eyes are heavy and dim!
Seam, and gusset, and band,
    Band, and gusset, and seam—
Till over the buttons I fall asleep,
    And sew them on in a dream!

"O Men, with sisters dear!
    O Men, with mothers and wives!
It is not linen you're wearing out,
    But human creatures' lives!

Stitch—stitch—stitch,
  In poverty, hunger, and dirt—
Sewing at once, with a double thread,
  A shroud as well as a Shirt!

"But why do I talk of Death—
  That phantom of grisly bone?
I hardly fear his terrible shape,
  It seems so like my own—
  It seems so like my own
  Because of the fasts I keep;
O God! that bread should be so dear,
  And flesh and blood so cheap!

"Work—work—work!
  My labour never flags;
And what are its wages? A bed of straw,
  A crust of bread—and rags!
That shattered roof—and this naked floor—
  A table—a broken chair—
And a wall so blank my shadow I thank
  For sometimes falling there!

"Work—work—work,
  From weary chime to chime!
Work—work—work,
  As prisoners work for crime!
Band, and gusset, and seam,
  Seam, and gusset, and band—
Till the heart is sick and the brain benumbed,
  As well as the weary hand.

"Work—work—work,
  In the dull December light!

And work—work—work,
    When the weather is warm and bright!—
While underneath the eaves
    The brooding swallows cling,
As if to show me their sunny backs,
    And twit me with the Spring.

"Oh! but to breathe the breath
    Of the cowslip and primrose sweet—
With the sky above my head,
    And the grass beneath my feet!
For only one short hour
    To feel as I used to feel,
Before I knew the woes of want
    And the walk that costs a meal!

"Oh! but for one short hour—
    A respite however brief!
No blessed leisure for Love or Hope,
    But only time for Grief!
A little weeping would ease my heart;
    But in their briny bed
My tears must stop, for every drop
    Hinders needle and thread!"

With fingers weary and worn,
    With eyelids heavy and red,
A woman sat, in unwomanly rags,
    Plying her needle and thread—
        Stitch! stitch! stitch!
    In poverty, hunger, and dirt;
And still, with a voice of dolorous pitch—
Would that its tone could reach the rich!—
    She sang this "Song of the Shirt!"

## THE BRIDGE OF SIGHS.

"Drowned! drowned!"—HAMLET.

ONE more unfortunate,
    Weary of breath,
Rashly importunate,
Gone to her death!

Take her up tenderly,
Lift her with care!
Fashioned so slenderly—
Young, and so fair!

Look at her garments,
Clinging like cerements,
Whilst the wave constantly
Drips from her clothing;
Take her up instantly—
Loving, not loathing!

Touch her not scornfully!
Think of her mournfully,
Gently and humanly—
Not of the stains of her;
All that remains of her
Now is pure womanly.

Make no deep scrutiny
Into her mutiny,
Rash and undutiful;
Past all dishonour,
Death has left on her
Only the beautiful.

Still, for all slips of hers—
One of Eve's family—
Wipe those poor lips of hers,
Oozing so clammily.

Loop up her tresses
Escaped from the comb—
Her fair auburn tresses—
Whilst wonderment guesses
Where was her home?

Who was her father?
Who was her mother?
Had she a sister?
Had she a brother?
Or was there a dearer one
Still, and a nearer one
Yet, than all other?

Alas for the rarity
Of Christian charity
Under the sun!
Oh, it was pitiful!
Near a whole city full,
Home she had none.

Sisterly, brotherly,
Fatherly, motherly
Feelings had changed—
Love, by harsh evidence,
Thrown from its eminence;
Even God's providence
Seeming estranged.

Where the lamps quiver
So far in the river,
With many a light
From window and casement,
From garret to basement,
She stood, with amazement,
Houseless by night.

The bleak wind of March
Made her tremble and shiver;
But not the dark arch,
Or the black flowing river:
Mad from life's history,
Glad to death's mystery,
Swift to be hurled—
Anywhere, anywhere
Out of the world!

In she plunged boldly—
No matter how coldly
The rough river ran—
Over the brink of it!
Picture it—think of it,
Dissolute Man!
Lave in it, drink of it,
Then, if you can!

Take her up tenderly—
Lift her with care!
Fashioned so slenderly—
Young, and so fair!

Ere her limbs, frigidly,
Stiffen too rigidly,

Decently, kindly,
Smooth and compose them;
And her eyes, close them,
Staring so blindly!
Dreadfully staring
Through muddy impurity,
As when, with the daring
Last look of despairing,
Fixed on futurity.

Perishing gloomily,
Spurred by contumely,
Cold inhumanity,
Burning insanity,
Into her rest!
Cross her hands humbly,
As if praying dumbly,
Over her breast!

Owning her weakness,
Her evil behaviour,
And leaving, with meekness,
Her sins to her Saviour!

---

## Mrs. Caroline Norton.

### TWILIGHT.

IT is the twilight hour,
　The daylight toil is done,
And the last rays are departing
　Of the cold and wintry sun.

It is the time when friendship
  Holds converse fair and free.
It is the time when children
  Dance round the mother's knee.
But my soul is faint and heavy,
  With a yearning sad and deep;
By the fireside lone and dreary
  I sit me down and weep!

Where are ye, merry voices,
  Whose clear and bird-like tone
Some other ear now blesses,
  Less anxious than my own?
Where are ye, steps of lightness,
  Which fell like blossom-showers?
Where are ye, sounds of laughter,
  That cheered the pleasant hours?
Through the dim light slow declining,
  Where my wistful glances fall,
I can see your pictures hanging
  Against the silent wall;—
They gleam athwart the darkness,
  With their sweet and changeless eyes,
But mute are ye, my children!
  No voice to mine replies.

Where are ye? Are ye playing
  By the stranger's blazing hearth;
Forgetting, in your gladness,
  Your old home's former mirth?
Are ye dancing? Are ye singing?
  Are ye full of childish glee?

Or do your light hearts sadden
    With the memory of me?
Round whom, oh! gentle darlings,
    Do your young arms fondly twine;
Does she press you to *her* bosom
    Who hath taken you from mine?

Oh! boys, the twilight hour
    Such a heavy time hath grown,—
It recalls with such deep anguish
    All I used to call my own,—
That the harshest word that ever
    Was spoken to me there,
Would be trivial—would be *welcome*—
    In this depth of my despair!
Yet no! Despair shall sink not,
    While life and love remain,—
Though the weary struggle haunt me,
    And my prayer be made in vain:
Though at times my spirit fail me,
    And the bitter tear-drops fall,
Though my lot be hard and lonely,
    Yet I hope—I hope through all!

When the mournful Jewish mother
    Laid her infant down to rest,
In doubt, and fear, and sorrow,
    On the water's changeful breast;
She knew not what the future
    Should bring the sorely tried:
That the high-priest of her nation
    Was the babe she sought to hide.

No! in terror wildly flying,
    She hurried on her path:
Her swoln heart full to bursting
    Of woman's helpless wrath;
Of that wrath so blent with anguish,
    When we seek to shield from ill
Those feeble little creatures
    Who *seem* more helpless still!
Ah! no doubt in such an hour
    Her thoughts were harsh and wild;
The fiercer burned her spirit
    The more she loved her child;
No doubt, a frenzied anger
    Was mingled with her fear,
When that prayer arose for justice
    Which God hath sworn to hear.
He heard it! From His heaven,
    In its blue and boundless scope,
He saw that task of anguish,
    And that fragile ark of hope;
When she turned from that lost infant
    Her weeping eyes of love,
And the cold reeds bent beneath it—
    *His* angels watched above!
She was spared the bitter sorrow
    Of her young child's early death,
Or the doubt where he was carried
    To draw his distant breath;
She was called his life to nourish
    From the well-springs of her heart,
God's mercy reuniting
    Those whom man had forced apart.

Nor was *thy* woe forgotten,
   Whose worn and weary feet
Were driven from thy homestead
   Through the red sand's parching heat;
Poor Hagar! scorned and banished,
   That another's son might be
Sole claimant on that father
   Who felt no more for thee.
Ah! when thy dark eye wandered,
   Forlorn Egyptian slave!
Across that lurid desert,
   And saw no fountain wave,—
When thy southern heart, despairing,
   In the passion of its grief,
Foresaw no ray of comfort,
   No shadow of relief,
But to cast the young child from thee,
   That thou might'st not *see* him die,
How sank thy broken spirit—
   But the Lord of Hosts was nigh!
He (He, too oft forgotten,
   In sorrow as in joy)
Had willed they should not perish—
   The outcast and her boy:
The cool breeze swept across them
   From the angel's waving wing,—
The fresh tide gushed in brightness
   From the fountain's living spring,—
And they stood—those two—forsaken
   By all earthly love or aid,
Upheld by God's firm promise,
   Serene and undismayed!

And thou, Nain's grieving widow!
　　Whose task of life seemed done,
When the pale corse lay before thee
　　Of thy dear and only son;
Though death, that fearful shadow,
　　Had veiled his fair young eyes,
There was mercy for thy weeping,
　　There was pity for thy sighs!
The gentle voice of Jesus
　　(Who the touch of sorrow knew)
The grave's cold claim arrested
　　Ere it hid him from thy view;
And those loving orbs reopened
　　And knew thy mournful face,—
And the stiff limbs warmed and bent them
　　With all life's moving grace,—
And his senses dawned and wakened
　　From the dark and frozen spell
Which death had cast around him
　　Whom thou didst love so well;
Till, like one returned from exile
　　To his former home of rest,
Who speaks not while his mother
　　Falls sobbing on his breast;
But with strange bewildered glances
　　Looks round on objects near,
To recognize and welcome
　　All that memory held dear,—
Thy young son stood before thee
　　All living and restored,
And they who saw the wonder
　　Knelt down to praise the Lord!

The twilight hour is over!
  In busier homes than mine
I can see the shadows crossing
  Athwart the taper's shine;
I hear the roll of chariots
  And the tread of homeward feet,
And the lamps' long rows of splendour
  Gleam through the misty street.
No more I mark the objects
  In my cold and cheerless room;
The fire's unheeded embers
  Have sunk—and all is gloom;
But I know where hang your pictures
  Against the silent wall,
And my eyes turn sadly towards them,
  Though I hope—I hope through all.
By the summons to that mother,
  Whose fondness fate beguiled,
When the tyrant's gentle daughter
  Saved her river-floating child;—
By the sudden joy which bounded
  In the banished Hagar's heart,
When she saw the gushing fountain
  From the sandy desert start;—
By the living smile which greeted
  The lonely one of Nain,
When her long last watch was over,
  And her hope seemed wild and vain;—
By all the tender mercy
  God hath shown to human grief,
When fate or man's perverseness
  Denied and barred relief,—

By the helpless woe which taught me
    To look to Him alone,
From the vain appeals for justice
    And wild efforts of my own,—
By thy light—thou unseen future,
    And thy tears—thou bitter past,
I will hope—though all forsake me—
    In His mercy to the last!

---

## "WE HAVE BEEN FRIENDS TOGETHER."

WE have been friends together,
    In sunshine and in shade,
Since first beneath the chestnut trees
    In infancy we played.
But coldness dwells within thy heart—
    A cloud is on thy brow;
We have been friends together—
    Shall a light word part us now?

We have been gay together;
    We have laughed at little jests:
For the fount of hope was gushing,
    Warm and joyous, in our breasts.
But laughter now hath fled thy lip,
    And sullen glooms thy brow:
We have been gay together—
    Shall a light word part us now?

We have been sad together—
    We have wept, with bitter tears,

O'er the grass-grown graves, where slumbered
    The hopes of early years.
The voices which are silent there
    Would bid thee clear thy brow;
We have been sad together—
    O! what shall part us now?

---

## THE FALLEN LEAVES.

WE stand among the fallen leaves,
    Young children at our play,
And laugh to see the yellow things
    Go rustling on their way:
Right merrily we hunt them down,
    The autumn winds and we,
Nor pause to gaze where snow-drifts lie,
    Or sunbeams gild the tree:
With dancing feet we leap along
    Where withered boughs are strown;
Nor past nor future checks our song—
    *The present* is our own.

We stand among the fallen leaves
    In youth's enchanted spring—
When hope (who wearies at the last)
    First spreads her eagle wing.
We tread with steps of conscious strength
    Beneath the leafless trees,
And the colour kindles in our cheek
    As blows the winter breeze;

While, gazing towards the cold gray sky,
  Clouded with snow and rain,
We wish the old year all passed by,
  And the young spring come again.

We stand among the fallen leaves
  In manhood's haughty prime—
When first our pausing hearts begin
  To love "the olden time;"
And, as we gaze, we sigh to think
  How many a year hath passed
Since 'neath those cold and faded trees
  Our footsteps wandered last;
And old companions—now perchance
  Estranged, forgot, or dead—
Come round us, as those autumn leaves
  Are crushed beneath our tread.

We stand among the fallen leaves
  In our *own* autumn day—
And, tottering on with feeble steps,
  Pursue our cheerless way.
We look not back—too long ago
  Hath all we loved been lost;
Nor forward—for we may not live
  To see our new hope crossed:
But on we go—the sun's faint beam
  A feeble warmth imparts—
Childhood without its joy returns—
  *The present* fills our hearts!

## Samuel Lover.

### RORY O'MORE; OR, GOOD OMENS.

YOUNG Rory O'More courted Kathleen bawn—
 He was bold as the hawk, and she soft as the dawn;
He wished in his heart pretty Kathleen to please,
And he thought the best way to do that was to tease.
"Now, Rory, be aisy," sweet Kathleen would cry,
Reproof on her lip, but a smile in her eye—
"With your tricks, I don't know, in throth, what I'm about;
Faith, you've teased till I've put on my cloak inside out."
"Och! jewel," says Rory, "that same is the way
You've thrated my heart for this many a day;
And 'tis plazed that I am, and why not, to be sure?
For 'tis all for good luck," says bold Rory O'More.

"Indeed, then," says Kathleen, "don't think of the like,
For I half gave a promise to soothering Mike;
The ground that I walk on he loves, I'll be bound"—
"Faith!" says Rory, "I'd rather love you than the ground."
"Now, Rory, I'll cry if you don't let me go;
Sure I dream every night that I'm hating you so!"
"Och!" says Rory, "that same I'm delighted to hear,
For dhrames always go by conthraries, my dear.
Och! jewel, keep dhraming that same till you die,
And bright morning will give dirty night the black lie!
And 'tis plazed that I am, and why not, to be sure?
Since 'tis all for good luck," says bold Rory O'More.

" Arrah, Kathleen, my darlint, you've teased me enough;
Sure I've thrashed, for your sake, Dinny Grimes and Jim
  Duff;
And I've made myself, drinking your health, quite a baste,
So I think, after that, I may talk to the priest."
Then Rory, the rogue, stole his arm round her neck,
So soft and so white, without freckle or speck;
And he looked in her eyes, that were beaming with light,
And he kissed her sweet lips—don't you think he was right?
" Now, Rory, leave off, sir—you'll hug me no more—
That's eight times to-day you've kissed me before."
" Then here goes another," says he, " to make sure,
For there's luck in odd numbers," says Rory O'More.

### THE ANGEL'S WHISPER.

A BABY was sleeping;
  Its mother was weeping;
For her husband was far on the wild raging sea;
  And the tempest was swelling
  Round the fisherman's dwelling;
And she cried, "Dermot, darling, oh come back to me!"

  Her beads while she numbered,
  The baby still slumbered,
And smiled in her face as she bended her knee:
  " O blest be that warning,
  My child, thy sleep adorning,
For I know that the angels are whispering with thee."

  " And while they are keeping
  Bright watch o'er thy sleeping,

Oh, pray to them softly, my baby, with me!
        And say thou wouldst rather
        They'd watch o'er thy father!
For I know that the angels are whispering to thee!"

        The dawn of the morning
        Saw Dermot returning,
And the wife wept with joy her babe's father to see;
        And closely caressing
        Her child with a blessing,
Said, "I knew that the angels were whispering with thee."

---

## Thomas Babington Macaulay.

### THE BATTLE OF IVRY.

NOW glory to the Lord of Hosts,
    From whom all glories are!
And glory to our sovereign liege,
    King Henry of Navarre!
Now let there be the merry sound
    Of music and the dance,
Through thy corn-fields green, and sunny vines,
    Oh, pleasant land of France!
And thou, Rochelle, our own Rochelle,
    Proud city of the waters,
Again let rapture light the eyes
    Of all thy mourning daughters.
As thou wert constant in our ills,
    Be joyous in our joy,

For cold, and stiff, and still are they
   Who wrought thy walls annoy.
Hurrah! hurrah! a single field
   Hath turned the chance of war;
Hurrah! hurrah! for Ivry,
   And King Henry of Navarre!

Oh! how our hearts were beating,
   When, at the dawn of day,
We saw the army of the League
   Drawn out in long array;
With all its priest-led citizens,
   And all its rebel peers,
And Appenzel's stout infantry,
   And Egmont's Flemish spears!
There rode the brood of false Lorraine,
   The curses of our land!
And dark Mayenne was in the midst,
   A truncheon in his hand;
And, as we looked on them, we thought
   Of Seine's empurpled flood,
And good Coligni's hoary hair
   All dabbled with his blood;
And we cried unto the living God,
   Who rules the fate of war,
To fight for his own holy name,
   And Henry of Navarre!

The king is come to marshal us,
   In all his armour dressed,
And he has bound a snow-white plume
   Upon his gallant crest.

He looked upon his people,
    And a tear was in his eye;
He looked upon the traitors,
    And his glance was stern and high.
Right graciously he smiled on us,
    As rolled from wing to wing,
Down all our line, in deafening shout,
    "God save our lord, the king!"
"And if my standard-bearer fall,
    As fall full well he may—
For never saw I promise yet
    Of such a bloody fray—
Press where ye see my white plume shine,
    Amidst the ranks of war,
And be your oriflamme, to-day,
    The helmet of Navarre!"

Hurrah! the foes are moving!
    Hark to the mingled din
Of fife, and steed, and trump, and drum,
    And roaring culverin!
The fiery Duke is pricking fast
    Across Saint Andre's plain,
With all the hireling chivalry
    Of Guelders and Almayne.
Now by the lips of those ye love,
    Fair gentlemen of France,
Charge for the golden lilies now,
    Upon them with the lance!
A thousand spurs are striking deep,
    A thousand spears in rest,
A thousand knights are pressing close

    Behind the snow-white crest;
And in they burst, and on they rushed,
    While, like a guiding star,
Amidst the thickest carnage blazed
    The helmet of Navarre!

Now, God be praised, the day is ours!
    Mayenne hath turned his rein;
D'Aumale hath cried for quarter—
    The Flemish Count is slain.
Their ranks are breaking like thin clouds
    Before a Biscay gale;
The field is heaped with bleeding steeds,
    And flags, and cloven mail;
And then we thought on vengeance,
    And all along our van,
"Remember Saint Bartholomew!"
    Was passed from man to man:
But out spake gentle Henry—
    "No Frenchman is my foe;
Down, down with every foreigner,
    But let your brethren go."
Oh! was there ever such a knight,
    In friendship or in war,
As our sovereign lord, King Henry,
    The soldier of Navarre!

Ho! maidens of Vienne!
    Ho! matrons of Lucerne!
Weep, weep, and rend your hair for those
    Who never shall return.
Ho! Philip, send, for charity,

                Thy Mexican pistoles,
            That Antwerp monks may sing a mass
                For thy poor spearmen's souls!
            Ho! gallant nobles of the League,
                Look that your arms be bright!
            Ho! burghers of Saint Genevieve,
                Keep watch and ward to-night!
            For our God hath crushed thy tyrant,
                Our God hath raised the slave,
            And mocked the counsel of the wise
                And the valour of the brave.
            Then glory to his holy name
                From whom all glories are;
            And glory to our sovereign lord,
                King Henry of Navarre!

---

### Mrs. Elizabeth Barrett Browning.
### THE CRY OF THE CHILDREN.

Do ye hear the children weeping, O my brothers!
    Ere the sorrow comes with years?
They are leaning their young heads against their mothers,
    And *that* cannot stop their tears.
The young lambs are bleating in the meadows,
    The young birds are chirping in the nest,
The young fawns are playing in the shadows,
    The young flowers are blowing from the west;
But the young, young children, O my brothers!
    They are weeping bitterly!

They are weeping in the playtime of the others,
   In the country of the free.

Do you question the young children in their sorrow,
   Why their tears are falling so?
The old man may weep for his to-morrow
   Which is lost in long ago.
The old tree is leafless in the forest,
   The old year is ending in the frost;
The old wound, if stricken, is the sorest,
   The old hope is hardest to be lost!
But the young, young children, O my brothers!
   Do you ask them why they stand
Weeping sore before the bosoms of their mothers,
   In our happy fatherland!

They look up with their pale and sunken faces,
   And their looks are sad to see;
For the man's grief abhorrent draws and presses
   Down the cheeks of infancy.
"Your old earth," they say, "is very dreary;"
   "Our young feet," they say, "are very weak!
Few paces have we taken, yet are weary—
   Our grave-rest is very far to seek!
Ask the old why they weep, and not the children,
   For the outside earth is cold,
And we young ones stand without, in our bewild'ring,
   And the graves are for the old."

"True," say the young children, "it may happen
   That we die before our time!
Little Alice died last year,—the grave is shapen
   Like a snow-ball, in the rime.

We looked into the pit prepared to take her,
  *Was no room for any work in the close clay!*
From the sleep wherein she lieth none will wake her,
  Crying—' Get up, little Alice, it is day!'
If you listen by that grave in sun and shower,
  With your ear down, little Alice never cries;
Could we see her face, be sure we should not know her,
  *For the smile has time for growing in her eyes.*
For merry go her moments, lulled and stilled in
  The shroud, by the kirk-chime!
It is good when it happens," say the children,
  " That we die before our time!"

Alas, the young children! they are seeking
  Death in life, as best to have!
They are binding up their hearts away from breaking,
  With a cerement from the grave.
Go out, children, from the mine and from the city,
  Sing out, children, as the little thrushes do!
Pluck your handfuls of the meadow cowslips pretty,
  Laugh aloud to feel your fingers let them through!
But they answer, " Are your cowslips of the meadows
  Like the weeds anear the mine?"[1]
Leave us quiet in the dark of our coal-shadows,
  From your pleasures fair and fine.

" For oh!" say the children, " we are weary,
  And we cannot run or leap:
*If we cared for any meadows, it were merely*
  *To drop down in them and sleep.*

---

[1] A commissioner mentions the fact of weeds being thus confounded with the idea of flowers.

Our knees tremble sorely in the stooping;
    We fall on our face, trying to go;
And underneath our heavy eyelids drooping,
    *The reddest flowers would look as pale as snow;*
For all day, we drag our burden tiring,
    Through the coal-dark underground,
Or, all day, we drive the wheels of iron
    In the factories round and round.

"For all day the wheels are droning, turning,
    Their wind comes in our faces!
Till our hearts turn, and our heads with pulses burning,
    And the walls turn in their places!
Turns the sky in the high window, blank and reeling,
    Turns the long light that droopeth down the wall;
Turn the black flies that crawl along the ceiling—
    Are all turning all the day, and we with all!
And all day the iron wheels are droning,
    And sometimes we could pray—
'O ye wheels (breaking out in a mad moaning),
    Stop! be silent for to-day!'"

Ay, be silent! let them hear each other breathing,
    For a moment, mouth to mouth;
Let them touch each other's hands, in a fresh wreathing
    Of their tender human youth;
Let them feel that this cold metallic motion
    Is not all the life God fashions or reveals;
Let them prove their inward souls against the notion
    That they live in you, or under you, O wheels!
Still, all day, the iron wheels go onward,
    Grinding life down from its mark!

And the children's souls, which God is calling sunward,
   Spin on blindly in the dark.

Now tell the poor young children, O my brothers!
   To look up to Him and pray,
So the blessed One who blesseth all the others,
   Will bless them another day.
They answer: "Who is God that He should hear us,
   While the rushing of the iron wheels is stirred?
When we sob aloud, the human creatures near us
   Pass unhearing—at least, answer not a word;
And we hear not (for the wheels in their resounding)
   Strangers speaking at the door:
Is it likely God, with angels singing round Him,
   Hears our weeping any more?

"Two words, indeed, of praying we remember;
   And at midnight's hour of harm,
'Our Father!' looking upward in the chamber,
   We say softly, for a charm.'[1]
We know no other words except 'Our Father!'
   And we think that, in some pause of angels' song,
God may pluck them with the silence sweet to gather,
   And hold both within His right hand, which is strong.
Our Father! If He heard us, He would surely—
   For they call him good and mild—
Answer, smiling down the steep world very purely,
   'Come and rest with me, my child.'

---

[1] The report of the commissioners presents repeated instances of children whose religious devotion is confined to the repetition of the first two words of the Lord's Prayer.

"But no," say the children, weeping faster,
  "He is speechless as a stone;
And they tell us, of His image is the master
  Who commands us to work on.
Go to!" say the children; "up in heaven,
  Dark, wheel-like, turning clouds are all we find!
Do not mock us! grief has made us unbelieving;
  We look up for God—*but tears have made us blind!*"
Do you hear children weeping and disproving,
  O my brothers, what ye preach?
For God's possible is taught by His world's loving,
  And the children doubt of each!

And well may the children weep before ye;
  *They are weary ere they run!*
They have never seen the sunshine, nor the glory
  Which is brighter than the sun!
They know the grief of man, but not the wisdom;
  They sink in man's despair, without its calm;
Are slaves without the liberty in Christdom—
  Are martyrs by the pang, without the palm!
Are worn as if with age; yet unretrievingly
  The harvest of its memories cannot keep;
*Are orphans of the earthly love and heavenly—*
  Let them weep, let them weep!

They look up, with their pale and sunken faces,
  And their look is dread to see;
For they mind you of their angels in their places,
  With eyes meant for Deity.
"How long," they say, "how long, O cruel nation!
  Will you stand, to move the world, on a child's heart?

Stifle down with mailèd heel its palpitation,
  And tread onward to your throne amid the mart?
Our blood splashes upward, O our tyrants!
  And your purple shows your path"—
*But the child's sob curseth deeper in the silence*
  *Than the strong man in his wrath!*

---

## Robert Browning.

### HOW THEY BROUGHT THE GOOD NEWS FROM GHENT TO AIX.

I SPRANG to the stirrup, and Joris and he:
  I galloped, Dirck galloped, we galloped all three;
"Good speed!" cried the watch, as the gate-bolts undrew
"Speed!" echoed the wall to us galloping through.
Behind shut the postern, the lights sank to rest,
And into the midnight we galloped abreast.

Not a word to each other; we kept the great pace—
Neck by neck, stride by stride, never changing our place
I turned in my saddle and made its girths tight,
Then shortened each stirrup and set the pique right,
Rebuckled the check-strap, chained slacker the bit,
Nor galloped less steadily Roland a whit.

'Twas moonset at starting; but, while we drew near
Lokernew, the cocks crew, and twilight dawned clear;
At Boom, a great yellow star came out to see;
At Duffield, 'twas morning as plain as could be,
And from Mecheln church-steeple we heard the half-chime
So Joris broke silence with, "Yet there is time!"

At Aerschot, up leaped of a sudden the sun,
And against him the cattle stood, black every one,
To stare through the mist at us galloping past;
And I saw my stout galloper, Roland, at last,
With resolute shoulders each butting away
The haze, as some bluff river headland its spray—

And his low head and crest, just one sharp ear bent back
For my voice, and the other pricked out on his track;
And one eye's black intelligence,—ever that glance
O'er its white edge at me, its own master, askance;
And the thick, heavy spume-flakes, which aye and anon
His fierce lips shook upward in galloping on.

By Hasselt Dirck groaned; and cried Joris, "Stay spur!
Your Roos galloped bravely, the fault's not in her;
We'll remember at Aix"—for one heard the quick wheeze
Of her chest, saw the stretched neck, and staggering knees,
And sunk tail, and horrible heave of the flank,
As down on her haunches she shuddered and sank.

So we were left galloping, Joris and I,
Past Looz and past Tongres, no cloud in the sky;
The broad sun above laughed a pitiless laugh;
'Neath our foot broke the brittle bright stubble like chaff;
Till over by Dalhem a dome-tower sprang white,
And "Gallop," cried Joris, "for Aix is in sight!"

"How they'll greet us!"—and all in a moment his roan
Rolled neck and croup over, lay dead as a stone;
And there was my Roland to bear the whole weight
Of the news which alone could save Aix from her fate,
With his nostrils like pits full of blood to the brim,
And with circles of red for his eye-socket's rim.

Then I cast loose my buff-coat, each holster let fall,
Shook off both my jack-boots, let go belt and all,
Stood up in the stirrup, leaned, patted his ear,
Called my Roland his pet-name, my horse without peer—
Clapped my hands, laughed and sung, any noise, bad or good,
Till at length into Aix Roland galloped and stood.

And all I remember is friends flocking round,
As I sate with his head 'twixt my knees on the ground;
And no voice but was praising this Roland of mine,
As I poured down his throat our last measure of wine,
Which (the burgesses voted by common consent)
Was no more than his due who brought good news from
    Ghent.

---

## THE STATUE AND THE BUST.

THERE'S a palace in Florence, the world knows well,
    And a statue watches it from the square;
And this story of both do the townsmen tell:

Ages ago, a lady there,
At the farthest window facing the east,
Asked, "Who rides by with the royal air?"

The bridesmaids' prattle around her ceased;
She leaned forth, one on either hand;
They saw how the blush of the bride increased—

They felt by its beats her heart expand—
As one at each ear and both in a breath
Whispered, "The Great-Duke Ferdinand."

That self-same instant, underneath,
The Duke rode past in his idle way,
Empty and fine like a swordless sheath.

Gay he rode, with a friend as gay,
Till he threw his head back—"Who is she?"
—"A bride the Riccardi brings home to-day."

Hair in heaps laid heavily
Over a pale brow spirit-pure,
Carved like the heart of the coal-black tree.

Crisped like a war-steed's encolure—
Which vainly sought to dissemble her eyes
Of the blackest black our eyes endure.

And lo! a blade for a knight's emprise
Filled the fine empty sheath of a man,—
The Duke grew straightway brave and wise.

He looked at her, as a lover can;
She looked at him, as one who awakes,—
The past was a sleep, and her life began.

As Love so ordered for both their sakes,
A feast was held that self-same night
In the pile which the mighty shadow makes.

(For Via Larga is three-parts light,
But the Palace overshadows one,
Because of a crime which may God requite!

To Florence and God the wrong was done,
Through the first republic's murder there
By Cosimo and his cursèd son.)

The Duke (with the statue's face in the square)
Turned, in the midst of his multitude,
At the bright approach of the bridal pair.

Face to face the lovers stood
A single minute and no more—
While the bridegroom bent as a man subdued—

Bowed till his bonnet brushed the floor—
For the Duke on the lady a kiss conferred,
As the courtly custom was of yore.

In a minute can lovers exchange a word?
If a word did pass, which I do not think,
Only one out of the thousand heard.

That was the bridegroom. At day's brink,
He and his bride were alone at last
In a bed-chamber by a taper's blink.

Calmly he said that her lot was cast,
That the door she had passed was shut on her
Till the final catafalk repassed.

The world meanwhile, its noise and stir,
Through a certain window facing the east
She might watch like a convent's chronicler.

Since passing the door might lead to a feast,
And a feast might lead to so much beside,
He, of many evils, chose the least.

"Freely I choose, too," said the bride;
"Your window and its world suffice."
So replied the tongue, while the heart replied—

"If I spend the night with that devil twice,
May his window serve as my loop of hell
Whence a damnèd soul looks on Paradise!

"I fly to the Duke, who loves me well,
Sit by his side and laugh at sorrow,
Ere I count another ave-bell.

"'Tis only the coat of a page to borrow,
And tie my hair in a horse-boy's trim,
And I save my soul—but not to-morrow—"

(She checked herself, and her eye grew dim)—
"My father tarries to bless my state:
I must keep it one day more for him.

"Is one day more so long to wait?
Moreover, the Duke rides past, I know—
We shall see each other, sure as fate."

She turned on her side and slept. Just so!
So we resolve on a thing, and sleep—
So did the lady, ages ago.

That night the Duke said, "Dear or cheap
As the cost of this cup of bliss may prove
To body or soul, I will drain it deep."

And on the morrow, bold with love,
He beckoned the bridegroom (close on call,
As his duty bade, by the Duke's alcove)—

And smiled: "'Twas a very funeral
Your lady will think, this feast of ours,—
A shame to efface, whate'er befall!

"What if we break from the Arno bowers,
And let Petraja, cool and green,
Cure last night's fault with this morning's flowers?"

The bridegroom, not a thought to be seen
On his steady brow and quiet mouth,
Said, "Too much favour for me so mean!

"Alas! my lady leaves the south.
Each wind that comes from the Apennine
Is a menace to her tender youth.

"No way exists, the wise opine,
If she quits her palace twice this year,
To avert the flower of life's decline."

Quoth the Duke, "A sage and a kindly fear.
Moreover, Petraja is cold this spring—
Be our feast to-night as usual here!"

And then to himself—"Which night shall bring
Thy bride to her lover's embraces, fool—
Or I am the fool, and thou art his king!

"Yet my passion must wait a night, nor cool—
For to-night the Envoy arrives from France,
Whose heart I unlock with thyself, my tool.

"I need thee still, and might miss perchance.
To-day is not wholly lost, beside,
With its hope of my lady's countenance—

"For I ride—what should I do but ride?
And passing her palace, if I list,
May glance at its window—well betide!"

So said, so done; nor the lady missed
One ray that broke from the ardent brow,
Nor a curl of the lips where the spirit kissed.

Be sure that each renewed the vow—
No morrow's sun should arise and set
And leave them as it left them now.

But next day passed, and next day yet,
With still fresh cause to wait one more
Ere each leaped over the parapet.

And still, as love's brief morning wore,
With a gentle start, half smile, half sigh,
They found love not as it seemed before.

They thought it would work infallibly,
But not in despite of heaven and earth—
The rose would blow when the storm passed by

Meantime they could profit in winter's dearth
By winter's fruits that supplant the rose.
The world and its ways have a certain worth;

And to press a point while these oppose
Were a simple policy—best wait,
And lose no friends and gain no foes.

Meanwhile, worse fates than a lover's fate
Who daily may ride, and lean, and look,
Where his lady watches behind the grate!

And she—she watched the square like a book
Holding one picture and only one,
Which daily to find she undertook.

When the picture was reached the book was done,
And she turned from it all night to scheme
Of tearing it out for herself next sun.

Weeks grew months, years—gleam by gleam
The glory dropped from youth and love,
And both perceived they had dreamed a dream;

Which hovered as dreams do, still above,—
But who can take a dream for truth?
Oh, hide our eyes from the next remove!

One day, as the lady saw her youth
Depart, and the silver thread that streaked
Her hair, and, worn by the serpent's tooth,

The brow so puckered, the chin so peaked,—
And wondered who the woman was,
So hollow-eyed and haggard-cheeked,

Fronting her silent in the glass!—
"Summon here," she suddenly said,
"Before the rest of my old self pass,

"Him, the carver, a hand to aid,
Who moulds the clay no love will change,
And fixes a beauty never to fade.

"Let Robbia's craft, so apt and strange,
Arrest the remains of young and fair,
And rivet them while the seasons range.

"Make me a face on the window there,
Waiting as ever, mute the while,
My love to pass below in the square!

"And let me think that it may beguile
Dreary days which the dead must spend
Down in their darkness under the aisle,

"To say,—'What matters at the end?
I did no more while my heart was warm,
Than does that image, my pale-faced friend.'

"Where is the use of the lip's red charm,
The heaven of hair, the pride of the brow,
And the blood that blues the inside arm—

"Unless we turn, as the soul knows how,
The earthly gift to an end divine?
A lady of clay is as good, I trow."

But long ere Robbia's cornice, fine
With flowers and fruits which leaves enlace,
Was set where now is the empty shrine—

(With, leaning out of a bright blue space,
As a ghost might, from a chink of sky,
The passionate pale lady's face—

Eying ever with earnest eye,
And quick-turned neck at its breathless stretch,
Some one who ever passes by)—

The Duke sighed like the simplest wretch
In Florence: "So, my dream escapes!
Will its record stay?" And he bade them fetch

Some subtle fashioner of shapes—
"Can the soul, the will, die out of a man
Ere his body find the grave that gapes?

"John of Douay shall work my plan,
Mould me on horseback here aloft,
Alive—(the subtle artisan!)

"In the very square I cross so oft!
That men may admire, when future suns
Shall touch the eyes to a purpose soft—

"While the mouth and the brow are brave in bronze—
Admire and say, 'When he was alive,
How he would take his pleasure once!'

"And it shall go hard but I contrive
To listen meanwhile, and laugh in my tomb
At indolence which aspires to strive."

---

So! while these wait the trump of doom,
How do their spirits pass, I wonder,
Nights and days in the narrow room?

Still, I suppose, they sit and ponder
What a gift life was, ages ago,
Six steps out of the chapel yonder.

Surely they see not God, I know,
Nor all that chivalry of His,
The soldier-saints who, row on row,

Burn upward each to his point of bliss—
Since, the end of life being manifest,
He had cut his way through the world to this.

I hear your reproach—"But delay was best,
For their end was a crime!"—Oh, a crime will do
As well, I reply, to serve for a test,

As a virtue golden through and through,
Sufficient to vindicate itself
And prove its worth at a moment's view.

Must a game be played for the sake of pelf?
Where a button goes, 'twere an epigram
To offer the stamp of the very Guelph.

The true has no value beyond the sham.
As well the counter as coin, I submit,
When your table's a hat, and your prize a dram.

Stake your counter as boldly every whit;
Venture as truly, use the same skill;
Do your best, whether winning or losing it,

If you choose to play—is my principle!
Let a man contend to the uttermost
For his life's set prize, be it what it will!

The counter our lovers staked was lost
As surely as if it were lawful coin;
And the sin I impute to each frustrate ghost

Was the unlit lamp and the ungirt loin,
Though the end in sight was a crime, I say.
You of the virtue (we issue join),
How strive you?   *De te, fabula!*

## Alfred Tennyson.

### LOCKSLEY HALL.

COMRADES, leave me here a little, while as yet 'tis early morn—
Leave me here, and when you want me, sound upon the bugle-horn.

'Tis the place, and all around it, as of old, the curlews call,
Dreary gleams about the moorland, flying over Locksley Hall;

Locksley Hall, that in the distance overlooks the sandy tracts,
And the hollow ocean-ridges roaring into cataracts.

Many a night from yonder ivied casement, ere I went to rest,
Did I look on great Orion sloping slowly to the West.

Many a night I saw the Pleiads, rising through the mellow shade,
Glitter like a swarm of fire-flies tangled in a silver braid.

Here about the beach I wandered, nourishing a youth sublime
With the fairy tales of science, and the long result of Time;

When the centuries behind me like a fruitful land reposed;
When I clung to all the present for the promise that it closed;

When I dipped into the future far as human eye could
see—
Saw the vision of the world, and all the wonder that would
be.

In the Spring a fuller crimson comes upon the robin's
breast;
In the Spring the wanton lapwing gets himself another
crest;
In the Spring a livelier Iris changes on the burnished dove;
In the Spring a young man's fancy lightly turns to thoughts
of love.

Then her cheek was pale and thinner than should be for
one so young,
And her eyes on all my motions with a mute observance
hung.

And I said, "My cousin Amy, speak, and speak the truth
to me;
Trust me, cousin, all the current of my being sets to thee."

On her pallid cheek and forehead came a colour and a
light,
As I have seen the rosy red flushing in the northern night.

And she turned—her bosom shaken with a sudden storm
of sighs—
All the spirit deeply dawning in the dark of hazel eyes—

Saying, "I have hid my feelings, fearing they should do
me wrong;"
Saying, "Dost thou love me, cousin?" weeping, "I have
loved thee long."

Love took up the glass of Time, and turned it in his glow-
    ing hands;
Every moment, lightly shaken, ran itself in golden sands.

Love took up the harp of Life, and smote on all the chords
    with might;
Smote the chord of Self, that, trembling, passed in music
    out of sight.

Many a morning on the moorland did we hear the copses
    ring,
And her whisper thronged my pulses with the fulness of the
    Spring.

Many an evening by the waters did we watch the stately
    ships,
And our spirits rushed together at the touching of the lips.

O my cousin, shallow-hearted! O my Amy, mine no
    more!
O the dreary, dreary moorland! O the barren, barren
    shore!

Falser than all fancy fathoms, falser than all songs have
    sung—
Puppet to a father's threat, and servile to a shrewish tongue!

Is it well to wish thee happy?—having known me; to
    decline
On a range of lower feelings and a narrower heart than
    mine!

Yet it shall be: thou shalt lower to his level day by day,
What is fine within thee growing coarse to sympathize with
    clay.

As the husband is, the wife is: thou art mated with a clown,
And the grossness of his nature will have weight to drag thee down.

He will hold thee, when his passion shall have spent its novel force,
Something better than his dog, a little dearer than his horse.

What is this? his eyes are heavy—think not they are glazed with wine.
Go to him; it is thy duty—kiss him; take his hand in thine.

It may be my lord is weary, that his brain is overwrought:
Soothe him with thy finer fancies,—touch him with thy lighter thought.

He will answer to the purpose, easy things to understand—
Better thou wert dead before me, though I slew thee with my hand.

Better thou and I were lying, hidden from the heart's disgrace,
Rolled in one another's arms, and silent in a last embrace.

Cursèd be the social wants that sin against the strength of youth!
Cursèd be the social lies that warp us from the living truth!

Cursèd be the sickly forms that err from honest Nature's rule!
Cursèd be the gold that gilds the straitened forehead of the fool!

Well—'tis well that I should bluster!—Hadst thou less unworthy proved,
Would to God—for I had loved thee more than ever wife was loved.

Am I mad, that I should cherish that which bears but bitter fruit?
I will pluck it from my bosom, though my heart be at the root.

Never! though my mortal summers to such length of years should come
As the many-wintered crow that leads the clanging rookery home.

Where is comfort? in division of the records of the mind?
Can I part her from herself, and love her, as I knew her, kind?

I remember one that perished: sweetly did she speak and move;
Such a one do I remember, whom to look at was to love.

Can I think of her as dead, and love her for the love she bore?
No—she never loved me truly; love is love for evermore.

Comfort? comfort scorned of devils! this is truth the poet sings,
That a sorrow's crown of sorrow is remembering happier things.

Drug thy memories, lest thou learn it, lest thy heart be put to proof,
In the dead, unhappy night, and when the rain is on the roof.

Like a dog, he hunts in dreams; and thou art staring at the wall,
Where the dying night-lamp flickers, and the shadows rise and fall.

Then a hand shall pass before thee, pointing to his drunken sleep,
To thy widowed marriage-pillows, to the tears that thou wilt weep.

Thou shalt hear the "Never, never," whispered by the phantom years,
And a song from out the distance in the ringing of thine ears;

And an eye shall vex thee, looking ancient kindness on thy pain.
Turn thee, turn thee on thy pillow; get thee to thy rest again.

Nay, but Nature brings thee solace; for a tender voice will cry;
'Tis a purer life than thine; a lip to drain thy trouble dry.

Baby-lips will laugh me down; my latest rival brings thee rest—
Baby-fingers, waxen touches, press me from the mother's breast.

Oh, the child, too, clothes the father with a dearness not his due;
Half is thine, and half is his—it will be worthy of the two.

Oh, I see thee, old and formal, fitted to thy petty part,
With a little hoard of maxims preaching down a daughter's heart:

"They were dangerous guides, the feelings—she herself was not exempt—
Truly, she herself had suffered."—Perish in thy self-contempt!

Overlive it—lower yet—be happy! wherefore should I care?
I myself must mix with action, lest I wither by despair.

What is that which I should turn to, lighting upon days like these?
Every door is barred with gold, and opens but to golden keys.

Every gate is thronged with suitors; all the markets overflow.
I have but an angry fancy: what is that which I should do?

I had been content to perish, falling on the foeman's ground,
When the ranks are rolled in vapour, and the winds are laid with sound.

But the jingling of the guinea helps the hurt that honour feels,
And the nations do but murmur, snarling at each other's heels.

Can I but relive in sadness? I will turn that earlier page.
Hide me from my deep emotion, O thou wondrous Mother-Age!

Make me feel the wild pulsation that I felt before the strife,
When I heard my days before me, and the tumult of my life;

Yearning for the large excitement that the coming years would yield—
Eager-hearted as a boy when first he leaves his father's field,

And at night along the dusky highway near and nearer drawn,
Sees in heaven the light of London flaring like a dreary dawn;

And his spirit leaps within him to be gone before him then,
Underneath the light he looks at, in among the throngs of men—

Men, my brothers, men the workers, ever reaping something new:
That which they have done but earnest of the things that they shall do;

For I dipped into the future, far as human eye could see—
Saw the vision of the world, and all the wonder that would be—

Saw the heavens fill with commerce, argosies of magic sails,
Pilots of the purple twilight, dropping down with costly bales—

Heard the heavens fill with shouting, and there rained a ghastly dew
From the nations' airy navies grappling in the central blue;

Far along the world-wide whisper of the south-wind rushing warm,
With the standards of the peoples plunging through the thunder-storm;

Till the war-drum throbbed no longer, and the battle-flags were furled
In the Parliament of man, the Federation of the world.

There the common sense of most shall hold a fretful realm in awe,
And the kindly earth shall slumber, lapped in universal law.

So I triumphed, ere my passion, sweeping through me, left me dry—
Left me with the palsied heart, and left me with the jaundiced eye—

Eye, to which all order festers, all things here are out of joint.
Science moves, but slowly, slowly, creeping on from point to point;

Slowly comes a hungry people, as a lion, creeping nigher,
Glares at one that nods and winks behind a slowly-dying fire.

Yet I doubt not through the ages one increasing purpose runs,
And the thoughts of men are widened with the process of the suns.

What is that to him that reaps not harvest of his youthful joys,
Though the deep heart of existence beat forever like a boy's?

Knowledge comes, but wisdom lingers; and I linger on the shore,
And the individual withers, and the world is more and more.

Knowledge comes, but wisdom lingers, and he bears a laden
    breast,
Full of sad experience moving toward the stillness of his
    rest.

Hark! my merry comrades call me, sounding on the bugle-
    horn—
They to whom my foolish passion were a target for their
    scorn;

Shall it not be scorn to me to harp on such a mouldered
    string?
I am shamed through all my nature to have loved so slight
    a thing.

Weakness to be wroth with weakness! woman's pleasure,
    woman's pain—
Nature made them blinder motions bounded in a shallower
    brain;

Woman is the lesser man; and all thy passions, matched
    with mine,
Are as moonlight unto sunlight, and as water unto wine—

Here, at least, where nature sickens, nothing. Ah, for
    some retreat
Deep in yonder shining Orient, where my life began to
    beat!

Where in wild Mahratta-battle fell my father, evil-starred;
I was left a trampled orphan, and a selfish uncle's ward.

Or to burst all links of habit—there to wander far away,
On from island unto island at the gateways of the day—

Larger constellations burning, mellow moons and happy skies,
Breadths of tropic shade and palms in cluster, knots of Paradise.

Never comes the trader, never floats a European flag—
Slides the bird o'er lustrous woodland, droops the trailer from the crag—

Droops the heavy-blossomed bower, hangs the heavy-fruited tree—
Summer isles of Eden lying in dark-purple spheres of sea.

There, methinks, would be enjoyment more than in this march of mind—
In the steamship, in the railway, in the thoughts that shake mankind.

There the passions, cramped no longer, shall have scope and breathing-space;
I will take some savage woman, she shall rear my dusky race.

Iron-jointed, supple-sinewed, they shall dive, and they shall run,
Catch the wild goat by the hair, and hurl their lances in the sun,

Whistle back the parrot's call, and leap the rainbows of the brooks,
Not with blinded eyesight poring over miserable books—

Fool, again the dream, the fancy! but I know my words are wild,
But I count the gray barbarian lower than the Christian child.

I to herd with narrow foreheads, vacant of our glorious gains,
Like a beast with lower pleasures, like a beast with lower pains!

Mated with a squalid savage—what to me were sun or clime?
I the heir of all the ages, in the foremost files of time—

I that rather held it better men should perish one by one,
Than that earth should stand at gaze like Joshua's moon in Ajalon!

Not in vain the distance beacons. Forward, forward let us range;
Let the great world spin forever down the ringing grooves of change.

Through the shadow of the globe we sweep into the younger day:
Better fifty years of Europe than a cycle of Cathay.

Mother-age (for mine I knew not), help me as when life begun—
Rift the hills and roll the waters, flash the lightnings, weigh the sun—

O, I see the crescent promise of my spirit hath not set;
Ancient founts of inspiration well through all my fancy yet.

Howsoever these things be, a long farewell to Locksley Hall!
Now for me the woods may wither, now for me the rooftree fall.

Comes a vapour from the margin, blackening over heath
    and holt,
Cramming all the blast before it, in its breast a thunderbolt.

Let it fall on Locksley Hall, with rain or hail, or fire or
    snow;
For the mighty wind arises, roaring seaward, and I go.

---

### THE MAY QUEEN.

#### I.

YOU must wake and call me early, call me early,
    mother dear;
To-morrow 'll be the happiest time of all the glad New
    year—
Of all the glad New-year, mother, the maddest, merriest
    day;
For I'm to be Queen o' the May, mother, I'm to be Queen
    o' the May.

#### II.

There's many a black, black eye, they say, but none so
    bright as mine;
There's Margaret and Mary, there's Kate and Caroline;
But none so fair as little Alice in all the land, they say:
So I'm to be Queen o' the May, mother, I'm to be Queen
    o' the May.

#### III.

I sleep so sound all night, mother, that I shall never wake
If you do not call me loud when the day begins to break;

But I must gather knots of flowers and buds, and garlands gay;
For I'm to be Queen o' the May, mother, I'm to be Queen o' the May.

### IV.

As I came up the valley, whom think ye should I see,
But Robin leaning on the bridge beneath the hazel-tree?
He thought of that sharp look, mother, I gave him yester day,—
But I'm to be Queen o' the May, mother, I'm to be Queen o' the May.

### V.

He thought I was a ghost, mother, for I was all in white;
And I ran by him without speaking, like a flash of light.
They call me cruel-hearted, but I care not what they say,
For I'm to be Queen o' the May, mother, I'm to be Queen o' the May.

### VI.

They say he's dying all for love—but that can never be;
They say his heart is breaking, mother—what is that to me?
There's many a bolder lad 'll woo me any summer day;
And I'm to be Queen o' the May, mother, I'm to be Queen o' the May.

### VII.

Little Effie shall go with me to-morrow to the green,
And you'll be there, too, mother, to see me made the Queen;
For the shepherd lads on every side 'll come from far away,

And I'm to be Queen o' the May, mother, I'm to be Queen o' the May.

### VIII.

The honeysuckle round the porch has woven its wavy bowers,
And by the meadow-trenches blow the faint sweet cuckoo-flowers;
And the wild marsh-marigold shines like fire in swamps and hollows gray,
And I'm to be Queen o' the May, mother, I'm to be Queen o' the May.

### IX.

The night-winds come and go, mother, upon the meadow-grass,
And the happy stars above them seem to brighten as they pass;
There will not be a drop of rain the whole of the livelong day,
And I'm to be Queen o' the May, mother, I'm to be Queen o' the May.

### X.

All the valley, mother, 'll be fresh and green and still,
And the cowslip and the crowfoot are over all the hill,
And the rivulet in the flowery dale 'll merrily glance and play,
For I'm to be Queen o' the May, mother, I'm to be Queen o' the May.

### XI.

So you must wake and call me early, call me early, mother dear,

To-morrow 'll be the happiest time of all the glad New-
    year:
To-morrow 'll be of all the year the maddest, merriest
    day,
For I'm to be Queen o' the May, mother, I'm to be Queen
    o' the May.

## NEW YEAR'S EVE.

### I.

If you're waking, call me early, call me early, mother
    dear,
For I would see the sun rise upon the glad New-year.
It is the last New-year that I shall ever see—
Then you may lay me low i' the mould, and think no more
    of me.

### II.

To-night I saw the sun set—he set and left behind
The good old year, the dear old time, and all my peace of
    mind;
And the New-year's coming up, mother; but I shall never
    see
The blossom on the blackthorn, the leaf upon the tree.

### III.

Last May we made a crown of flowers; we had a merry
    day—
Beneath the hawthorn on the green they made me Queen
    of May;
And we danced about the May-pole and in the hazel
    copse,
Till Charles's Wain came out above the tall white chim-
    ney-tops.

#### IV.

There's not a flower on all the hills—the frost is on the pane;
I only wish to live till the snowdrops come again.
I wish the snow would melt and the sun come out on high—
I long to see a flower so before the day I die.

#### V.

The building rook 'll caw from the windy tall elm-tree,
And the tufted plover pipe along the fallow lea,
And the swallow 'll come back again with summer o'er the wave,
But I shall lie alone, mother, within the mouldering grave.

#### VI.

Upon the chancel-casement, and upon that grave of mine,
In the early, early morning the summer sun 'll shine,
Before the red cock crows from the farm upon the hill—
When you are warm asleep, mother, and all the world is still.

#### VII.

When the flowers come again, mother, beneath the waning light
You'll never see me more in the long gray fields at night;
When from the dry dark wold the summer airs blow cool
On the oat-grass and the sword-grass, and the bulrush in the pool.

#### VIII.

You'll bury me, my mother, just beneath the hawthorn shade,
And you'll come sometimes and see me where I am lowly laid.

I shall not forget you, mother; I shall hear you when you pass,
With your feet above my head in the long and pleasant grass.

### IX.

I've been wild and wayward, but you'll forgive me now;
You'll kiss me, my own mother, upon my cheek and brow;
Nay, nay, you must not weep, nor let your grief be wild;
You should not fret for me, mother—you have another child.

### X.

If I can, I'll come again, mother, from out my resting-place;
Though you'll not see me, mother, I shall look upon your face;
Though I cannot speak a word, I shall hearken what you say,
And be often, often with you when you think I'm far away.

### XI.

Good-night! good-night! when I have said good-night for evermore,
And you see me carried out from the threshold of the door,
Don't let Effie come to see me till my grave be growing green—
She'll be a better child to you than ever I have been.

### XII.

She'll find my garden-tools upon the granary floor.
Let her take 'em—they are hers; I shall never garden more.

But tell her, when I'm gone, to train the rose-bush that I set
About the parlour window, and the box of mignonnette.

### XIII.

Good-night, sweet mother! Call me before the day is born.
All night I lie awake, but I fall asleep at morn;
But I would see the sun rise upon the glad New-year—
So, if you're waking, call me, call me early, mother dear.

## CONCLUSION.

### I.

I THOUGHT to pass away before, and yet alive I am;
And in the fields all round I hear the bleating of the lamb.
How sadly, I remember, rose the morning of the year!
To die before the snowdrop came, and now the violet's here.

### II.

O sweet is the new violet, that comes beneath the skies;
And sweeter is the young lamb's voice to me that cannot rise;
And sweet is all the land about, and all the flowers that blow;
And sweeter far is death than life, to me that long to go.

### III.

It seemed so hard at first, mother, to leave the blessed sun,
And now it seems as hard to stay; and yet, His will be done!
But still I think it can't be long before I find release;
And that good man, the clergyman, has told me words of peace.

### IV.

O blessings on his kindly voice, and on his silver hair!
And blessings on his whole life long, until he meet me there!
O blessings on his kindly heart and on his silver head!
A thousand times I blest him, as he knelt beside my bed.

### V.

He showed me all the mercy, for he taught me all the sin;
Now, though my lamp was lighted late, there's One will let me in.
Nor would I now be well, mother, again, if that could be;
For my desire is but to pass to Him that died for me.

### VI.

I did not hear the dog howl, mother, or the death-watch beat—
There came a sweeter token when the night and morning meet;
But sit beside my bed, mother, and put your hand in mine,
And Effie on the other side, and I will tell the sign.

### VII.

All in the wild March-morning I heard the angels call—
It was when the moon was setting, and the dark was over all;
The trees began to whisper, and the wind began to roll,
And in the wild March-morning I heard them call my soul.

### VIII.

For lying broad awake, I thought of you and Effie dear;
I saw you sitting in the house, and I no longer here;
With all my strength I prayed for both—and so I felt resigned,
And up the valley came a swell of music on the wind.

### IX.

I thought that it was fancy, and I listened in my bed;
And then did something speak to me—I know not what was said;
For great delight and shuddering took hold of all my mind,
And up the valley came again the music on the wind.

### X.

But you were sleeping; and I said, "It's not for them—it's mine;"
And if it comes three times, I thought, I take it for a sign.
And once again it came, and close beside the window-bars—
Then seemed to go right up to Heaven and die among the stars.

### XI.

So now I think my time is near; I trust it is. I know
The blessed music went that way my soul will have to go.
And for myself, indeed, I care not if I go to-day;
But Effie, you must comfort her when I am past away.

### XII.

And say to Robin a kind word, and tell him not to fret;
There's many worthier than I would make him happy yet.
If I had lived—I cannot tell—I might have been his wife;
But all these things have ceased to be, with my desire of life.

### XIII.

O look! the sun begins to rise! the heavens are in a glow;
He shines upon a hundred fields, and all of them I know.
And there I move no longer now, and there his light may shine—
Wild flowers in the valley for other hands than mine.

### XIV.

O sweet and strange it seems to me, that ere this day is done,
The voice that now is speaking may be beyond the sun—
Forever and forever with those just souls and true—
And what is life, that we should moan? why make we
    such ado?

### XV.

Forever and forever, all in a blessed home,
And there to wait a little while till you and Effie come—
To lie within the light of God, as I lie upon your breast—
And the wicked cease from troubling, and the weary are at
    rest.

---

### LADY CLARA VERE DE VERE.

Lady Clara Vere de Vere,
  Of me you shall not win renown:
You thought to break a country heart
  For pastime, ere you went to town.
At me you smiled, but unbeguiled
  I saw the snare, and I retired:
The daughter of a hundred Earls,
  You are not one to be desired.

Lady Clara Vere de Vere,
  I know you proud to bear your name,
Your pride is yet no mate for mine,
  Too proud to care from whence I came.
Nor would I break for your sweet sake
  A heart that dotes on truer charms.

A simple maiden in her flower
    Is worth a hundred coats-of-arms.

Lady Clara Vere de Vere,
    Some meeker pupil you must find,
For were you queen of all that is,
    I could not stoop to such a mind.
You sought to prove how I could love,
    And my disdain is my reply.
The lion on your old stone gates
    Is not more cold to you than I.

Lady Clara Vere de Vere,
    You put strange memories in my head.
Not thrice your branching limes have blown
    Since I beheld young Laurence dead.
Oh your sweet eyes, your low replies:
    A great enchantress you may be;
But there was that across his throat
    Which you had hardly cared to see.

Lady Clara Vere de Vere,
    When thus he met his mother's view,
She had the passions of her kind,
    She spake some certain truths of you.
Indeed I heard one bitter word
    That scarce is fit for you to hear;
Her manners had not that repose
    Which stamps the caste of Vere de Vere.

Lady Clara Vere de Vere,
    There stands a spectre in your hall:

The guilt of blood is at your door:
    You changed a wholesome heart to gall.
You held your course without remorse,
    To make him trust his modest worth,
And, last, you fixed a vacant stare,
    And slew him with your noble birth.

Trust me, Clara Vere de Vere,
    From yon blue heavens above us bent,
The grand old gardener and his wife
    Smile at the claims of long descent.
Howe'er it be, it seems to me,
    'Tis only noble to be good.
Kind hearts are more than coronets,
    And simple faith than Norman blood.

I know you, Clara Vere de Vere:
    You pine among your halls and towers:
The languid light of your proud eyes
    Is wearied of the rolling hours.
In glowing health, with boundless wealth,
    But sickening of a vague disease,
You know so ill to deal with time,
    You needs must play such pranks as these.

Clara, Clara Vere de Vere,
    If Time be heavy on your hands,
Are there no beggars at your gate,
    Nor any poor about your lands?
Oh! teach the orphan-boy to read,
    Or teach the orphan-girl to sew,
Pray heaven for a human heart,
    And let the foolish yeoman go.

### EXTRACTS FROM "IN MEMORIAM."

I ENVY not, in any moods,
   The captive void of noble rage,
   The linnet born within the cage,
That never knew the summer woods.

I envy not the beast that takes
   His license in the field of time,
   Unfettered by the sense of crime,
To whom a conscience never wakes;

Nor, what may count itself as blest,
   The heart that never plighted troth,
   But stagnates in the weeds of sloth—
Nor any want-begotten rest.

I hold it true, whate'er befall—
   I feel it, when I sorrow most—
   'Tis better to have loved and lost
Than never to have loved at all.

---

WITH trembling fingers did we weave
   The holly round the Christmas hearth;
   A rainy cloud possessed the earth
And sadly fell our Christmas eve.

At our old pastimes in the hall
   We gambolled, making vain pretence
   Of gladness, with an awful sense
Of one mute Shadow watching all.

We paused; the winds were in the beech—
   We heard them sweep the winter land;
   And in a circle hand in hand
Sat silent, looking each at each.

Then echo-like our voices rang;
   We sang, though every eye was dim—
   A merry song we sang with him
Last year: impetuously we sang;

We ceased. A gentler feeling crept
   Upon us; surely rest is meet;
   "They rest," we said; "their sleep is sweet."
And silence followed, and we wept.

Our voices took a higher range;
   Once more we sang: "They do not die,
   Nor lose their mortal sympathy,
Nor change to us, although they change:

"Rapt from the fickle and the frail,
   With gathered power, yet the same,
   Pierces the keen seraphic flame
From orb to orb, from veil to veil.

"Rise, happy morn! rise, holy morn!
   Draw forth the cheerful day from night!
   O Father! touch the east, and light
The light that shone when Hope was born!"

---

Dost thou look back on what hath been,
   As some divinely gifted man,
   Whose life in low estate began,
And on a simple village green?

Who breaks his birth's invidious bar,
   And grasps the skirts of happy chance,
   And breasts the blows of circumstance,
And grapples with his evil star;

Who makes by force his merit known,
   And lives to clutch the golden keys—
   To mould a mighty state's decrees,
And shape the whisper of the throne;

And moving up from high to higher,
   Becomes on Fortune's crowning slope
   The pillar of a people's hope,
The centre of a world's desire;

Yet feels, as in a pensive dream,
   When all his active powers are still,
   A distant dearness in the hill,
A secret sweetness in the stream,

The limit of his narrower fate,
   While yet beside its vocal springs
   He played at counsellors and kings,
With one that was his earliest mate;

Who ploughs with pain his native lea,
   And reaps the labor of his hands,
   Or in the furrow musing stands:
"Does my old friend remember me?"

---

WITCH-ELMS, that counterchange the floor
   Of this flat lawn with dusk and bright;
   And thou, with all thy breadth and height
Of foliage, towering sycamore;

How often, hither wandering down,
  My Arthur found your shadows fair,
  And shook to all the liberal air
The dust and din and steam of town!

He brought an eye for all he saw;
  He mixed in all our simple sports;
  They pleased him, fresh from brawling courts
And dusky purlieus of the law.

O joy to him, in this retreat,
  Immantled in ambrosial dark,
  To drink the cooler air, and mark
The landscape winking through the heat.

O sound to rout the brood of cares,
  The sweep of scythe in morning dew,
  The gust that round the garden flew,
And tumbled half the mellowing pears!

O bliss, when all in circle drawn
  About him, heart and ear were fed,
  To hear him, as he lay and read
The Tuscan poets on the lawn;

Or in the all-golden afternoon
  A guest, or happy sister, sung,
  Or here she brought the harp, and flung
A ballad to the brightening moon!

Nor less it pleased, in livelier moods,
  Beyond the bounding hill to stray,
  And break the livelong summer day
With banquet in the distant woods;

Whereat we glanced from theme to theme,
   Discussed the books to love or hate,
   Or touched the changes of the state,
Or threaded some Socratic dream.

But if I praised the busy town,
   He loved to rail against it still,
   For, "ground in yonder social mill,
We rub each other's angles down,

"And merge," he said, "in form and gloss
   The picturesque of man and man."
   We talked; the stream beneath us ran,
The wine-flask lying couched in moss,

Or cooled within the glooming wave;
   And last, returning from afar,
   Before the crimson-circled star
Had fallen into her father's grave,

And brushing ankle-deep in flowers,
   We heard behind the woodbine veil
   The milk that bubbled in the pail,
And buzzings of the honeyed hours.

---

Thy converse drew us with delight,
   The men of rathe and riper years;
   The feeble soul, a haunt of fears,
Forgot his weakness in thy sight.

On thee the loyal-hearted hung,
   The proud was half disarmed of pride;
   Nor cared the serpent at thy side
To flicker with his treble tongue.

The stern were mild when thou wert by;
   The flippant put himself to school
   And heard thee; and the brazen fool
Was softened, and he knew not why;

While I, thy dearest, sat apart,
   And felt thy triumph was as mine;
   And loved them more, that they were thine,
The graceful tact, the Christian art;

Not mine the sweetness or the skill,
   But mine the love that will not tire,
   And, born of love, the vague desire
That spurs an imitative will.

———

Dear friend, far off, my lost desire,
   So far, so near, in woe and weal;
   O, loved the most when most I feel
There is a lower and a higher;

Known and unknown, human, divine!
   Sweet human hand and lips and eye,
   Dear heavenly friend that canst not die,
Mine, mine, forever, ever mine!

Strange friend, past, present, and to be,
   Loved deeplier, darklier understood;
   Behold I dream a dream of good
And mingle all the world with thee.

———

Thy voice is on the rolling air;
   I hear thee where the waters run;
   Thou standest in the rising sun,
And in the setting thou art fair.

What art thou, then? I cannot guess;
　But though I seem in star and flower
　To feel thee, some diffusive power,
I do not therefore love thee less:

My love involves the love before;
　My love is vaster passion now;
　Though mixed with God and Nature thou.
I seem to love thee more and more.

Far off thou art, but ever nigh;
　I have thee still, and I rejoice.
　I prosper, circled with thy voice;
I shall not lose thee, though I die.

---

### THE BUGLE SONG.

THE splendour falls on castle walls
　　And snowy summits old in story;
The long light shakes across the lakes,
　　And the wild cataract leaps in glory.
Blow, bugle, blow! set the wild echoes flying:
Blow, bugle; answer, echoes—dying, dying, dying!

　O hark, O hear! how thin and clear,
　　And thinner, clearer, further going!
　O sweet and far, from cliff and scar,
　　The horns of Elfland faintly blowing!
Blow! let us hear the purple glens replying:
Blow, bugle; answer, echoes—dying, dying, dying!

O love, they die in yon rich sky;
  They faint on hill or field or river:
Our echoes roll from soul to soul,
  And grow forever and forever.
Blow, bugle, blow! set the wild echoes flying,
And answer, echoes, answer—dying, dying, dying!

---

## COME INTO THE GARDEN, MAUD.

### I.

COME into the garden, Maud—
  For the black bat, night, has flown!
Come into the garden, Maud,
  I am here at the gate alone;
And the woodbine spices are wafted abroad,
  And the musk of the roses blown.

### II.

For a breeze of morning moves,
  And the planet of Love is on high,
Beginning to faint in the light that she loves
  On a bed of daffodil sky,
To faint in the light of the sun she loves,
  To faint in his light, and to die.

### III.

All night have the roses heard
  The flute, violin, bassoon;
All night has the casement jessamine stirred
  To the dancers dancing in tune—
Till a silence fell with the waking bird,
  And a hush with the setting moon.

#### IV.

I said to the lily, "There is but one
   With whom she has heart to be gay.
When will the dancers leave her alone?
   She is weary of dance and play."
Now half to the setting moon are gone,
   And half to the rising day;
Low on the sand and loud on the stone
   The last wheel echoes away.

#### V.

I said to the rose, "The brief night goes
   In babble and revel and wine.
O young lord-lover, what sighs are those,
   For one that will never be thine!
But mine, but mine," so I sware to the rose,
   "For ever and ever, mine!"

#### VI.

And the soul of the rose went into my blood,
   As the music clashed in the hall;
And long by the garden lake I stood,
   For I heard your rivulet fall
From the lake to the meadow and on to the wood—
   Our wood, that is dearer than all—

#### VII.

From the meadow your walks have left so sweet,
   That wherever a March-wind sighs,
He sets the jewel-print of your feet,
   In violets blue as your eyes,
To the woody hollows in which we meet,
   And the valleys of Paradise.

### VIII.

The slender acacia would not shake
  One long milk-bloom on the tree;
The white lake-blossom fell into the lake,
  As the pimpernel dozed on the lea;
But the rose was awake all night for your sake,
  Knowing your promise to me;
The lilies and roses were all awake,
  They sighed for the dawn and thee.

### IX.

Queen rose of the rosebud garden of girls,
  Come hither, the dances are done,
In gloss of satin and glimmer of pearls,
  Queen lily and rose in one;
Shine out, little head, sunning over with curls,
  To the flowers, and be their sun.

### X.

There has fallen a splendid tear
  From the passion-flower at the gate.
She is coming, my dove, my dear!
  She is coming, my life, my fate!
The red rose cries, "She is near, she is near;"
  And the white rose weeps, "She is late;"
The larkspur listens, "I hear, I hear;"
  And the lily whispers, "I wait."

### XI.

She is coming, my own, my sweet!
  Were it ever so airy a tread,
My heart would hear her and beat,
  Were it earth in an earthy bed;

My dust would hear her and beat,
    Had I lain for a century dead—
Would start and tremble under her feet,
    And blossom in purple and red.

---

## THE CHARGE OF THE LIGHT BRIGADE, AT BALAKLAVA.

### I.

HALF a league, half a league,
    Half a league onward,
All in the valley of Death,
    Rode the Six Hundred.
"Charge!" was the captain's cry;
Theirs not to reason why,
Theirs not to make reply,
Theirs but to do and die;
Into the valley of Death
    Rode the Six Hundred.

### II.

Cannon to right of them,
Cannon to left of them,
Cannon in front of them,
    Volleyed and thundered.
Stormed at with shot and shell,
Boldly they rode and well;
Into the jaws of Death,
Into the mouth of hell,
    Rode the Six Hundred.

### III.

Flashed all their sabres bare,
Flashed all at once in air,
Sabring the gunners there,
Charging an army, while
　All the world wondered.
Plunged in the battery smoke,
Fiercely the line they broke;
Strong was the sabre-stroke,
Making an army reel,
　Shaken and sundered;
Then they rode back, but not—
　Not the Six Hundred.

### IV.

Cannon to right of them,
Cannon to left of them,
Cannon behind them,
　Volleyed and thundered.
Stormed at with shot and shell,
They that had struck so well
Rode through the jaws of Death
Half a league back again—
Up from the mouth of hell
All that was left of them—
　Left of Six Hundred.

### V.

Honour the brave and bold!
Long shall the tale be told,
Yes, when our babes are old—
How they rode onward.

## IDYLS OF THE KING.

### VIVIEN.

A STORM was coming, but the winds were still,
And in the wild woods of Broceliande,
Before an oak so hollow huge and old
It looked a tower of ruined masonwork,
At Merlin's feet the wily Vivien lay.

The wily Vivien stole from Arthur's court:
She hated all the knights, and heard in thought
Their lavish comment when her name was named.
For once, when Arthur, walking all alone,
Vexed at a rumour rife about the Queen,
Had met her, Vivien, being greeted fair,
Would fain have wrought upon his cloudy mood
With reverent eyes mock-loyal, shaken voice,
And fluttered adoration, and at last
With dark sweet hints of some who prized him more
Than who should prize him most; at which the King
Had gazed upon her blankly and gone by:
But one had watched, and had not held his peace:
It made the laughter of an afternoon
That Vivien should attempt the blameless King.
And after that, she set herself to gain
Him, the most famous man of all those times,
Merlin, who knew the range of all their arts,
Had built the King his havens, ships, and halls,
Was also Bard, and knew the starry heavens;
The people called him Wizard; whom at first

She played about with slight and sprightly talk,
And vivid smiles, and faintly-venomed points
Of slander, glancing here and grazing there;
And yielding to his kindlier moods, the Seer
Would watch her at her petulance, and play,
Ev'n when they seemed unlovable, and laugh
As those that watch a kitten; thus he grew
Tolerant of what he half disdained, and she,
Perceiving that she was but half disdained,
Began to break her sports with graver fits,
Turn red or pale, would often when they met
Sigh fully, or all-silent gaze upon him
With such a fixed devotion, that the old man,
Though doubtful, felt the flattery, and at times
Would flatter his own wish in age for love,
And half believe her true: for thus at times
He wavered; but that other clung to him,
Fixed in her will, and so the seasons went.
Then fell upon him a great melancholy;
And leaving Arthur's court he gained the beach;
There found a little boat, and stepped into it;
And Vivien followed, but he marked her not.
She took the helm and he the sail; the boat
Drave with a sudden wind across the deeps,
And touching Breton sands, they disembarked.
And then she followed Merlin all the way,
Ev'n to the wild woods of Broceliande.
For Merlin once had told her of a charm,
The which if any wrought on any one
With woven paces and with waving arms,
The man so wrought on ever seemed to lie
Closed in the four walls of a hollow tower,

From which was no escape for evermore;
And none could find that man for evermore,
Nor could he see but him who wrought the charm
Coming and going, and he lay as dead
And lost to life and use and name and fame.
And Vivien ever sought to work the charm
Upon the great Enchanter of the Time,
As fancying that her glory would be great
According to his greatness whom she quenched.

  \*  \*  \*  \*  \*

She mused a little, and then clapped her hands
Together with a wailing shriek, and said:
"Stabbed through the heart's affections to the heart!
Seethed like the kid in its own mother's milk!
Killed with a word worse than a life of blows!
I thought that he was gentle, being great:
O God, that I had loved a smaller man!
I should have found in him a greater heart.
Oh, I, that flattering my true passion, saw
The knights, the court, the king, dark in your light,
Who loved to make men darker than they are,
Because of that high pleasure which I had
To seat you sole upon my pedestal
Of worship—I am answered, and henceforth
The course of life that seemed so flowery to me
With you for guide and master, only you,
Becomes the sea-cliff pathway broken short,
And ending in a ruin—nothing left,
But into some low cave to crawl, and there,
If the wolf spare me, weep my life away,
Killed with unutterable unkindliness."

She paused, she turned away, she hung her head,
The snake of gold slid from her hair, the braid
Slipped and uncoiled itself, she wept afresh,
And the dark wood grew darker toward the storm
In silence, while his anger slowly died
Within him, till he let his wisdom go
For ease of heart, and half believed her true:
Called her to shelter in the hollow oak,
"Come from the storm," and having no reply,
Gazed at the heaving shoulder, and the face
Hand-hidden, as for utmost grief or shame;
Then thrice essayed, by tenderest-touching terms
To sleek her ruffled peace of mind, in vain.
At last she let herself be conquered by him,
And as the cageling newly flown returns,
The seeming-injured simple-hearted thing
Came to her old perch back, and settled there.
There while she sat, half falling from his knees,
Half nestled at his heart, and since he saw
The slow tear creep from her closed eyelid yet,
About her, more in kindness than in love,
The gentle wizard cast a shielding arm.
But she dislinked herself at once and rose,
Her arms upon her breast across, and stood
A virtuous gentlewoman deeply wronged,
Upright and flushed before him: then she said:

"There must be now no passages of love
Betwixt us twain henceforward evermore.
Since, if I be what I am grossly called,
What should be granted which your own gross heart
Would reckon worth the taking? I will go.

In truth, but one thing now—better have died
Thrice than have asked it once—could make me stay—
That proof of trust—so often asked in vain!
How justly, after that vile term of yours,
I find with grief! I might believe you then,
Who knows? once more. Oh, what was once to me
Mere matter of the fancy, now has grown
The vast necessity of heart and life.
Farewell: think kindly of me, for I fear
My fate or fault, omitting gayer youth
For one so old, must be to love you still.
But ere I leave you let me swear once more
That if I schemed against your peace in this,
May yon just Heaven that darkens o'er me, send
One flash, that, missing all things else, may make
My scheming brain a cinder, if I lie."

Scarce had she ceased, when out of heaven a bolt
(For now the storm was close above them) struck,
Furrowing a giant oak, and javelining
With darted spikes and splinters of the wood
The dark earth round. He raised his eyes and saw
The tree that shone white-listed through the gloom.
But Vivien, fearing Heaven had heard her oath,
And dazzled by the livid-flickering fork,
And deaféned with the stammering cracks and claps
That followed, flying back and crying out,
"O Merlin, though you do not love me, save,
Yet save me!" clung to him and hugged him close;
And called him dear protector in her fright,
Nor yet forgot her practice in her fright,
But wrought upon his mood and hugged him close.

The pale blood of the wizard at her touch
Took gayer colours, like an opal warmed.
She blamed herself for telling hearsay tales:
She shook from fear, and for her fault she wept
Of petulancy; she called him lord and liege,
Her seer, her bard, her silver star of eve,
Her God, her Merlin, the one passionate love
Of her whole life; and ever overhead
Bellowed the tempest, and the rotten branch
Snapped in the rushing of the river-rain
Above them; and in change of glare and gloom
Her eyes and neck glittering went and came;
Till now the storm, its burst of passion spent,
Moaning and calling out of other lands,
Had left the ravaged woodland yet once more
To peace; and what should not have been had been—
For Merlin, overtalked and overworn,
Had yielded, told her all the charm, and slept.

 Then, in one moment, she put forth the charm
Of woven paces and of waving hands,
And in the hollow oak he lay as dead,
And lost to life and use and name and fame.

 Then crying, "I have made his glory mine,"
And shrieking out, "O fool!" the harlot leaped
Adown the forest, and the thicket closed
Behind her, and the forest echoed, "Fool!"

## Mary Howitt.

### CORNFIELDS.

WHEN on the breath of autumn breeze,
    From pastures dry and brown,
Goes floating like an idle thought
    The fair white thistle-down,
Oh then what joy to walk at will
Upon the golden harvest hill!

What joy in dreamy ease to lie
    Amid a field new shorn,
And see all round on sun-lit slopes
    The piled-up stacks of corn;
And send the fancy wandering o'er
All pleasant harvest-fields of yore!

I feel the day—I see the field,
    The quivering of the leaves,
And good old Jacob and his house
    Binding the yellow sheaves;
And at this very hour I seem
To be with Joseph in his dream.

I see the fields of Bethlehem,
    And reapers many a one,
Bending under their sickles' stroke—
    And Boaz looking on;
And Ruth, the Moabite, so fair,
Among the gleaners stooping there.

Again I see a little child,
   His mother's sole delight,—
God's living gift unto
   The kind, good Shunammite;
To mortal pangs I see him yield,
And the lad bear him from the field

The sun-bathed quiet of the hills,
   The fields of Galilee,
That eighteen hundred years ago
   Were full of corn, I see;
And the dear Saviour takes his way
'Mid ripe ears on the Sabbath day.

O golden fields of bending corn,
   How beautiful they seem!
The reaper-folk, the piled-up sheaves,
   To me are like a dream.
The sunshine and the very air
Seem of old time, and take me there.

---

# William Motherwell.

### JEANIE MORRISON.

I'VE wandered east, I've wandered west,
   Through mony a weary way;
But never, never can forget
   The luve o' life's young day!
The fire that's blawn on Beltane e'en
   May weel be black gin Yule;
But blacker fa' awaits the heart
   Where first fond luve grows cule.

O dear, dear Jeanie Morrison,
  The thochts o' bygane years
Still fling their shadows ower my path,
  And blind my een wi' tears:
They blind my een wi' saut, saut tears,
  And sair and sick I pine,
As memory idly summons up
  The blithe blinks o' langsyne.

'Twas then we luvit ilk ither weel,
  'Twas then we twa did part;
Sweet time—sad time! twa bairns at scule,
  Twa bairns, and but ae heart!
'Twas then we sat on ae laigh bink,
  To leir ilk ither lear;
And tones and looks and smiles were shed,
  Remembered evermair.

I wonder, Jeanie, aften yet,
  When sitting on that bink,
Cheek touchin' cheek, loof locked in loof,
  What our wee heads could think.
When baith bent doun ower ae braid page,
  Wi' ae buik on our knee,
Thy lips were on thy lesson, but
  My lesson was in thee.

O, mind ye how we hung our heads,
  How cheeks brent red wi' shame,
Whene'er the scule-weans, laughin', said
  We cleeked thegither hame?
And mind ye o' the Saturdays
  (The scule then skail't at noon),

When we ran off to speel the braes,—
　　The broomy braes o' June?

My head rins round and round about—
　　My heart flows like a sea,
As ane by ane the thochts rush back
　　O' scule-time and o' thee.
O mornin' life! O mornin' luve!
　　O lichtsome days and lang,
When hinnied hopes around our hearts
　　Like simmer blossoms sprang!

O, mind ye, luve, how aft we left
　　The deavin' dinsome toun,
To wander by the green burnside,
　　And hear its waters croon?
The simmer leaves hung ower our heads,
　　The flowers burst round our feet,
And in the gloamin o' the wood
　　The throssil whusslit sweet;—

The throssil whusslit in the wood,
　　The burn sang to the trees—
And we, wi' Nature's heart in tune,
　　Concerted harmonies;
And on the knowe abune the burn
　　For hours thegither sat
In the silentness o' joy, till baith
　　Wi' very gladness grat.

Ay, ay, dear Jeanie Morrison,
　　Tears trinkled doun your cheek
Like dew-beads on a rose, yet nane
　　Had ony power to speak!

That was a time, a blessed time,
   When hearts were fresh and young,
When freely gushed all feelings forth,
   Unsyllabled—unsung!

I marvel, Jeanie Morrison,
   Gin I hae been to thee
As closely twined wi' earliest thochts
   As ye hae been to me?
O, tell me gin their music fills
   Thine ear as it does mine!
O, say gin e'er your heart grows grit
   Wi' dreamings o' langsyne?

I've wandered east, I've wandered west,
   I've borne a weary lot;
But in my wanderings, far or near,
   Ye never were forgot.
The fount that first burst frae this heart
   Still travels on its way;
And channels deeper, as it rins,
   The luve o' life's young day.

O dear, dear Jeanie Morrison,
   Since we were sindered young
I've never seen your face, nor heard
   The music o' your tongue;
But I could hug all wretchedness,
   And happy could I die,
Did I but ken your heart still dreamed
   O' bygane days and me!

## MY HEID IS LIKE TO REND, WILLIE.

MY heid is like to rend, Willie—
   My heart is like to break;
I'm wearin' aff my feet, Willie—
   I'm dyin' for your sake!
O, lay your cheek to mine, Willie,
   Your hand on my briest-bane,—
O, say ye'll think on me, Willie,
   When I am deid and gane!

It's vain to comfort me, Willie—
   Sair grief maun ha'e its will;
But let me rest upon your briest
   To sab and greet my fill.
Let me sit on your knee, Willie—
   Let me shed by your hair,
And look into the face, Willie,
   I never sall see mair!

I'm sittin' on your knee, Willie,
   For the last time in my life,—
A puir heart-broken thing, Willie,
   A mither, yet nae wife.
Ay, press your hand upon my heart,
   And press it mair and mair,—
Or it will burst the silken twine,
   Sae strang is its despair.

O, wae's me for the hour, Willie,
   When we thegither met,—
O, wae's me for the time, Willie,
   That our first tryst was set!

O, wae's me for the loanin' green
    Where we were wont to gae,—
And wae's me for the destinie
    That gart me luve thee sae!

O, dinna mind my words, Willie—
    I downa seek to blame;
But O, it's hard to live, Willie,
    And dree a warld's shame!
Het tears are hailin' ower your cheek,
    And hailin' ower your chin;
Why weep ye sae for worthlessness,
    For sorrow, and for sin?

I'm weary o' this warld, Willie,
    And sick wi' a' I see;
I canna live as I ha'e lived,
    Or be as I should be.
But fauld unto your heart, Willie,
    The heart that still is thine,—
And kiss ance mair the white, white cheek
    Ye said was red langsyne.

A stoun' gaes through my heid, Willie—
    A sair stoun' through my heart;
O, haud me up and let me kiss
    Thy brow ere we twa pairt.
Anither, and anither yet!—
    How fast my life-strings break!—
Fareweel! fareweel! through yon kirkyard
    Step lichtly for my sake!

The lav'rock in the lift, Willie,
    That lilts far ower our heid,

Will sing the morn as merrilie
 Abune the clay-cauld deid;
And this green turf we're sittin' on,
 Wi' dew-draps shimmerin' sheen,
Will hap the heart that luvit thee
 As warld has seldom seen.

But O, remember me, Willie,
 On land where'er ye be—
And O, think on the leal, leal heart,
 That ne'er luvit ane but thee!
And O, think on the cauld, cauld mools
 That file my yellow hair,—
That kiss the cheek and kiss the chin
 Ye never sall kiss mair!

---

## Mrs. Caroline Anne Southey.

### THE MARINER'S HYMN.

LAUNCH thy bark, mariner!
 Christian, God speed thee!
Let loose the rudder-bands—
 Good angels lead thee!
Set thy sails warily,
 Tempests will come;
Steer thy course steadily,
 Christian, steer home!

Look to the weather-bow,
 Breakers are round thee;

Let fall the plummet now,
   Shallows may ground thee.
Reef in the foresail there!
   Hold the helm fast!
So—let the vessel wear—
   There swept the blast.

"What of the night, watchman?
   What of the night?"
"Cloudy—all quiet—
   No land yet—all's right!"
Be wakeful, be vigilant—
   Danger may be
At an hour when all seemeth
   Securest to thee.

How! gains the leak so fast?
   Clear out the hold—
Hoist up thy merchandise,
   Heave out thy gold;—
There—let the ingots go—
   Now the ship rights;
Hurra! the harbour's near—
   Lo, the red lights!

Slacken not sail yet
   At inlet or island;
Straight for the beacon steer,
   Straight for the highland;
Crowd all thy canvas on,
   Cut through the foam—
Christian! cast anchor now—
   Heaven is thy home!

## THE PAUPER'S DEATH-BED.

TREAD softly—bow the head—
   In reverent silence bow—
No passing bell doth toll—
Yet an immortal soul
   Is passing now.

Stranger! however great,
   With lowly reverence bow;
There's one in that poor shed—
One by that paltry bed—
   Greater than thou.

Beneath that beggar's roof,
   Lo! Death does keep his state;
Enter—no crowds attend—
Enter—no guards defend
   *This* palace gate.

That pavement, damp and cold,
   No smiling courtiers tread;
One silent woman stands,
Lifting with meagre hands
   A dying head.

No mingling voices sound—
   An infant wail alone;
A sob suppressed—again
That short, deep gasp, and then
   The parting groan.

O change!—O wondrous change!—
   Burst are the prison bars—

This moment *there*, so low,
So agonized, and now
   Beyond the stars!

O change!—stupendous change!
   There lies the soulless clod;
The Sun eternal breaks—
The new immortal wakes—
   Wakes with his God.

---

## Eliza Cook.

### THE OLD ARM-CHAIR.

I LOVE it, I love it; and who shall dare
   To chide me for loving that old arm-chair?
I've treasured it long as a sainted prize,
I've bedewed it with tears, and embalmed it with sighs;
'Tis bound by a thousand bands to my heart;
Not a tie will break, not a link will start.
Would ye learn the spell? a mother sat there,
And a sacred thing is that old arm-chair.

In childhood's hour I lingered near
The hallowed seat with listening ear;
And gentle words that mother would give,
To fit me to die and teach me to live.
She told me shame would never betide,
With truth for my creed and God for my guide;
She taught me to lisp my earliest prayer,
As I knelt beside that old arm-chair.

I sat and watched her many a day,
When her eye grew dim, and her locks were gray;
And I almost worshipped her when she smiled
And turned from her Bible to bless her child.
Years rolled on, but the last one sped—
My idol was shattered, my earth-star fled;
I learnt how much the heart can bear,
When I saw her die in that old arm-chair.

'Tis past! 'tis past! but I gaze on it now
With quivering breath and throbbing brow:
'Twas there she nursed me, 'twas there she died;
And memory flows with lava tide.
Say it is folly, and deem me weak,
While the scalding drops start down my cheek;
But I love it, I love it, and cannot tear
My soul from a mother's old arm-chair.

## SONG OF THE HEMPSEED.

AY, scatter me well, 'tis a moist Spring day,
   Wide and far be the hempseed sown,
And bravely I'll stand on the Autumn land
   When the rains have dropp'd and the winds have blown.
Man shall carefully gather me up,
   His hand shall rule and my form shall change,
Not as a mate for the purple of state,
   Nor into aught that is "rich and strange."
But I will come forth all woven and spun,
   With my fine threads curled in serpent length,
And the fire-wrought chain, and the lion's thick mane,
   Shall be rivalled by me in mighty strength.

I have many a place in the busy world,
   Of triumph and fear, of sorrow and joy;
I carry the freeman's flag unfurled,
   I am linked to childhood's darling toy.
Then scatter me wide, and hackle me well,
For a varied tale can the hempseed tell.

Bravely I swing in the anchor ring
   Where the foot of the proud man cometh not,
Where the dolphin leaps, and the sea-weed creeps
   O'er the rifted sand and coral grot.
Down, down below I merrily go
   When the huge ship takes her rocking rest;
The waters may chafe, but she dwelleth as safe
   As the young bird in its woodland nest.
I wreathe the spars of that same fair ship
   Where the gallant sea-hearts cling about,
Springing aloft with a song on the lip,
   Putting their faith in the cordage stout.
I am true when the blast sways the giant mast,
   Straining and stretched in a nor'west gale;
I abide with the bark, in the day and the dark,
   Lashing the hammock and reefing the sail.
Oh, the billows and I right fairly cope,
And the wild tide is stemmed by the cable rope.

Sons of evil, bad and bold,
   Madly ye live and little ye reck,
Till I am noosed in a coiling fold
   Ready to hug your felon neck.
The yarn is smooth and the knot is sure
   I will be firm to the task I take;

Thinly they twine the halter line,
   Yet when does the halter hitch or break?
My leaves are light and my flowers are bright—
   Fit for an infant hand to clasp;
But what think ye of me 'neath the gibbet-tree,
   Dangling high in the hangman's grasp?
Oh, a terrible thing does the hempseed seem
'Twixt the hollow floor and stout cross-beam!

The people rejoice, the banners are spread;
   There is frolic and feasting in cottage and hall;
The festival shout is echoing out
   From trellised porch and Gothic wall;
Merry souls hie to the belfry tower,
   Gayly they laugh when I am found,
And rare music they make, till the quick peals shake
   The ivy that wraps the turret round:
The hempseed lives with the old church-bell,
And helpeth the holiday ding-dong-dell.

The sunshine falls on a new-made grave!
   The funeral train is long and sad;
The poor man has come to the happiest home
   And easiest pillow he ever had.
I shall be there to lower him down
   Gently into his narrow bed;
I shall be there, the work to share,
   To guard his feet, and cradle his head.
I may be seen on the hillock green,
   Flung aside with the bleaching skull,
While the earth is thrown with worm and bone,
   Till the sexton has done, and the grave is full.

Back to the gloomy vault I'm borne,
  Leaving coffin and nail to crumble and rust,
There I am laid with the mattock and spade,
  Moistened with tears and clogged with dust:
Oh, the hempseed cometh in doleful shape,
With the mourner's cloak and sable crape.


Harvest shall spread with its glittering wheat;
  The barn shall be opened, the stack shall be piled;
Ye shall see the ripe grain shining out from the wain,
  And the berry-stained arms of the gleaner-child.
Heap on, heap on, till the wagon-ribs creak,
  Let the sheaves go towering to the sky,
Up with the shock till the broad wheels rock,
  Fear not to carry the rich freight high.
For I will infold the tottering gold,
  I will fetter the rolling load;
Not an ear shall escape my binding hold,
  On the furrowed field or jolting road:
Oh, the hempseed hath a fair place to fill,
With the harvest band on the corn-crown'd hill.


My threads are set in the heaving net,
  Out with the fisher-boy far at sea,
While he whistles a tune to the lonely moon,
  And trusts for his morrow's bread to me.
Toiling away through the dry summer-day,
  Round and round I steadily twist,
And bring from the cell of the deep old well
  What is rarely prized but sorely missed.
In the whirling swing—in the peg-top string,
  There am I, a worshipped slave.

On ocean and earth I'm a goodly thing,
  I serve from the play-ground to the grave.
I have many a place in the busy world,
  Of triumph and fear, of sorrow and joy;
I carry the freeman's flag unfurled,
  And am linked to childhood's darling toy:
Then scatter me wide, and hackle me well,
And a varied tale shall the hempseed tell.

---

## Charles Kingsley.

### SONG OF THE RIVER.

  CLEAR and cool, clear and cool,
    By laughing shallow and dreaming pool;
  Cool and clear, cool and clear,
    By shining shingle, and foaming wear;
Under the crag where the ouzel sings,
And the ivied wall where the church-bell rings,
    Undefiled, for the undefiled;
Play by me, bathe in me, mother and child.

  Dank and foul, dank and foul,
    By the smoke-grimed town in its murky cowl;
  Foul and dank, foul and dank,
    By wharf and sewer and slimy bank;
Darker and darker the further I go,
Baser and baser the richer I grow;
    Who dare sport with the sin-defiled?
Shrink from me, turn from me, mother and child.

> Strong and free, strong and free,
> The floodgates are open, away to the sea.
> Free and strong, free and strong,
> Cleansing my streams as I hurry along
> To the golden sands and the leaping bar,
> And the taintless tide that awaits me afar,
> As I lose myself in the infinite main,
> Like a soul that has sinned and is pardoned again.
> Undefiled, for the undefiled,
> Play by me, bathe in me, mother and child.

---

## Alexander Smith.

### A SONG

#### (From a Life-Drama).

> In Winter, when the dismal rain
>    Comes down in slanting lines,
> And Wind, that grand old harper, smote
>    His thunder-harp of pines,
>
> A Poet sat in his antique room,
>    His lamp the valley kinged,
> 'Neath dry crusts of dead tongues he found
>    Truth, fresh and golden-winged.
>
> When violets came and woods were green,
>    And larks did skyward dart,
> A Love alit and white did sit,
>    Like an angel on his heart.

From his heart he unclasped his love
   Amid the trembling trees,
And sent it to the Lady Blanche
   On wingèd poesies.

The Lady Blanche was saintly fair,
   Nor proud, but meek her look;
In her hazel eyes her thoughts lay clear
   As pebbles in a brook.

Her father's veins ran noble blood,
   His hall rose 'mid the trees;
Like a sunbeam she came and went
   'Mong the white cottages.

The peasants thanked her with their tears,
   When food and clothes were given,—
"This is a joy," the Lady said,
   "Saints cannot taste in Heaven!"

They met—the Poet told his love,
   His hopes, despairs, his pains,—
The Lady with her calm eyes mocked
   The tumult in his veins.

He passed away—a fierce song leapt
   From cloud of his despair,
As lightning, like a bright, wild beast
   Leaps from its thunder-lair.

He poured his frenzy forth in song,—
   Bright heir of tears and praises!
Now resteth that unquiet heart
   Beneath the quiet daisies.

The world is old,—Oh! very old,—
　The wild winds weep and rave;
The world is old, and gray, and cold,
　Let it drop into its grave!

---

## Jean Ingelow.

### THE BRIDES OF ENDERBY; OR, THE HIGH TIDE.

THE old mayor climbed the belfry tower,
　　The ringers ran by two, by three;
"Pull, if ye never pulled before;
　Good ringers, pull your best," quoth he.
"Play uppe, play uppe, O Boston bells!
Ply all your changes, all your swells,
　Play uppe 'The Brides of Enderby.'"

Men say it was a stolen tyde—
　The Lord that sent it, He knows all;
But in myne ears doth still abide
　The message that the bells let fall:
And there was naught of strange, beside
The flights of mews and peewits pied
　By millions crouched on the old sea wall.

I sat and spun within the doore,
　My thread brake off, I raised myne eyes;
The level sun, like ruddy ore,
　Lay sinking in the barren skies;

And dark against day's golden heath
She moved where Lindis wandereth,
My sonne's faire wife, Elizabeth.

"Cusha! Cusha! Cusha!" calling,
Ere the early dews were falling,
Farre away I heard her song.
"Cusha! Cusha!" all along;
Where the reedy Lindis floweth,
    Floweth, floweth,
From the meads where melick groweth,
Faintly came her milking song.—

"Cusha! Cusha! Cusha!" calling,
"For the dews will soone be falling;
Leave your meadow grasses mellow,
    Mellow, mellow;
Quit your cowslips, cowslips yellow;
Come uppe Whitefoot, come uppe Lightfoot;
Quit the stalks of parsley hollow,
    Hollow, hollow;
Come uppe Jetty, rise and follow,
From the clovers lift your head;
Come uppe Whitefoot, come uppe Lightfoot,
Come uppe Jetty, rise and follow,
Jetty, to the milking shed."

If it be long, aye, long ago,
  When I beginne to think howe long,
Againe I hear the Lindis flow,
  Swift as an arrowe, sharpe and strong;
And all the aire it seemeth mee

Bin full of floating bells (sayth shee),
That ring the tune of Enderby.

Alle fresh the level pasture lay,
   And not a shadowe mote be seene,
Save, where full fyve good miles away
   The steeple towered from out the greene;
And lo! the great bell farre and wide
Was heard in all the country side
That Saturday at eventide.

The swannerds where their sedges are
   Moved on in sunset's golden breath,
The shepherd lads I heard afarre,
   And my sonne's wife, Elizabeth;
Till floating o'er the grassy sea
Came downe that kyndly message free,
"The Brides of Mavis Enderby."

Then some looked uppe into the sky,
   And all along where Lindis flows
To where the goodly vessels lie,
   And where the lordly steeple shows.
They sayde, "And why should this thing be,
What danger lowers by land or sea?
They ring the tune of Enderby!

"For evil news from Mablethorpe,
   Of pyrate galleys warping down;
For shippes ashore beyond the scorpe,
   They have not spared to wake the towne:
But while the west bin red to see,
And storms be none, and pyrates flee,
Why ring 'The Brides of Enderby?'"

I looked without, and lo! my sonne
   Came riding downe with might and main:
He raised a shout as he drew on,
   Till all the welkin rang again,
"Elizabeth! Elizabeth!"
(A sweeter woman ne'er drew breath
Than my sonne's wife, Elizabeth.)

"The olde sea wall (he cried) is downe,
   The rising tide comes on apace,
And boats adrift in yonder towne
   Go sailing uppe the market-place."
He shook as one that looks on death:
"God save you, mother!" straight he saith;
"Where is my wife, Elizabeth?"

"Good sonne, where Lindis winds away
   With her two bairns I marked her long;
And ere yon bells beganne to play,
   Afar I heard her milking song."
He looked across the grassy sea,
To right, to left, "Ho Enderby!"
They rang "The Brides of Enderby!"

With that he cried and beat his breast;
   For lo! along the river's bed
A mighty eygre reared his crest,
   And uppe the Lindis raging sped.
It swept with thunderous noises loud;
Shaped like a curling snow-white cloud,
Or like a demon in a shroud.

And rearing Lindis backward pressed,
   Shook all her trembling bankes amaine;

Then madly at the eygre's breast
  Flung uppe her weltering walls again.
Then bankes came downe with ruin and rout—
Then beaten foam flew round about—
Then all the mighty floods were out.

So farre, so fast the eygre drave,
  The heart had hardly time to beat,
Before a shallow seething wave
  Sobbed in the grasses at oure feet:
The feet had hardly time to flee
Before it brake against the knee,
And all the world was in the sea.

Upon the roofe we sate that night,
  The noise of bells went sweeping by:
I marked the lofty beacon light
  Stream from the church tower, red and high—
A lurid mark and dread to see;
And awsome bells they were to mee,
That in the dark rang "Enderby."

They rang the sailor lads to guide
  From roofe to roofe who fearless rowed;
And I—my sonne was at my side,
  And yet the ruddy beacon glowed:
And yet he moaned beneath his breath,
"O come in life, or come in death!
O lost! my love, Elizabeth."

And didst thou visit him no more?
  Thou didst, thou didst, my daughter deare;
The waters laid thee at his doore,
  Ere yet the early dawn was clear.

Thy pretty bairns in fast embrace,
The lifted sun shone on thy face,
Downe drifted to thy dwelling-place.

That flow strewed wrecks about the grass,
   That ebbe swept out the flocks to sea;
A fatal ebbe and flow, alas!
   To manye more than myne and me:
But each will mourn his own (she saith).
And sweeter woman ne'er drew breath
Than my sonne's wife, Elizabeth.

  I shall never hear her more
  By the reedy Lindis shore,
  "Cusha, Cusha, Cusha!" calling,
  Ere the early dews be falling;
  I shall never hear her song,
  "Cusha, Cusha!" all along,
  Where the sunny Lindis floweth,
     Goeth, floweth;
  From the meads where melick groweth,
  When the water winding down,
  Onward floweth to the town.

  I shall never see her more
  Where the reeds and rushes quiver,
     Shiver, quiver;
  Stand beside the sobbing river,
  Sobbing, throbbing, in its falling,
  To the sandy lonesome shore;
  I shall never hear her calling,
  "Leave your meadow grasses mellow,
     Mellow, mellow;

Quit your cowslips, cowslips yellow;
Come uppe Whitefoot, come uppe Lightfoot;
Quit your pipes of parsley hollow,
    Hollow, hollow;
Come uppe Lightfoot, rise and follow;
    Lightfoot, Whitefoot,
From your clovers lift the head;
Come uppe Jetty, follow, follow,
Jetty, to the milking shed."

---

## Edwin Arnold.

### THE KNIGHT'S GRAVE.

#### I.

UNDER painted cross and chalice,
    In the flood of light,
Lies in marble, with Dame Alice,
    Andrew Welldon, Knight;
Side by side, the legend sayeth,
    These two lived and died,
And carvèd stone o'er mingled bone
    Showeth them side by side.

#### II.

Nothing here, above or under,
    Of fanatic gloom;
No fool's fear of death's deep wonder
    Spoils their simple tomb:
Seems it that the sculptor graved it
    Only for to show

What the Knight and what his Dame were
  Now they are not so.

### III.

Merry cheeps of madcap swallows
  Reach them, darting by,
Changeful shadows from the sallows
  On their white brows lie;
Changeful shadows from the sallows,
  Constant from the limes;
For light friends go, if winds do blow,
  As in their ancient times.

### IV.

Certes, lovely was the Lady!
  Eyes, I guess, whose blue,
Calm and cold, but gleaming steady,
  Tender was and true.
Of a noble presence surely,
  Dutiful and staid,
Worthinesse was glad before her,
  Worthlessnesse afraid.

### V.

Read beneath, in golden letters,
  Proudly written down,
Names of all her "sonnes and daughteres,"
  Each a matron crown:
Deftly cut in ruff and wimple,
  Kneeling figures show
Small heads over smaller rising,
  In a solemn row.

VI.

These her triumphs. Sterner token
    Chronicles her lord:
Hangs above him, grim and broken,
    Gilded helm and sword.
Sometimes, when with quire and organ
    All the still air swings,
Red with the rust and gray with the dust,
    Low rattles that blade, and rings.

VII.

Time was, Knight, that tiny treble
    Should have stirred thy soul
More than drums and trumpets rebel
    Braying health to Noll.
No more fight now!—nay, nor flight now!
    The rest that thou hast given
In chancel shade to that good blade
    God gives thy soul in heaven.

VIII.

Somewhere on this summer morning,
    In this English isle,
Blooms a cheek whose rich adorning
    Herits, Dame, thy smile:
Some one in the realm whose fathers
    Suffered much, and long,
Owes that sword and its good lord
    Thanks for a righted wrong.

IX.

Therefore for that maiden say I:
    "Dame, God thee assoil;"

Therefore for that freeman pray I:
"Knight, God quit thy toil;"
And for all Christian men and me
Grace from the gracious Lord
To write our name with no more shame,
And sheathe as clean a sword.

---

## Gerald Massey.

### THE KINGLIEST KINGS.

HO! ye who in noble work
Win scorn, as flames draw air,
And in the way where lions lurk,
God's image bravely bear;
Though trouble-tried and torture-torn,
The kingliest Kings are crowned with thorn.

Life's glory, like the bow in heaven,
Still springeth from the cloud;
And soul ne'er soared the starry seven,
But pain's fire-chariot rode.
They've battled best who've boldest borne,
The kingliest Kings are crowned with thorn.

The martyr's fire-crown on the brow
Doth into glory burn;
And tears that from love's torn heart flow,
To pearls of spirit turn:
Our dearest hopes in pangs are born,
The kingliest Kings are crowned with thorn.

As beauty in Death's cerement shrouds,
    And stars bejewel night,
God-splendours live in dim heart-clouds,
    And suffering worketh might.
The murkiest hour is mother o' morn,
The kingliest Kings are crowned with thorn.

---

### Sydney Dobell.

#### "HOW'S MY BOY?"

"Ho, sailor of the sea!
    How's my boy—my boy?"
"What's your boy's name, good wife,
And in what good ship sailed he?"

"My boy John—
He that went to sea—
What care I for the ship, sailor?
My boy's my boy to me.

"You come back from sea,
And not know my John?
I might as well have asked some landsman,
Yonder down in the town.
There's not an ass in all the parish
But knows my John.

"How's my boy—my boy?
And unless you let me know,

I'll swear you are no sailor,
Blue jacket or no—
Brass buttons or no, sailor,
Anchor and crown or no—
Sure his ship was the 'Jolly Briton'"—
"Speak low, woman, speak low!"

"And why should I speak low, sailor,
About my own boy John?
If I was loud as I am proud
I'd sing him over the town!
Why should I speak low, sailor?"—
"That good ship went down."

"How's my boy—my boy?
What care I for the ship, sailor—
I was never aboard her.
Be she afloat or be she aground,
Sinking or swimming, I'll be bound
Her owners can afford her!
I say, how's my John?"—
"Every man on board went down,
Every man aboard her."

"How's my boy—my boy?
What care I for the men, sailor?
I'm not their mother—
How's my boy—my boy?
Tell me of him and no other!
How's my boy—my boy?"

## Walter Thornbury.

### THE TWO NORSE KINGS.

#### A YORKSHIRE LEGEND.

TWO galleys, each with crimson sail,
Plough fast the green bath of the whale.

A fierce king stands on either prow,
A gold band round his knotty brow.

A bronze axe and an ivory horn
Are by each wrath king proudly borne.

A torque of twisted gold one wore—
That brooch Jarls from the walrus tore.

The raven banner's blowing black,
Their red prows cast a flaming track.

Clashing the gold links on his chest,
Each bids his rowers do their best.

The Saxon land is fair and green—
Broad meadows with a stream between.

Both galleys, with an equal beak,
Touch at one bound the sandy peak.

Both Norse kings leap at once to land,
Like sunbeams spring forth either hand.

Gunthron kneels down to kiss the earth,
Bonthron laughs loud with cruel mirth.

Then helm meets helm, and shield meets shield,
Red grows the sand, and red the field.

Gather, ye eagles, on the crag,
Swarm, ravens, on each chalky jag.

Notched splints of steel and shreds of gold
Are scattered on the Saxon mould.

Bright mail is cloven, flags are torn,
Dear are the shouts to Odin borne.

But all the fight, this narrow verse
May not, if it could, rehearse.

This I know, a burial mound
Rises o'er that battle-ground;

And to this day the Saxon boor
Calls it in legends "Bonthron's Moor."

---

## Robert Buchanan.-

### THE STORY OF PYGMALION.

BLUE night. I threw the lattice open wide,
   Drinking the odorous air; and from my height
I saw the watch-fires of the town, and heard
The gradual dying of the murmurous day.
Then, as the twilight deepened, on her limbs
The silver lances of the stars and moon
Were shattered, and the shining fragments fell
Like jewels at her feet. The Cyprian star
Quivered to liquid emerald where it hung
On the ribb'd ledges of the darkening hills,
Gazing upon her; and, as in a dream,

Methought the marble, underneath that look,
Stirred—like a bank of milky asphodels
Kissed into tumult by a wind of light.

Whereat there swam upon me utterly
A drowsy sense wherein my holy dream
Was melted, as a pearl in wine: bright-eyed,
Keen, haggard, passionate, with languid thrills
Of insolent unrest, I watched the stone,
And lo, I loved it; not as men love fame,
Not as the warrior loves his laurel wreath,
But with prelusion of a passionate joy
That threw me from the height whereon I stood
To grasp at Glory, and with impiousness
Of sweet communing with some living Soul
Chambered in that cold bosom. As I gazed,
There was a buzz of revel in mine ears,
And tinkling fragments of a ditty of love,
Warbled by wantons over wine-cups, swam
Like bees within the brain.—Then I was shamed
By her pale beauty, and I scorned myself,
And standing at the lattice dark and cool
Watched the dim winds of twilight enter in,
And draw a veil about that loveliness
White, dim, and breathed on by the common air.

But, like a snake's moist eye, the dewy star
Of lovers drew me; and I watched it grow
Large, soft, and tremulous; and as I gazed
In fascinated impotence of heart,
I prayed the lifeless silence might assume
A palpable life, and soften into flesh,

And be a beautiful and human joy
To crown my love withal; and thrice the prayer
Blackened across my pale face with no word.
But through the woolly silver of a cloud
The cool star dripping emerald from the baths
Of Ocean brightened in upon my tower,
And touched the marble forehead with a gleam
Soft, green, and dewy; and I said, "The prayer
Is heard!"
        The livelong night, the breathless night,
I waited in a darkness, in a dream,
Watching the snowy figure faintly seen,
And ofttimes shuddering when I seemed to see
Life, like a taper burning in a skull,
Gleam through the rayless eyes: yea, wearily
I hearkened through the dark and seemed to hear
The low warm billowing of a living breast,
Or the slow motion of anointed limbs
New-stirring into life; and, shuddering,
Fearing the thing I hoped for, awful eyed,
On her cold breast I placed a hand as cold
And sought a fluttering heart.—But all was still,
And chill, and breathless; and she gazed right on
With rayless orbs, nor marvelled at my touch:
White, silent, pure, ineffable, a shape
Rebuking human hope, a deathless thing,
Sharing the wonder of the Sun who sends
His long bright look through all futurity.

  When Shame lay heavy on me, and I hid
My face, and almost hated her, my work,
Because she was so fair, so human fair,

Yea not divinely fair as that pure face
Which, when mine hour of loss and travail came,
Haunted me, out of heaven.   Then the Dawn
Stared in upon her: when I opened eyes,
And saw the gradual Dawn encrimson her
Like blood that blushed within her,—and behold
She trembled—and I shrieked!

        With haggard eyes
I gazed on her, my fame, my work, my love!
Red sunrise mingled with the first bright flush
Of palpable life—she trembled, stirred, and sighed—
And the dim blankness of her stony eyes
Melted to azure.   Then, by slow degrees,
She tingled with the milky warmth of blood:
Her eyes were vacant of a seeing soul,
But dewily the bosom rose and fell,
The lips caught sunrise, parting, and the breath
Fainted through pearly teeth.

       I was as one
Who gazes on a goddess serpent-eyed,
And cannot fly, and knows to look is death.
O apparition of my work and wish!
The weight of awe oppressed me, and the air
Swung as the Seas swing around drowning men.

   \*   \*   \*   \*

 Then sat we, side by side.   She, queenly stoled,
Amid the gleaming fountains of her hair,
With liquid azure orbs and rosy lips
Gorgeous with honeyed kisses; I like a man
Who loves fair eyes and knows they are a fiend's,
And in them sees a heaven he knows is hell.
For, like a glorious beast, she ate and drank,

Staining her lips in crimson wine, and laughed
To feel the vinous bubbles froth and burst
In veins whose sparkling blood was meet to be
An angel's habitation.   Cup on cup
I drained in fulness—careless as a god—
A haggard bearded head upon a breast
In tumult like a sun-kissed bed of flowers.
  *  *  *  *  *
Three days and nights the vision dwelt with me,
Three days and nights we dozed in dreadful state,
Looked piteously upon by sun and star;
But the third night there passed a homeless sound
Across the city underneath my tower,
And lo! there came a roll of muffled wheels,
A shrieking and a hurrying to and fro
Beneath, and I gazed forth.   Then far below
I heard the people shriek, "A pestilence!"
  *  *  *  *  *
 I turned to her, the partner of my height:
She, with bright eyeballs sick with wine, and hair
Gleaming in sunset, on a couch asleep.
And lo! a horror lifted up my scalp,
The pulses plunged upon the heart, and fear
Froze my wide eyelids.   Peacefully she lay
In purple stole arrayed, one little hand
Bruising the downy cheek, the other still
Clutching the dripping goblet, and the light,
With gleams of crimson on the ruinous hair,
Spangling a blue-veined bosom, whence the robe
Fell back in rifled folds; but dreadful change
Grew pale and hideous on the waxen face,
And in her sleep she did not stir, nor dream.

## Richard Chenevix Trench.

### BE PATIENT.

BE patient! O, be patient! Put your ear against the earth;
Listen there how noiselessly the germ o' the seed has birth—
How noiselessly and gently it upheaves its little way,
Till it parts the scarcely broken ground, and the blade stands up in the day.

Be patient! O, be patient! The germs of mighty thought
Must have their silent undergrowth, must underground be wrought;
But as sure as there's a power that makes the grass appear,
Our land shall be green with liberty, the blade-time shall be here.

Be patient! O, be patient!—go and watch the wheat-ears grow—
So imperceptibly that ye can mark nor change nor throe—
Day after day, day after day, till the ear is fully grown,
And then again day after day, till the ripened field is brown.

Be patient! O, be patient!—though yet our hopes are green,
The harvest-fields of freedom shall be crowned with sunny sheen.
Be ripening! be ripening!—mature your silent way,
Till the whole broad land is tongued with fire on freedom's harvest day!

## Miss Adelaide Anne Proctor.

### A DOUBTING HEART.

WHERE are the swallows fled?
     Frozen and dead,
Perchance, upon some bleak and stormy shore.
     O doubting heart!
    Far over purple seas,
    They wait, in sunny ease,
    The balmy southern breeze,
To bring them to their northern home once more.

Why must the flowers die?
     Prisoned they lie
In the cold tomb, needless of tears or rain.
     O doubting heart!
    They only sleep below
    The soft white ermine snow,
    While winter winds shall blow,
To breathe and smile upon you soon again.

The sun has hid its rays
     These many days:
Will dreary hours never leave the earth?
     O doubting heart!
    The stormy clouds on high
    Veil the same sunny sky
    That soon (for spring is nigh)
Shall wake the summer into golden mirth.

Fair hope is dead, and light
    Is quenched in night.
What sound can break the silence of despair?
    O doubting heart!
    The sky is overcast,
    Yet stars shall rise at last,
    Brighter for darkness past,
And angels' silver voices stir the air.

*THE END.*